# THE
# ROAD TO HEL

To

NORA CHADWICK

who has given me so much

# THE
# ROAD TO HEL

*A Study of the Conception of the Dead in Old Norse Literature*

BY

HILDA RODERICK ELLIS
M.A., Ph.D.

*Sometime Marion Kennedy Research Student of Newnham College
Assistant Lecturer in English, Royal Holloway College*

CAMBRIDGE
AT THE UNIVERSITY PRESS
1943

CAMBRIDGE UNIVERSITY PRESS
Cambridge, New York, Melbourne, Madrid, Cape Town,
Singapore, São Paulo, Delhi, Mexico City

Cambridge University Press
The Edinburgh Building, Cambridge CB2 8RU, UK

Published in the United States of America by Cambridge University Press, New York

www.cambridge.org
Information on this title: www.cambridge.org/9781107632349

First published 1943
First paperback edition 2013

*A catalogue record for this publication is available from the British Library*

ISBN 978-1-107-63234-9 Paperback

Cambridge University Press has no responsibility for the persistence or
accuracy of URLs for external or third-party internet websites referred to in
this publication, and does not guarantee that any content on such websites is,
or will remain, accurate or appropriate.

# Contents

# Preface

In the literature of Old Scandinavia we meet with something unique in mediaeval Europe: a great and rich literature composed before the thirteenth century; clear incisive prose, and poetry whose stormy music can deal fittingly with the tales of gods and heroes; and a remarkable clarity of vision, showing itself in understanding of human strength and weakness and full awareness of the greatness of the issues involved. Comparison with the literature of Ancient Greece is not unfitting; the mingling of humour and tragedy in the Icelandic Sagas recalls the world of Homer while it foreshadows Shakesperian drama. But the appreciation of mighty issues in the lives of simple folk which we find in them is something as new as the perfect mastery of a narrative prose style; neither was to appear again in Europe for centuries.

The religion of a people who could produce such a literature as this must be worthy of study, especially as we can see the results of northern heathenism developing until the end of the tenth century without interference either from Christian thought or from the Latin culture so closely bound up with it. The doors between Scandinavia and the East were still open when this literature came into being, and memories of a pre-Christian Celtic culture yet remained alive. It is a setting of another kind from that to which we have grown accustomed, that of Mediterranean influences impinging early on the Germanic world; and there are great riches awaiting the explorers of the realm of thought in that complex and vigorous age about which all too little is known. Of men's attitude to life the literature tells us much, and we must recognise the strength and sanity of it; how much can it tell us of their thoughts concerning death and the soul? This work is an attempt to begin the answer to this question, and if it can reveal something of the variety and richness of the lost religion of the North it will have served its purpose.

Originally this book formed part of a thesis accepted in 1940 for the degree of Ph.D. in the University of Cambridge. It was while holding a research studentship from Newnham College that I completed the greater part of the work, and my first acknowledgment must be to the College for the generous help it has provided. To

Professor and Mrs Chadwick I owe more than can be easily expressed: the discovery of both the inspiration and discipline of research, and unfailing help, both with practical advice and encouragement, the whole of the way. I would like also to thank Mr and Mrs J. M. de Navarro and Mr G. N. Garmonsway for many suggestions and for their sympathetic interest; and Miss G. D. Willcock, who read the book in manuscript, and Miss Helen Brown, who read the proofs and assisted with the index, for their helpful criticism and support. Finally my thanks are due to the Syndics of the University Press for undertaking the publication of this book despite the difficulties of war-time, and to its Staff for the courtesy and efficiency they have shown throughout.

H. R. ELLIS

*December 1942*

## ABBREVIATIONS

| | |
|---|---|
| *A.f.n.O.* | *Aarböger for nordisk Oldkyndighed og Historie.* |
| *Ark.f.n.F.* | *Arkiv for nordisk Filologi.* |
| *Ebert* | *Reallexicon der Vorgeschichte.* Berlin, 1924–32. |
| *F.A.S.* | *Fornaldar Sögur Nordrlanda.* Ásmundarson: Reykjavík. |
| *Litt. Hist.* | F. Jónsson, *Oldnorske og Oldislandske Litteraturs Historie.* Copenhagen, 1894. |
| *Lndn.* | *Landnámabók.* Ásmundarson: Reykjavík, 1902. |
| *M.o.M.* | *Maal og Minne.* Norske Studier. |
| Saxo | Saxo Grammaticus, *Danish History*, i–ix (trans. Elton, London, 1894). |
| *Z.d.V.f.V.* | *Zeitschrift der Vereins für Volkskunde.* |

# Introduction

'Have you no desire to be like that king who was victorious against all whom
he fought, who was handsome also, and accomplished in all things, so that in all
the northern lands there was never his like? He who could grant victory to
others in battle as well as to himself, and who found poetry came as easily to
him as speech to other men?' Then the king sat up and seized a prayer-book
on the bed, and made to hurl it at the stranger's head, exclaiming 'Least of all
would I be like you—you wicked Othin!'

(*Óláfs Saga Helga: Flateyjarbók*, II, 56.)

It is typical of Old Norse literature that King Olaf Tryggvason and
his successor Olaf the Holy, striving hard to establish the Christian
faith firmly in Norway, had many such interviews as this with the
old gods recorded of them. Even in the eleventh century the power
of the gods was not destroyed, and both the might and the beauty
of the old religion still remained a potent force in men's minds. This
one-eyed stranger, of whom we are told, won his way to the king's
bedside by the wisdom of his speech and by the wealth of stories
which he could tell of the rulers and heroes of old time, and it is the
irresistible fascination which the storied past held for the men of
Scandinavia in the centuries following the Conversion that has resulted in the rich treasury of heathen traditions which Old Norse
literature has preserved for us. Even such an earnest young fanatic as
King Olaf the Holy could not close his ears entirely to the blandish-
ments of Othin.

Yet for all the rich poetry and humour of the mythology, for
all the information vouchsafed to us about heathen practices and
beliefs, the pre-Christian religion of Scandinavia remains paradoxi-
cally a subject about which we know very little. It is true that
Christianity came late into the north and was only accepted by the
Icelandic Assembly in the year A.D. 1000, four centuries after the
coming of St Augustine to Kent and considerably more than four
centuries after the time when the first missionaries reached Scotland
and Ireland. It is true also that the devotion to the past which is so
characteristic of Norse literature has left us such a record as is offered
by no other early literature in North-West Europe. But against this
must be set the fact that those who recorded the prose and poetry of
Scandinavia were men who lived after the coming of Christianity,

and that for them it was no longer a living faith which they chronicled but old lore from an age that had passed. It may happen that they know much concerning the heathen religion and never guess that their readers will not inevitably share that knowledge, with the result that they leave gaps which we find it hard to bridge, or hints which in our ignorance we are unable to follow up. Or frequently their interest lies in a different direction from ours, and chance allusions are made merely to tantalise the curious reader. But all too often it means that they themselves know little of what they are recording, so that they either present us with a confused mass of incomprehensible details to sort out for ourselves, or, more commonly, try to supply an explanation from the background of thought of their own time. Or if they are themselves creative writers, as was Snorri Sturlason to whom we owe the great account of Norse mythology in the *Prose Edda*, it is likely that they may choose to build up a new structure from old material, as imagination and the desire for consistency directs them; this has resulted in some of the finest conceptions in Norse literature, but has proved perhaps the most misleading path of all to those who attempt to discover the nature of Norse heathen thought.

In this book an attempt has been made to collect the evidence concerned with one important aspect of Norse heathenism: ideas about the fate of man after death. The conception which has made the strongest appeal to popular imagination is that of the warrior paradise, Valhalla; and it is surprising at first to have to realise that this is only one of many conflicting pictures of the realm of the dead, and one moreover which occupies only a very small section of the prose and poetry which has come down to us. One of the many problems which still awaits an answer is whether from the vast accumulation of evidence relating to the dead it is possible to make out any definite and consistent presentation of the other world, and of the fate of man beyond the grave. In attempting to find a solution of this problem, we may gain help from the fact that archaeology as well as literature has evidence to offer us, in particular about funeral customs; and no more dramatic introduction could be desired than that presented by the heathen graves which have been explored in Scandinavia, with their rich implications of ship-funeral and human sacrifice. Beside the study of funeral customs, such a survey as this must include all that can be discovered about the conception of a realm or realms of the dead, any traces of a cult of the dead which have been recorded, and any indication which the literature can give as to the nature of survival after death according to heathen thought. Finally, in the concluding chapters we shall pass on to certain conceptions which appear to be of some importance, those connected with the relationship between the world of the living and that of the dead. Here there are two main aspects to be considered: the consultation of the dead by the living, and the entry of the living soul into the world of the dead to learn its secrets.

The primary object of such a survey is to take stock of the material which Old Norse literature offers us on these subjects, and to see if it is possible to discern any consistent body of pre-Christian ideas about the life after death and the relation between the dead and the living. Secondly, to discover whether any connection exists between the practices recorded in the prose literature and the poems in the Edda which deal with mythological subjects. In spite of a great deal of valuable textual and critical work done on these poems, they still remain for the most part obscure to us, and it is possible that an approach by way of the information gained from the prose literature might serve to throw new light on them. It will at once be realised that the main difficulty is that of distinguishing between literary traditions and records of actual practice and belief. Clearly a wide knowledge of the history and evolution of the literary forms as well as of the historical background of the heathen period in Scandinavia and the neighbouring lands must be necessary before any final decision is given. This work claims to give no such decision; it is no more than an introduction, to clear the ground for further investigation, and in it I shall do little more than attempt to sift and arrange the available evidence and to see whether any main lines of agreement may be discerned.

Moreover, even did we possess the means to trace back such poems of the Edda, for instance, as are likely to have been composed in heathen times to their original form, our problem would by no means be solved for us. It is certain that we should still be faced with conflicting and contradictory evidence, with complexities and inconsistencies, for at no time during the heathen period did the old faith attain to such unity in the North as to bequeath to us an unshakeable body of truths or a logical whole. There are no Thirty-nine Articles of heathen belief lurking behind the obscurities of Norse mythology or the welter of strange practices recorded in the sagas. There are, it is true, certain distinctions to be made in assessing the value of the evidence the literature offers; in particular the skaldic poetry, whose authorship and date for the most part can be determined with something approaching accuracy and which in some cases indubitably goes back to the time of the heathen king Harald the Fairhaired, is an all-important source for our knowledge of heathen thought towards the close of the Viking Age. But having allowed for this, it is possible to lay too great emphasis on the fact that most of the sources which we possess have in their present form only been recorded in Christian times, in the thirteenth century or later. The Conversion of the North meant that a new and absorbing interest came into literature, although the power of the new classical learning and philosophy was never as potent and all-conquering in Scandinavia as in Anglo-Saxon England, and the old lore, besides, had been granted four precious centuries to develop and establish itself more deeply. It meant also that fresh complications were now added to the already complicated material, as has already been emphasised. But two things must be remembered: first, that with the coming of Christian culture the heathen literature was for the first time recorded in writing, and so caught and fixed in permanent form; and secondly, that there was never any question of the Conversion shattering into fragments a structure already in existence as a perfect whole. All through the heathen period belief and thought was shifting and fluid, varying according to local cultures, developing in accordance with particular influences in separate localities; and the oral literature that reflected it was shifting and developing too. The necessary first step in rediscovering the nature of heathen thought in Scandinavia is to discover how much has been caught up and preserved in the literature we possess, and to assess carefully the extent of the wealth at our disposal before we trace out its origins. After that it should be possible to carry the quest further, and in the course of this book I hope to indicate the most fruitful lines of later study. For the moment it seems to me that the first great test to be applied is that of consistency.

Consistency between different sources may be established in a number of ways. There may be close verbal echoes, parallel statements and repetitions of the same motif, such as are likely to indicate literary borrowings by one source from another, or a deliberate use of certain set fashions in style. When on the other hand we find a number of sources differing widely in style, content, detail and treatment, which seem nevertheless to be drawing on the same body of traditions, memories and ideas, then we have some right to claim an agreement which is stronger than mere imitation, and which may be held to reflect in some degree the thought of an earlier time recorded, perhaps unconsciously, in later literature. In such a case there will be contradictions, misunderstandings and minor inconsistencies, but it should be possible to perceive a deeper agreement on general lines which outweighs these. This is by no means to argue for a subjective approach to early literature; on the contrary the approach will have to be strictly objective and the evidence stand or fall strictly on its own merit without forcing or twisting the information gained; otherwise this test of consistency will be a mockery. It is necessary, too, to examine a large amount of evidence before coming to any conclusion as to the general direction in which it is tending; but as far as Old Norse literature is concerned there is little reason to complain of the scantiness of the field, which is bewildering by its richness rather than depressing by its barrenness.

This approach is particularly important in dealing with incidents from the Icelandic sagas which have to do with the supernatural. While it is universally recognised that the majority of these are based on the doings of historic persons and on reliable local tradition, passages which bring in the supernatural element are apt to be eyed with suspicion and dismissed as fictitious interpolations to enliven the story. Moreover, the high literary quality of the sagas as a whole means that a form and unity have been given to their plots which could never have resulted from the mere slavish recording of accurate facts; and how much then of the heathen background is to be attributed to the creative imagination and shaping hand of the storytellers who have worked on the original traditions about local heroes? It remains to be seen whether the evidence for heathen practices given in these tales gives us reason to believe that they are based on actual customs and genuine traditions remembered from the heathen period. The test of a consistent picture agreeing not in small details and forms of narrative but in the fundamental outline, which remains recognisable and convincing, seems the most satisfactory guide to demand here. As regards the *Fornaldar Sögur*, the 'sagas of old time', the date of these in their present form is late, and it is impossible to base any conclusions on their evidence alone. But they are of great value for purposes of comparison, and it will be found that passages from them sometimes serve to illumine evidence gained from more reliable sources, suggesting that a good deal of the material they contain is composed from genuine traditions, albeit imperfectly remembered, from heathen times.

There are two additional ways in which a check may be kept on the reliability of literary records. The first is by comparing them with archaeological evidence, which can sometimes supply us with information about early history when other sources fail, and which provides a record of funeral customs in the heathen period particularly significant for any study connected with beliefs about the dead; of this, as already stated, full use will be made. The other method, to be used with caution, is that of comparison with heathen practices outside the region under discussion. Occasionally the records of modern anthropologists give us information about non-Christian practices in other parts of the world which afford a striking comparison with those described or alluded to in Old Norse literature, and thus offer additional justification for regarding certain features in the literary evidence as valuable. Both the archaeological and anthropological material may be dangerous if applied too freely and uncritically, but I believe that neither up till now has been sufficiently taken into consideration in approaching the subject of Norse heathen thought. Unquestionably however it is literature alone which can reveal to us something of what passed through the minds of the men of a former faith and of a different age, and particularly the work of the poets. I would echo with conviction the words with which Snorri Sturlason, the first to attempt a systematic record of the heathen religion of his people, closes the preface to his *Ynglinga Saga:* 'The poems, as it seems to me, can least of all be set aside, provided that they are well and truly rendered and are interpreted with wisdom.'

# Chapter I

## FUNERAL CUSTOMS: THE EVIDENCE
## OF ARCHAEOLOGY

Time which antiquates antiquity and hath an art to make dust of all things hath yet
spared these minor monuments.          Sɪʀ Tʜᴏᴍᴀs Bʀᴏᴡɴᴇ, *Urn Burial.*

### Tʜᴇ Dɪsᴘᴏsᴀʟ ᴏꜰ ᴛʜᴇ Dᴇᴀᴅ ɪɴ Hᴇᴀᴛʜᴇɴ Tɪᴍᴇs

If we desire to know what ideas men held in heathen times about the
life beyond the grave, it is natural to turn first to the evidence of
archaeology. The grave is an uncontrovertible witness; changes of
custom, trivial or sweeping, the importance of funeral ritual in the
disposal of the dead, the choice of goods to lay beside or destroy with
the body—all these it preserves for us, as definite facts that cannot be
questioned. Any collection of literary evidence about the future
life must benefit by a preliminary survey of these facts, to act as
a touchstone by which the vague or contradictory statements of
literary records may be tested.

But archaeology may only be regarded as a science as long as it
remains purely descriptive; once we begin to interpret the sure
standards give way. It is not only a question of uncertainty because
all the facts are not yet known; for when we leave the customs and
turn to the beliefs behind them we are dealing with the whims
and reactions of the human mind, capricious from its infancy. Moreover, though the mentality of the people whose customs are being
examined may be at an early stage of development, there is possible
contact with other peoples at different mental stages to be considered,
and outside influences may play strange tricks such as no logical
scheme anticipates. We cannot hope then that from the evidence
which archaeology can give us from heathen Scandinavia we shall
have material for a definite answer to the question of what was
believed to happen to the dead. But a summary made as briefly as
possible from the rich and complex evidence at our disposal is likely
to prove the most profitable introduction to an investigation of
heathen beliefs about the life beyond the grave.

We may begin as far back as the opening of the Bronze Age, that is, Period I of Montelius. At this time the practice of burying groups of people together in one grave was giving place to that of separate burials, with the bodies laid in the earth in crouched position. In the first phase of the middle Bronze Age (Montelius II) coffins of stone or oak were much used, but throughout all this period while inhumation was the prevailing rite, the normal form of grave was a stone cist within a barrow. Then in Period III came an abrupt change, and in certain districts the dead were burned and not buried. The new custom was destined to live long in Scandinavia, for not until the conversion of the North to Christianity, about two thousand years later, did it die out altogether. It appears to have come northward through Germany, spreading slowly but with such startling thoroughness that finally the old practice of inhumation which had so long been the only one was, in Period III b of Montelius, completely replaced by the new.[1] When cremation first appeared (Period III a) the burnt remains were still placed in a man-length stone cist; but during the next period (III b), as cremation became the universal rite, the grave altered accordingly, and the stone chamber which had held the body now shrank to a smaller, box-like stone cist to contain the urn. Mounds, when erected, were smaller; sometimes the urns were placed in barrows of an earlier period, and sometimes in the late Bronze Age (Montelius IV onwards) buried in flat graves.

But although at the end of the Bronze Age the change from burial to burning seemed to be complete, certain graves which date from the transition period between the Bronze and Iron Ages prove a puzzling exception to the general rule, and show that in certain parts burial of the dead had either never been entirely abandoned or that it was now introduced again. In Gotland certain graves of early Iron Age date have been found to hold unburned bodies;[2] it is thought that these may be due to Celtic influence, but since they were never scientifically excavated no definite conclusions can be reached. A few similar graves from the late Bronze Age have been found on the East Baltic coast in Estonia,[3] and there is a probable one from Billerbeck in Pomerania.[4] Most puzzling of all are the ship-form graves found in Gotland.[5] Some of these are cremation and some inhumation graves, but in either case the remains, in urn, stone cist or coffin, are laid in a grave enclosed by upright stones in the

1 M. Ebert, *Praehistorische Zeitschrift*, 1922, XIII–XIV, p. 15.
2 O. Almgren, *Die ältere Eisenzeit Gotlands* (Stockholm, 1923), p. 3.
3 Ebert, XIII, p. 5.        4 *Ibid.* II, p. 23 f.        5 *Ibid.* IV, p. 408 f.

form of a ship. The date of these graves seems to vary from the late Bronze Age to the early Iron Age, the ones containing skeletons being on the whole later than the cremation graves. For other ship-form graves in Bornholm[1] and Latvia[2] a late Bronze Age date has been suggested, though the evidence is not conclusive.

Apart from such local exceptions as these, cremation remains the general rule throughout the early Iron Age. Some changes in the treatment of the remains, however, must be noticed. Formerly the bones had been removed from the remains of the funeral pyre after burning and washed before they were placed in the urn, but now the grave goods were burned together with the body on the pyre, and the confused mass of the remains put into the urn and heaped round it without attempt at separation.[3] This practice too seems to have reached Scandinavia from Germany by way of Bornholm. As might be expected, the next step was to dispense with the urn.[4] In certain Pomeranian graves the remains were left in a little heap without an urn to hold them, and a still further development was to scatter the residue of the pyre throughout the grave. The new custom travelled by the usual road, and was fully established in Bornholm by the second period of La Tène culture. It also became usual to bend or roll up weapons burned on the pyre with the dead before placing them in the grave.

In the Roman period, beginning in the first century A.D., Roman culture and Roman fashions touched even far-off Scandinavia, and under the new influences burial of the dead came back once more into the North. The Roman idea of an elaborate burial was to leave the dead man lying in the earth surrounded by everything necessary for a magnificent banquet, so that the graves of this period are supplied with cups, vessels and stores of food and drink rather than swords and shields and the panoply of the warrior. This was par-ticularly true of Denmark, where the richer districts were more open to the influences of Southern culture than Norway and Sweden, and from this time Danish funeral customs tended to develop on a line of their own apart from the rest of Scandinavia; an instance of this is the fact that grave-mounds and memorial stones now came into use again in Norway and Sweden, while graves in Denmark remained for the most part flat. Cremation meanwhile continued throughout the period side by side with burial.

1 Ebert, II, p. 117.
2 *Ibid.* XIII, p. 6.
3 'Brandschüttungsgräber', *ibid.* II, p. 122 f.
4 'Brandgrubengräber', *op. cit.*

As the Migration period succeeded the Roman one the cleavage between Denmark and the rest of Scandinavia became more marked, and in Norway and parts of Sweden the mounds became larger and the dead were laid within them fully clothed, with the weapons of the men and the full household equipment of the women beside them. Perhaps the most impressive graves found are those of Vendel in Sweden, where a line of chiefs has been buried, for the most part in their ships, in a series of graves which seem to date in unbroken succession from the sixth century to the tenth. Nor were the cremation graves neglected, for the splendid tombs of the kings of Old Uppsala belong to this period, and again seem to include ships among the possessions burned with the dead. Ship-funeral is found in both types of graves from about A.D. 500. During the seventh century there was a tendency towards simpler funeral customs, possibly due to Merovingian influences;[1] and in Denmark there was no reversal from this. In Norway and Sweden, however, the Viking Age reveals a movement in the opposite direction. Not only the princely dead but men and women throughout the country were provided with both personal possessions and all the familiar objects of daily life, so that farming implements, smiths' tools, kitchen objects and all necessary for spinning and weaving and the work of the house were placed in the grave, and horses and dogs were sacrificed to bear their owners company. It is to this period that the elaborate ship-burials of Gokstad and Oseberg, which will be described later, belong.

The favourite method of interment of either cremation or inhumation burials throughout the Viking Age was the howe, but it was by no means the invariable form of grave; there are a good many examples of stone-formed graves too, and there are also cases of flat graves dug down into the earth with no howe above. In certain localities the timbered chambers, found in East Norway in the Migration period, continued into the Viking Age, with or without a howe; in these the dead seem to have been sometimes placed sitting upright.[2]

Meanwhile cremation continued in Scandinavia until late in the Viking Age. When Iceland was colonised at the end of the ninth century we find no evidence for cremation graves among the early

---

1 Shetelig and Falk, *Scandinavian Archaeology* (trans. Gordon, Oxford, 1937), p. 261 f.
2 Almgren, 'Vikingatidens grafskick i verkligheten och i den fornordiska litteraturen' (*Nordiska Studier til. A. Noreen*, Uppsala, 1904), p. 310 f.

settlers, and we might therefore be tempted to assume that the custom was no longer widespread at the time. But the position varied greatly in different parts of Scandinavia.[1] In Denmark inhumation was practically universal throughout the Viking Age, with the exception of Jylland, where a few cremation graves may be due to settlers from Norway or Sweden. In Gotland inhumation is predominant; in Öland the numbers of cremation and inhumation graves are perhaps equal; in Sweden, however, cremation is in the ascendancy, except for Skåne, and the same may be said for Norway as a whole, although here there are wide local differences. A study of archaeological records from the inland regions there, made by E. S. Engelstad in 1926,[2] shows that in these parts cremation graves were still in the majority in the tenth century, although by this time the number of inhumation graves had increased considerably. In the eleventh century the numbers were nearly equal, with the cremation graves still slightly in the majority. Taking the Viking Age as a whole we find that the number of cremation graves exceeds that of inhumation ones, but the difference is much more marked in the inland districts than in the west coastal region,[3] where inhumation rapidly became popular. There are also differences in orientation; Shetelig, in his survey of the western region, found that most of the skeletons lay with their heads to the north, but in the inland region the usual procedure was to place the bodies facing westward until Christian orientation was adopted in the tenth and eleventh centuries, and there must, as Engelstad points out, be two different cultures involved. Although the western region was the first to be converted to Christianity, many of its inhumation graves are undoubtedly heathen ones, as may be seen from the large numbers facing north, and since it was from this region where cremation was dying out more rapidly that Iceland was mainly colonised, we have a reasonable explanation for the lack of cremation graves there.

Cremation in Norway, then, continued as late as the eleventh century. There is also evidence for it up to the tenth century in Swedish settlements in North Russia,[4] where in certain cemeteries

1 Almgren, *op. cit.* p. 318 f.
2 Engelstad, *Bergens Museums Aarbok*, 1926, p. 40 f.
3 Statistics as follows: in Western Norway, 107 cremation graves to 73 inhumation; in Central Norway 110 cremation graves to 20 inhumation (Engelstad, p. 62).
4 Arne, *La Suède et l'Orient* (Uppsala, 1914), p. 23 f.

the transition from cremation to inhumation can be clearly seen. A record of an elaborate cremation ceremony comes from an Arab traveller who claims to have witnessed it on the Volga in the year 921, in what presumably was a Scandinavian settlement.[1] Evidently the practice of burning the dead went on in the North until Christianity was so firmly established that inhumation once more became the universal custom. The evidence of Norway and Iceland shows that by the ninth century it no longer formed an essential part of the heathen religion, but the position evidently varied in different parts of Scandinavia. Almgren[2] comments on the fact that it is in the more progressive and richer regions of Scandinavia on the whole that inhumation was adopted on the largest scale, and he suggests that this may be due to the influence of Christian countries farther south, felt in Scandinavia in burial customs long before Christianity itself made its way there. The question of identifying Christian graves at the end of the Viking Age is in any case an extremely difficult one, as there seems no doubt that grave-goods continued to be buried with the dead after their conversion to Christianity, as has also been found to be the case in Anglo-Saxon England.[3] Almgren suggests that the flat, stone-lined graves in which the dead were laid in coffins, found at Björkö and elsewhere, may be the first distinctively Christian interments.

From this rapid survey of funeral customs, certain changes in practice stand out clearly, suggesting that new ideas about the after-life and the grave must have reached those who instituted them. The first and the most striking is that from inhumation to burning in the Bronze Age. Was this inspired by the wish to free the spirit of the dead from the clogging prison of the body, or by anxiety to protect the living from the harmful influence of the corpse while it still remained undecayed? Was it, in short, born of love or fear of the dead or of a combination of the two? And did the new practice reflect a new conception, that of another world to which the untrammelled spirit might journey? These are questions which have been long and widely discussed, and practices in many parts of the world have been quoted in support of the various theories; but nothing conclusive has yet been said.[4] The evidence for linking cremation with the burnt

1 See p. 45 below.                    2 Almgren, *op. cit.* p. 319.
3 Lethbridge, *Camb. Antiq. Soc.* (N.S.), III, p. 82.
4 For a summary of recent work on the subject see Almgren, *Nordische Felszeich-nungen als religiöse Urkunden* (Frankfurt, 1934), p. 304 f.

offering on the one hand, and with the cult of the sun god on the other, is perhaps the most suggestive. It is very likely that no one answer alone is sufficient, and that many different influences are involved; we can only be sure that so radical a change adopted with such unanimity throughout Europe must have satisfied the deepest desires and beliefs about the dead held by widely scattered peoples, while at the same time it presupposes close bonds between practice and belief in far separated regions. Archaeology alone can never tell us the meaning of cremation to those who practised it; we shall see later on whether literary evidence can go any further.

At the beginning of the Iron Age there is a further change in funeral ritual to be considered, when the custom came in of preserving the whole residue of the pyre and burying it in the grave without attempting to separate bones from grave-goods.[1] Such a step might imply mere carelessness, but on the other hand it might also mean the very opposite, a more scrupulous care to prevent anything from being overlooked and thrown away, either lest the dead should suffer or lest a slight to them should bring harm to the living. Such meticulous care over the burning of the body is attributed to the Estonians at a much later date by a traveller who visited King Alfred:[2] 'There is a custom among the Estonians,' he says, 'that in every tribe dead men shall be burned; and if a single bone be found unburned there, heavy atonement shall be made for it.'

Whether the reintroduction of inhumation in the Roman period came about through a change of belief seems more doubtful; it may have been part of the wave of Southern fashions due to contact with the ancient world, entering the more easily because cremation no longer represented definite ideas about the after-life. In any case the two practices continued side by side, with wide local differences, as in Norway later on.

The last change to be noticed is one which took place late in the heathen period, during the Viking Age, when the simplicity which had marked funeral rites in the seventh and eighth centuries was suddenly replaced in Norway and Sweden by a new elaboration in the choice of grave-goods for all classes of people. The dead were given as complete an equipment as possible of personal possessions, weapons, tools and household equipment, while animals were sacri-

1 Ebert, II, p. 122 f.
2 Inserted by Alfred in his translation of Orosius. Relevant extracts given in
   A. J. Wyatt, *Anglo-Saxon Reader* (Cambridge, 1925), p. 15.

ficed to accompany them; and in the funerals of the greatest folk, whether men or women, the array of treasures and the sacrifices were on a magnificent scale. It seems probable that human beings were sacrificed as well as animals, but we have no definite proof of this. So sudden and extensive a change, which involved so much trouble and cost, can hardly be explained by anything but a new and strong interest in the after-life, and a desire to provide the dead with everything needful in it. Possibly, as Shetelig suggested,[1] the elaborate funerals of the Christian Merovingian kings filled the heathen rulers of Norway with the desire to emulate them. But we do not find such rich graves in Denmark, and the increase in grave-goods is not restricted to the upper classes, so that the impression gained is that the supply of possessions to the dead had become a necessity in heathen thought. Whether any new ideas could have come from the southeast, by way of trade-routes through Russia, is perhaps a question worth considering. It is noteworthy that in the tenth century we have a ship-funeral described on the Volga whose elaborate ceremonial gives a picture like that suggested by the treasures of the Oseberg ship.

At this point a brief survey of the evidence for human sacrifice may be helpful. It seems to have been known during the Bronze Age; the evidence of two elaborate howe-burials from the late period is at the least highly suggestive. In 'King Björn's Howe' at Uppsala[2] the burnt remains of a man lay in a man-length tree coffin inside a barrow, and outside the coffin were the unburnt bones of at least three other adult persons, one of them certainly a woman. Here as well as the possibility of suttee we have the more gruesome one of cannibalism, for one of the human bones was split lengthwise as though to extract the marrow. The grave-goods enable the date of the interment to be assigned to Period IV of the Bronze Age, although the man-length coffin holding the burnt remains and the richness of the objects are a link with an earlier period. In the second howe, at Seddin in Brandenburg,[3] the grave-goods suggest a similar date, and Period IV-V has been agreed upon. In this case we have the cremated remains of a man in a fine bronze urn contained in an outer one of clay, while two other clay urns held the remains of two women, one between twenty and thirty and one younger. The suggestion of human sacrifice given by these graves is strengthened by

1 *Osebergfundet* (Brøgger, Falk, Shetelig: Christiania, 1917), I, p. 249 f.
2 Ebert, VII, p. 133 f.                    3 *Ibid.* XI, p. 444 f.

a discovery at Vemmerlöv in Sweden,[1] in a peat bog. Two artificial pools, originally enclosed with sharpened stakes, were found to hold the bones of many animals, and human bones of at least four persons were included among them. The fact that only parts of the larger animals were found suggests that the rest was consumed at a sacrificial meal, and if this is true it seems that the same fate overtook the human beings also, for the skeletons were not complete and their bones lay mixed with the rest. Although such a find can hardly be dated accurately, examination of the soil proves it to be earlier than the Iron Age, while the marks of metal weapons on the stakes argues against the Neolithic period; and the fact that Bronze Age rock engravings are found nearby is an additional reason for assigning it to the same period.

The sacrifice of animals on a large scale at the funeral is again found in Sweden at the time of the Vendel graves, for the chieftains there were provided with many domestic animals, horses, dogs, hawks and other birds. Again, in the Viking Age many animals, and particularly horses, were buried with the dead, as the Gokstad and Oseberg ship-burials show. We have, however, no conclusive evidence for human sacrifice. Two women were apparently laid in the Oseberg ship, and it is possible that one of them may have been a servant slain to accompany her mistress, but the disturbed state of the burial makes it absolutely impossible to prove this. There are also a number of graves to be taken into account where the grave-goods suggest a double interment, since in them weapons and tools and characteristically masculine possessions are found mixed with those generally associated with women's graves, weaving implements, ornaments and the like. This might mean that occasionally in the Viking Age a widow was sacrificed at her husband's funeral. Shetelig made a list of all such graves known in 1908,[2] and his results are certainly suggestive; it may be noticed that all his examples are cremation ones, and of Viking Age date, and it has since been pointed out[3] that they are mostly graves of the tenth century. But Scandinavia has no definite evidence to equal that of the Gaulish cemetery of the early Iron Age at Thuizy,[4] where, out of sixty-four graves, twenty-eight contained double interments, with the man and woman

1 Ebert, XIV, p. 112 f.
2 Viking Club Saga Book, VI, 1909, p. 180 f.
3 Engelstad, Bergens Museums Aarbok, III, 1927, p. 60.
4 Déchelette, Manuel d'Archéologie (Paris, 1908–1914), II, p. 1035 f.

placed in a close embrace. The evidence as it stands is however worth taking into account to compare with that of the literature later on.

## THE FUNERAL SHIP

Archaeological records can supply nothing to bridge the gap in time between the ship-graves in Gotland at the beginning of the Iron Age and the graves which contain the buried or burnt remains of ships, for which we have evidence in Scandinavia from about A.D. 500. There is always the possibility that before this ships may have been made without rivets, as indeed is the case with one recovered from a bog,[1] and so could leave no trace when the wood decayed or after being burned; if this were the case, then ship-funeral in the North might go back earlier than our records. On the other hand, Lind-qvist[2] has made the disquieting suggestion that the rivets found in the early graves are not necessarily from ships at all, and are more likely to come from great chests burned or buried with the dead. He will accept no example of ship-funeral as definite before that of the earliest of the Vendel graves, which he dates at about A.D. 600.

The graves at Vendel[3] certainly offer a striking example of ship-funeral. Two out of the fourteen graves excavated were in too poor a condition for anything definite to be said, but in all except one of the others the contents were certainly placed within a ship. The lack of actual human remains is rather disappointing; in many cases these were completely missing, possibly because the grave had been plundered, while other graves contained only a few fragments of human bones. The only graves which held anything approaching a skeleton were number IX, thought to be of tenth-century date, where the remains of a man sitting upright on a chair were found, and one of the earliest of the graves, number XIV, where enough remained to show that the chieftain was again seated in full war-gear in the stern of the ship with his horse beside him. This is the grave which Lindqvist believes to be the oldest of all, and dates at 600 or a little earlier. Although the human remains are scanty, the graves held a large number of animal bones. Usually domestic animals—sheep, cattle, pigs—were found, some lying in the ship and some out; and there were a great many skeletons of horses, especially in the early

---

1 *Nordiske Fortidsminder*, III, 1, 1937, p. 72 f. ('Hjortspringfundet').
2 Lindqvist, *Fornvännen*, 1921, p. 106 f.
3 Stolpe and Arne, *La Nécropole de Vendel* (Stockholm, 1927), p. 8 f.

graves, where a number were sometimes found in a row on the starboard side with their heads towards the prow. There were a number of dogs too, large and small, a few hawks, and at least one duck and one goose. The warriors seem to have been provided with all their weapons, and in the forepart of the ship there were cauldrons, cooking utensils and so on. In grave XIV the dead man had evidently been deliberately supplied with food, for instead of the usual whole skeletons of animals the remains of a joint, a ham and a sheep's head were found.

There were again remains of animals in the cremation graves of the kings at Uppsala, although Lindqvist contends,[1] on account of the size and shape of the rivets found, that no ship could have been burned there. The dead whose ashes rest in these graves appear to have been burned in a rude hut or burial chamber, whose supporting posts left clear traces when they burned to the ground. Lindqvist points out that there is a striking resemblance between this and the custom of setting up burial chambers on ships buried in the earth, as was done in the case of the three great ships of the Viking Age excavated in Norway.

These three ships, from Oseberg, Gokstad and Tuna, mark the culmination of the practice of ship-burial, and fortunately the nature of the soil and the fact that they were discovered at a late enough date to allow them to be scientifically moved and restored has preserved them for us with some of their contents. All three had been plundered, but enough of the grave-goods of the Oseberg and Gokstad ships remain to give an idea of the richness and elaborate ceremonial of the funeral. On each ship a burial chamber was set up, built roughly of timber, before the ship and its contents were covered with a large burial mound.

In the Oseberg ship[2] a great wealth of grave-goods remained, although the most valuable treasures and in particular the jewels and personal adornments of the woman buried there must have been removed by the robbers. The burial chamber had suffered most from their attentions, but some of its contents remained. There was a chest containing wild apples and corn and another full of small articles like iron clamps, combs and so on; the scattered remains of one or possibly two beds, with a quantity of soft material which very likely formed bed-coverings or hangings for the wall; four carved posts in

1 Lindqvist, *Fornvännen*, 1921, pp. 106 f., 187 f.
2 *Osebergfundet* (Brøgger, Falk, Shetelig: Christiania, 1917), I, p. 17 f.

the shape of animal heads, of beautiful and intricate workmanship; a number of buckets, one holding wild apples; and a stool and equipment for weaving. The after-part of the ship was fitted up like a kitchen and well equipped with cooking utensils, a grindstone and the like. In the fore-part there were various objects belonging to the ship, such as a gangway, tubs and balers, and also an exquisite little wagon, with a bed laid on top, and four sledges. The wagon must from its position have been one of the first objects to be brought on to the ship, and since this and three of the sledges were of delicate and elaborate workmanship they were probably intended for ceremonial use only, and employed in the funeral procession when the bodies were brought on board. The remains of many animals were found in the ship; the body of an ox lay in the after-part, four dogs in the fore-ship, and beside the last a heap of horse skeletons, showing that at least ten animals must have been slain there. The heads of the horses and dogs had all been severed from their bodies, while the head of the ox was found, oddly enough, resting on the great bed in the fore-ship.

The ship was moored within the mound by a great stone, and a number of other stones had been thrown into her and around her before she was covered with earth. Yet in contrast to this, some of the oars had been placed in position, though others again lay to the east of the grave chamber and were not quite completed. The problem of who the dead woman was for whom this magnificent setting was prepared remains unsolved. The bones in the grave chamber had been ruthlessly scattered by the robbers.[1] Apparently two women had been laid there; one, whose skeleton was complete except for certain bones of the right hand and left arm, was a woman of between forty and fifty years of age. Of the other, few bones remained; parts of the skull suggest a younger woman of between twenty-five and thirty. The missing bones from the hand and arm of the one woman might well be accounted for by the fact that the robbers had carried them away along with the rings and bracelets which enriched them, but whether the other was so richly adorned that practically the whole body was taken is a question to which there seems little likelihood of finding an answer. Nor is it possible to say whether either of the two was a servant attending on her mistress, or whether this was a double burial of two members of the same family. No recognisable traces of clothes were found, except

1 *Osebergfundet*, I, p. 147 f.

the sole of a shoe which the robbers may have dropped, a further pair of shoes in the grave chamber, and a sandal in the fore-part. In the Gokstad ship [1] no rich articles remained, except one sledge which may have been used at the funeral. There were a number of wooden fittings belonging to the ship, including a finely carved tiller, some kitchen vessels, a large copper cauldron, the remains of what seems to be a gaming board, and a few bronze buckles and ornaments from the clothes of the dead man. Remains of the skeleton indicate that the burial was that of a man of at least fifty years of age and possibly older, who had suffered from chronic rheumatism which must have made him practically a cripple at the time of death, and it has been suggested that he might be identified with Olaf of Geirstaðr, the king of Vestfold who died of 'leg-pains' (*fótverkr*) about 840.[2] At least twelve horses and a number of dogs had been killed at the funeral, and were placed in the mound outside the ship, but the remains of a peacock were discovered inside. An interesting feature about this burial is that apparently deliberate damage had been done to some of the objects placed in the ship, such as cannot be attributed to the pillagers of the burial chamber. In particular the sledge had been broken into fragments, and these scattered about the ship.

Of the third ship-burial, from Tuna,[3] excavated as early as 1867, very little was preserved. The ship contained a cremation burial, and a horse seems to have been laid inside the grave chamber. It is thought from the report of these finds that the burial was that of a man, but practically nothing has survived. The grave had been robbed like the other two.

The use of the burial chamber in these three ships, in which, as we know from the Oseberg ship, beds might be set up for the dead to rest on, contrasts with the Vendel graves, in which the practice seems to have been to set the dead warrior upright in the stern; so indeed does the practice of burying women in this way at all. The fact that the Oseberg ship was not an isolated case, however, is suggested by finds from Tuna, in the district of Alsike,[4] where a number of boat-graves from the Viking Age or a little earlier were excavated, and found to resemble in many ways the cemetery at Vendel, and the

1 N. Nicolaysen, *Langskibet fra Gokstad* (Christiania, 1882).
2 *Ibid.* p. 70.
3 Montelius, 'Högsättning i skepp under Vikingatiden', *Svensk fornminnesforen. tidskrift*, VI.
4 Stolpe, 'Tuna-fyndet', *Ymer*, 1895, p. 219 f.

remains of women were found among them; unfortunately the state of the graves was very poor indeed, and the earth had been much disturbed, so that details about the individual graves are uncertain. As far as could be ascertained, the dead lay or sat in their ships as in the Vendel graves.

Lindqvist is anxious to establish a connection between the burial chamber in the three big ship-burials discussed above and the rough chambers supported on wooden posts in which the dead seem to have been burned at the graves at Old Uppsala. Apart from this feature, however, the personal possessions round the body, the kitchen utensils in the after-part of the ship, and the number of animals slain—some inside the ship and others out—are characteristic also of the Vendel and Tuna graves, though the beheading of the animals appears to be a new practice.

Besides Scandinavia proper, in which as long ago as 1906 Shetelig [1] reckoned in four figures the number of graves containing ships, there is evidence for the same practice in lands colonised from Norway and Sweden in the Viking Age. Burnt vessels are found in graves in Finland from the seventh century; [2] they have been recorded from Swedish settlements in North Russia, [3] and several funeral ships have been found in Iceland, although none of these graves is on such an elaborate scale as those which have previously been described. Strangely enough there has been little evidence for ship-funeral from Denmark, although in 1935 a rich burial in a ship was excavated at Ladby on the Isle of Fyen near Odense. [4] Certain features recall the great Norwegian burials, for the ship held the skeletons of eleven horses and some dogs with their trappings. The body was missing, and some of the richest and most interesting grave-goods had probably been removed, but a piece of bronze coupling for leashing the dogs was decorated in the Jellinge style of ornament which flourished in the early tenth century. In Brittany a large barrow containing the grave of a chief burned in his ship was excavated about 1909, [5] and proved to hold a large number of grave-goods and some animal bones; it is thought from the human remains—in poor condition—that it may have held two persons. A smaller ship-burial, which

1 Shetelig, *Viking Club Saga Book*, iv, 1906, p. 326 f.
2 Hackman, *Om likbränning i båtar....i Finland* (Finskt Museum, 1897).
3 Arne, *La Suède et l'Orient* (Uppsala, 1914), pp. 32-33.
4 E. M. Hardy, *Mariner's Mirror*, xxv, 2, April 1939 (Review of original report).
5 Chatellier and Pontois, *Viking Club Saga Book*, vi, 1909, p. 123 f.

contained the remains of a horse, was found in the Isle of Man in 1928.[1] On the whole however the Viking settlements in the British Isles have produced disappointingly little evidence for ship-funeral, and only a small number of graves in the Hebrides and the Orkneys contain rivets which indicate that ships were burned or buried there.[2]

Examples of ship-funeral from an earlier period have however been found in South-East England. The first discovery was that of a ship buried in a tumulus at Snape Common, near Aldeburgh.[3] When a group of barrows was excavated here in 1862, the remains of a clinker-built boat about 48 ft. long was found in the undisturbed soil under the largest barrow. Nothing more was found inside, unfortunately, than two masses of what was thought to be human hair, fragments of a green glass goblet of early Anglo-Saxon style, and a gold ring of the late Roman period. The glass and the ring made an early date in the Anglo-Saxon period probable, and the burial was therefore thought to be of sixth-century or even fifth-century date. This made it stand absolutely alone, since no other ship-burial was recorded in the British Isles before the Viking Age. However in the summer of 1939 this early dating was to a large extent confirmed by the spectacular discovery made at Sutton Hoo, near Woodbridge in Suffolk. A number of mounds stand on a high piece of ground above the river Deben, and in 1938 two of the smaller ones were excavated, when it was found that one contained traces of a boat 18 to 20 ft. long, with a rounded stern. Only a few gold fragments were left inside, and evidently the goods had been removed. The second mound held cremated remains, with associated objects suggesting a sixth- or seventh-century date, but insufficient to allow definite conclusions to be drawn. The third and largest of the group of mounds was opened in the summer of the following year, and this revealed a truly astonishing find, an Anglo-Saxon ship-burial on a royal scale.[4] The vessel in the mound had been dragged up from the river some half mile away and lowered into its resting-place from above, like a coffin; although the wood had rotted away, the outline could be clearly seen, and was that of a clinker-built boat, for thirty-eight rowers, with a length of 85 ft. A burial chamber had been placed amidships, built quite roughly of oak boards and with a gable-ended roof probably ridged with turf. An attempt made to

1 Kermode, *Journal of Society of Antiquaries*, 1930, p. 126 f.    2 *Ibid.* p. 133.
3 Smith, *Victoria County History of Suffolk*, p. 325.
4 *Antiquity*, March 1940, 'The Sutton Hoo Ship-burial'.

rob the barrow had providentially failed owing to the depth at which the ship was buried, and the only damage to the contents was that caused by the fall of the roof of the burial chamber many years after the burial, when the weight of the sand above was too much for it. Thus we have an almost unique opportunity to examine a ship-burial on a grand scale, in fairly good condition, and undisturbed by human agency from the day when it was laid in the earth.

The grave-goods were found lying on the floor of the chamber, though possibly some may have been hanging on the wall before it collapsed. There were a great number of very varied objects. Some seemed as though they must have formed part of the ceremonial regalia of a king; there was, for example, the boss of a mighty shield, too huge for normal use; a vast iron object decorated with bulls' heads, which may have been a portable flambeau intended to be stuck in the ground or else a symbolic structure to be borne before the king; and a great whetstone with each end decorated with strange human heads, beautifully carved in low relief. There were also weapons: a sword in its sheath, a magnificent helmet with a bronze face-piece and enriched with gold and silver, an iron-bladed weapon of some kind, an iron axe, and a number of other axes, angons and socketed spear-heads thrust through the handle of a bronze bowl. There was also some chain mail, in very bad condition. Among the other treasures there were a set of nine silver bowls, seven of them excellently preserved; two silver spoons and a number of horns with silver mounts, crushed beyond restoration but still recognisable; a great dish of silver of Byzantine workmanship, with a smaller one beneath it; six bottles made from gourds; a silver dipper and small bowl; and two bronze hanging bowls, perhaps fallen from the roof. There was also a wooden tub, and three bronze cauldrons and iron tackle to support them. Finally, there were what might be called personal possessions: a small musical instrument, a mysterious little tray of fine wood decorated with garnets, two rich gold clasps in cloisonné work which might have been intended for the shoulders of a cuirass, the gold frame of a purse, two buckles, some gold plaques, a strap-end, and other small objects of a similar kind. All these ornaments, except for the largest buckle, lay in a position which suggested that they had been hung up on the walls. A large leather bag with a silver handle and another smaller one were found among a mass of remains of textiles and leather, and finally there were forty Merovingian gold coins which had fallen out of the purse.

The most important of the grave-goods and all the personal equipment were placed at the west end of the burial chamber. At the east end were the cauldrons and various household vessels, while objects like the dishes and the horns lay between the two. The body might have been expected to lie at the west end of the chamber, but absolutely no trace of human remains of any kind were discovered, and there were no signs of burned bones or of any vessel that could have held cremated remains; nor did the position of the buckles, helmet and so on give the impression that they might have been placed on a dead man. It is not the first time that a grave has been found mysteriously empty; a number of the Vendel graves contained no human remains, and none were found in the Danish ship-burial at Fyen or in the ship excavated at Snape Common.[1] However, in these cases either the grave had been entered by robbers or else was in such a poor condition that no definite conclusions could be reached as to whether the body had been there or not. The grave at Sutton Hoo, however, had never been entered from the time when it was closed at the funeral, and the archaeologists who examined it are confident that human remains could not have disappeared without leaving some trace. It has been suggested that the mound may have been erected as a cenotaph, in memory of a king who was lost at sea; and perhaps in view of the other graves left mysteriously without an occupant there may be more Scandinavian examples of the same practice than have been previously recognised. Certainly one definite example is recorded from the Farmanns barrow in Norway, probably erected as a monument for one or more members of the Vestfold royal family to which King Harald the Fair-haired belonged. Brøgger, in his account of the grave, mentions other examples of howes in Scandinavia in which no human remains have been found.[2] Among the graves from the Christian period excavated in the Viking settlement in Greenland one was found to contain a stick carved in runes, which appears to have been buried to represent the dead person, whose body had been lost at sea.[3]

Mr Phillips has pointed out that another example of an elaborate burial from Saxon times, the Broomfield grave, seems from the records to have been empty of human remains, since the carbon and

1 It is likely that the mass thought to be human hair may have been animal fur of some kind (Phillips, *Antiquity, op. cit.* p. 6).
2 A. V. Brøgger, *A.f.n.O.* 1921, p. 117 f.
3 P. Norlund, *Viking Settlers in Greenland* (Cambridge, 1936), p. 51 f.

soot then thought to indicate a possible cremation are more likely to be traces of decayed woodwork. Another very puzzling feature of the Sutton Hoo burial was the basin of rough clay which seems to have been placed above the roof of the burial chamber, and which it is suggested may have been intended for libations.

The evidence of the finds dates the grave in the early part of the seventh century. The numismatists are disposed from the evidence of the coins to select a date about the middle of the century, or at any rate after 630. But such late dating is most improbable, since we know that by 640 Christianity was well established in East Anglia, and a burial such as this would necessitate a reversion to heathen customs for which we have no evidence. If a date between 600 and 640 is accepted, it seems probable that the cenotaph, if cenotaph it is, is that of Redwald, who ruled East Anglia from about 593 to 617, and was the only one of its kings to hold the title of High King of Britain, which belonged to him for some years before he died. This is Chadwick's suggestion,[1] supported by Bede's picture of the king as a man who never wholly gave up his heathen beliefs, and by the probability that Rendlesham, only four miles from this group of barrows, was Redwald's palace. It seems likely that a king with well-known tendencies towards the old faith, and who moreover was survived by a wife who supported it with enthusiasm, was the person in whose honour the barrow was raised; and this is rendered more probable by the fact that at the end of his reign he must have been the richest king in England.[2]

The barrows at Sutton Hoo, two of which have proved to be ship-graves, evidently formed part of a cemetery which goes back into the heathen period, and of which the chief grave has remained, miraculously, untouched. Excavation of the remaining barrows may throw more light on the date of the treasure. But we have undoubtedly here an example of an elaborate ship-burial in Anglo-Saxon times in the kingdom of East Anglia, corresponding in date with that of the Vendel graves in Sweden. Here, moreover, the erection of a burial chamber above the ship provides a parallel to the later ship-graves of the Viking period, and probably too with the burial chamber of which traces have been left in the Uppsala grave-mounds. The barrows at Snape, where the other ship-burial was found, indicate a second cemetery a little farther along the East Anglian coast; if the earlier date suggested for this burial is correct,

1 Chadwick, *Antiquity, op. cit.* p. 76 f.
2 Bede, *Historia Ecclesiastica* (ed. Plummer, vol. 1), II, 5; III, 22; II, 15.

we have ship-funeral in the British Isles as early as any recorded up to the present in Scandinavia. Shetelig's emphasis on the close cultural link between England and Scandinavia is confirmed by the treasure of Sutton Hoo, and the resemblance between it and the objects from the Vendel graves will probably become increasingly clear when the finds have been restored and examined further.

Our evidence for ship-funeral then may be briefly summed up as follows: We find in the North graves made in the shape of ships at the beginning of the Iron Age; then a long gap while cremation graves and later inhumation graves after the Roman fashion were the rule; and then, by the seventh century for certain and possibly in both cremation and inhumation graves for a century or more earlier, ship-funeral on an elaborate scale practised in Scandinavia and Anglo-Saxon England. This wide gap in time is puzzling, and even more so is the isolation of the ship-form graves in Gotland and the other side of the Baltic in the early Iron Age. Their isolation is not however so complete if we turn from grave forms alone to the ship as a symbol, and to what we know of religion in the Bronze Age in Northern Europe.

Our knowledge of it is based mainly on the pictures and symbols left by its people on the great walls of rock in the mountainous districts of Scandinavia. These drawings are not naturalistic sketches of animals and hunting scenes like those from the caves of the Paleolithic period, but consist of symbolic figures and groups, recurring many times both on the same rock face and in widely separated regions, depicted geometrically and conventionally though often they are spirited and graphic enough. The favourite figures employed are wheels, soles of feet, snakes, ploughs, axes and ships, while human figures are combined with all these to form processions, marriage groups and battle-scenes, or else are shown dancing, leaping, riding or fighting. There has been much discussion as to the purpose of these figures on the rocks. It is now generally accepted that their significance is a religious and ritual one, and convincing arguments have been put forward by Almgren[1] to the effect that they depict actual ceremonies, supported by evidence from art and ritual in other parts of the world and periods of civilisation. Traces of ritual fires and slain animals found near the rock-engravings in Sweden help to confirm this. It seems clear that the pictures are based on a fertility religion connected with the worship of the sun, and possibly including, as Almgren believes, the conception of rebirth; such ideas, arising in the East, can be seen fully developed in the art and religion

1 Almgren, *Nordische Felszeichnungen als religiöse Urkunden* (Frankfurt, 1934).

of Egypt, and seem to have travelled northward to reach Scandinavia during the Bronze Age. In this ritual the ship evidently played an important part, for it is shown continually, sometimes together with wheels and sun-discs, trees, snakes, horned animals, or men dancing, leaping or worshipping; the human figures are sometimes in the ship itself, sometimes forming a group with it, and occasionally seem to be carrying it in their hands.

Certain of the symbols found on the rock, and the ship among them, are found also on the walls of tombs, on gravestones, and in the neighbourhood of graves; and the ship and the axe in particular are found in Central Europe confined to graves alone. There has been much controversy as to whether an early cult of the dead, connected with sun-worship and with beliefs about fertility, developed until it became primarily a religion of the living away from the grave; or whether the earliest cult was one of fertility and sun-worship and later came to include beliefs and practices connected with the dead, passing on from the principle of rebirth in the world of nature to that of man after death. Almgren[1] supports the second view; he admits that the close connection of certain symbols with graves is evidence in the other direction, but proves on the other hand that rock-engravings in Sweden are not, as some have claimed, found only in the neighbourhood of burial places. The evidence is insufficient for definite conclusions to be established, but certainly the development of sun-worship in Egypt, where fuller records of it have been left than anywhere else in the world, is a good argument on Almgren's side.

All that we can learn of Bronze Age ritual and religion is likely to be important for our better understanding of ship-funeral; first because the ship symbol played so important a part in it, and moreover in Central Europe is confined to graves alone; and secondly because in Gotland there are rock-engravings near the ship-form graves, which may go some way to explain their mysterious origin there. No doubt there is also a link with the boat-offerings recovered from bogs, dating from the Iron Age, and recorded by Caesar as thank-offerings for victory.[2] If we knew definitely what was the significance

---

1 *Op. cit.* p. 280 f.
2 *Ibid.* p. 64; Caesar, *De Bello Gallico*, vi, 17. An example of such a sacrifice is the discovery at Hjortspring (*Nordiske Fortidsminder*, iii, 1, 1937), dated between the fourth and second centuries b.c. Many animal bones and weapons were found lying about a large ship, clearly an offering of some kind.

of the ship in the rock-engravings, we should then be more than
halfway towards understanding the meaning of the funeral ship.
Was it originally the ship of the sun-god, moving across the heavens,
as in Egypt? And was it afterwards believed that the dead might
travel with the god into another life? Or was it merely a symbol
of the sun, and therefore of fertility and rebirth, without any conception of a journey made by the dead within it?

The problem of whether the ship in the grave is based on any real
belief in a voyage of the dead is one of the most tantalising of all those
presented by Scandinavian funeral customs. There is so much evidence for ship-funeral, and yet nothing that gives us a direct answer.
Two other customs found for the most part outside Scandinavia may
have a connection with this problem; these are the practice of laying
coins in the mouth of the dead, and that of burying wagons in the
grave with them. The first was frequent at the time of the Roman
Empire, and was taken up by the Teutonic peoples in many parts of
Germany. Stjerna[1] laid great emphasis on this, and argued that the
custom taken from the Greeks of providing the dead with fares for
Charon developed in the North into the more elaborate practice of
giving boats to the dead that they might make the journey independently to the other shore. This of course does not take into account
the interest in the ship symbol before the Iron Age. On this point the
arguments put forward by Ebert[2] are very relevant. He claims that
by the time the Germans could have come into contact with the
Greeks there would no longer be any vital belief in Charon and his
boat to be passed on, since such naive ideas about the next world had
been replaced by Asiatic mystery cults and their teaching. Either the
coins laid in the mouth of the dead were nothing more than a fashion
imitated from the South, or they had some different meaning and
might, as Almgren suggests, be intended either as symbols of the
possessions of the dead or as protective amulets for them. The other
practice is more likely to be significant. Wagons were buried with
the dead in Scythian, Thracian and Celtic graves, and probably, like
that in the Oseberg ship, were those used to carry the body to the
tomb. But when war-chariots came to be buried in graves of the La
Tène period among the Celts we seem to be faced with a different
conception, that of providing the dead with what he will need in the

1 Stjerna, *Essays on Beowulf* (Viking Club, Coventry, 1912), p. 101 f.
2 Ebert, 'Die Bootfahrt ins Jenseits', *Praehist. Zeit.* 1919, XI–XII, p. 179 f.

next world. And when we find a gravestone depicting the dead in a chariot leaving the earth, then Ebert claims that we have a new idea coming in, that of the chariot as a means of reaching another world. Wagons are first found in Northern graves in the transition period between the Bronze and Iron Ages, that is at the same time as the ship-form graves first appear in Gotland. It seems possible then that at this period the conception of a death journey may have entered the North, and that the wagon and chariot used by an inland people were naturally replaced by the boat and ship among a people to whom travel meant primarily a journey by sea. This is Almgren's opinion; [1] Ebert is inclined to think that we find traces of the idea earlier still in the coffins of wood, formed from the hollowed-out trunk of a tree, in which the dead were laid in the middle Bronze Age; these were introduced independently of the practice of cremation and at about the same time as the rock-engravings begin, so that there may be a connection between the two.

But even if we decide that the conception of a journey made by the dead came in some time during the Bronze Age from the south of Europe, this does not necessarily mean that the ship-funerals which began in the sixth and seventh centuries were inspired by the same belief. The orientation of the graves rather suggests, it is true, that the second introduction of the ship was not unconnected with the first, [2] for, just as in the Gotland graves the dead lie with head to the north and feet to the south, so the same is true of the earliest of the Norwegian boat-graves. But the gap in time is enormous, and the evidence for the conception of a journey to another world behind the Northern boat graves of the Migration period and the Viking Age is hard to establish. Lindqvist [3] believes that the introduction of the ship in the grave arose out of the desire to provide the dead with as complete an equipment as possible, influenced partly by the example of Merovingian funeral rites on the continent. He instances the stones weighing down the Oseberg ship in its mound, and the mooring of it to the great stone with a rope. The burial chamber is another argument against any belief in a journey taken by the dead; we have a good many examples of it in Scandinavia, and in one grave from Karmø in Norway the timbered grave chamber was not even in the ship, but had its roof resting on two parallel stone walls built outside it. On the other hand, it is well to remember that

1 Almgren, *op. cit.* p. 195.                    2 *Ibid.* p. 201.
3 Lindqvist, *Fornvännen*, 1921, p. 175 f.

some of the oars in the Oseberg ship were laid in position as though waiting for the rowers.

It may prove misleading to concentrate too much on the most elaborate graves; it is the amazing popularity of the custom among all sections of the people that is perhaps the most impressive feature, and this can hardly be explained by changing fashions at court. Moreover Ebert's survey of the evidence for ship-funeral brought him to a different conclusion from that of Lindqvist.[1] The ships and the gravestones with ships depicted on them which precede the burials in Scandinavia, and the incomplete models of ships and ship-forms in stone which seem to mark the decadence of the custom late in the Viking Age, give the impression that a clear development can be traced,[2] and that the symbolism of the ship in the graves of the late heathen period was something more important than the mere desire to give the dead all that he had enjoyed in life for his sojourn in the grave.

But although our knowledge of religion in the Bronze Age in the North is confined to the inarticulate carvings on the rocks and to grave-goods buried in the earth, the late heathen period has left other records to which we may turn. Before attempting to draw any conclusions from the archaeological evidence regarding the dead, we must see what ideas concerning them are left in the literature of the North which preserves memories of heathen times.

1 Ebert, *Praehist. Zeit., op. cit.*
2 Almgren, 'Vikingatidens grafskick...' (*Nordiska Studier til. A. Noreen*, Uppsala, 1904), p. 317, quotes an interesting example of transition: the shape of a boat formed by upright stone slabs inside a howe, containing burned bones, weapons, and rivets, the last presumably from a burned boat, in a grave at Ølbǿr near Stavanger.

# Chapter II

## FUNERAL CUSTOMS: THE EVIDENCE
## OF LITERATURE

> Him will I
> Bury. So doing, nobly shall I die,
> Beloved shall I repose with him I love
> Having wrought a holy crime; since I must please
> The dead below far longer than the living,
> For there shall I dwell alway.
>
> SOPHOCLES, *Antigone* (Trevelyan's translation).

### CREMATION AND INHUMATION

Already in the thirteenth century Snorri Sturlason had considered the problem of the relationship between funeral practice and the belief in the after-life. He gives us some of his conclusions in the often quoted prologue of the *Ynglinga Saga:*

> The first age is called the Age of Burning; all dead men then had to be burned, and memorial stones were put up to them. But after Freyr had been laid in a howe at Uppsala, many chiefs raised howes as often as memorial stones in memory of their kinsmen. And after Dan the Proud, the Danish king, had a howe built for himself, and commanded that he should be carried there after death in his king's apparel with war-gear and horse and saddle-trappings and much wealth besides, then afterwards many of his descendants did likewise and the Age of Howes began there in Denmark; although among the Swedes and Norsemen the Age of Burning continued for a long time after.

Snorri's account makes an apt enough preface to the archaeological evidence, with the transition from burning to howe-burial, and the acceptance of inhumation in Denmark while cremation went on in Norway and Sweden. He can hardly be referring however to the change in practice which came in in the Roman period, a thousand years earlier; while the allusion to Freyr shows that he is here concerned with a change which first affected Sweden. The context may afford us some help here, for this paragraph does not occur in the midst of a dissertation on funeral customs, but in a brief account of the sources which he used for the history of the kings of Norway.

Some of these sources he mentions explicitly: Þjóðólfr's poem *Ynglingatal*, an account of the ancestors of King Rögnvaldr, and the similar work *Háleygjatal* composed by Eyvindr for Jarl Hákon; the work of the court poets of Harald Hárfagr and his successors; and the prose work of the Icelander Ari the Wise. Besides these, he tells us, he has relied also on the tales of wise men well versed in the past, and on genealogies which have been taught to him. It is in the midst of this account that the remarks about funeral practice occur. Now from what we possess of the *Ynglingatal* and the *Háleygjatal* we know that the chief interest of the poets is apparently the manner of death and the place of burial of the kings, so that Snorri is presumably pausing to sum up what he has learned of the burial customs of the past from these and other sources, including those from which he later takes the account of the first kings of the Swedes. He does not, however, mention Dan the Proud again, and evidently learned about him from some source not relevant for his history, perhaps from the oral traditions which he mentions at the opening of his preface.

Lindqvist[1] is of the opinion that the tradition about Dan is a genuine one, founded on actual practice in a certain part of Denmark. The description given by Snorri answers to that of a number of graves excavated in Fyen and Jylland, where cremation graves are found to be replaced about the year 800 by howe-burial; within the howes the dead are laid in grave chambers with their equipment and sometimes with their horses accompanying them, in the way described by Snorri. Probably these graves were modelled on that of Charles the Great, who like King Dan had his grave prepared according to his plan before he died, and was placed in it with all his regalia, sitting on a throne. If Snorri knew of this change of practice from Danish sources—and the fact that a similar passage about Dan is found in the *Skjöldunga Saga* is significant—he may well be inserting it here to compare with the parallel change from burning to burial in a howe which he found in the traditions about the early Swedish kings.

Danish sources are certainly of importance in the *Ynglinga Saga*, but in the first ten chapters, before Snorri proceeds to the material supplied by Þjóðólfr's poem, the centre of interest is neither Denmark nor Norway, but Sweden. The saga begins by placing 'Sweden the Great'—that is, Sweden itself and the Swedish settlements in Russia —in the middle of the known world, and in the story of Othin and

1 Lindqvist, *Fornvännen*, 1920, p. 56 f.

the religion which he established in the North the chief setting throughout is Sweden. There, at *fornu Sigtúnir*, Othin after his wanderings through Asia, Russia, Germany and Denmark finally settled; and the very choice of the name *fornu* instead of merely *Sigtúnir* implies, as Lindqvist points out,[1] a Swedish source and a fairly late one. Moreover the practices which he describes as characteristic of the followers of Othin are such as seem, from archaeological records, to belong to South-East Sweden in particular. We are told that Othin taught his followers to burn their dead, promising that

every man should enter Valhöll with as much wealth as he had on his pyre, and should also enjoy everything which he himself had buried in the earth; and the ashes should be borne out to sea or buried in the earth; but over men of renown a howe should be raised as memorial, and over all men who acquitted themselves manfully memorial stones should be raised; and this continued for a long time afterwards.

The practice of burying treasure was known in Scandinavia in the Migration period, but was nowhere as popular as in South-East Sweden; this is confirmed by the fact that later on, although Anglo-Saxon money must have been just as plentiful farther west, it is only in this region that hoards of it are found, together with quantities of Arabic coins and all kinds of silver. It is in Uppland too that we find the largest number of memorial stones, and these sometimes in sets of two or three, bearing out the use of the plural in Snorri's description.[2]

Evidently then it is to Sweden that we must look for the source of the traditions about Othin and cremation and Othin and magic; about the second there will be much to say later, and it is perhaps significant that the two are here introduced side by side as new institutions which came into Sweden with the worship of the god. This Swedish Othin, unlike the leader of the gods who perished at Ragnarrökr, dies in his bed; he is marked with a spear-point before death, since by means of weapons only can entry be gained into the world of the gods; and he is burned on a funeral pyre, in accordance with his teaching:

The burning was carried out in very splendid wise. It was then believed that the higher the smoke rose in the air, the loftier would his position be in heaven whose burning it was; and the more possessions were burned with him, the richer he would be (*Ynglinga Saga*, ix).

1 Lindqvist, *op. cit.* p. 104.    2 *Ibid.* p. 76 f.

Othin's successor Njörðr was also burned, but Freyr, who ruled after him, was laid in howe when he died, and sacrifices were made to him while he lay there so that good seasons might continue in Sweden. For the kings who follow Freyr, Snorri is content for the most part to adopt the version of their deaths given by Þjóðólfr, adding a story, usually of a fantastic nature, to explain the verse. Sometimes, as in the case of Fjölnir and Sveigðir, we are told the manner of their deaths but not of their funerals. Of those of whom information is given, Vanlandi, Dómarr and Agni are definitely said to have been burned after death, in each case on the bank of a river; while Vísburr, Eysteinn and Ingjaldr are said to have been burned in their halls, the first by his sons and the other two by enemies. Snorri himself does not look on this as cremation, but after a detailed examination of the poetic diction of Þjóðólfr Lindqvist[1] is convinced that the original tradition recorded a funeral ceremony at which the kings were burned, and borne away by the fire or by a Valkyrie to Othin. He holds that the original account has been misunderstood, partly by Þjóðólfr himself, working from a Swedish source, and still more by Snorri, who has cheerfully added to the confusion by concocting stories to explain the poem's obscurities. If he is correct, we have six kings out of the list cremated. In any case, whether we accept this or not, it is certainly significant that both Snorri and Þjóðólfr before him associate cremation of the dead with Swedish and not Norwegian kings. From little details which Snorri adds independently about the locality of the graves of a number of kings it seems likely that he had some additional information from a Swedish source, perhaps the same which furnished him with the account of the coming of Othin. As to the significance of ship-funeral Snorri is completely silent. He only tells us, in one of the passages where he is using material outside the poems, how Haki went to his death in a blazing ship (*Ynglinga Saga*, XXIII).

Outside the *Ynglinga Saga* Snorri gives us a detailed description of a cremation in a mythological setting, when he describes the funeral of Balder in the *Prose Edda*. There is also reference to the practice as an established one after battle in the work of the Danish historian, Saxo Grammaticus; there is an account of death in a blazing ship in

---

1 Lindqvist, *Fornvännen*, 1921, p. 138 f. Noreen (*Mytiska Beståndsdelar i Ynglingatal*, Uppsala, 1892, p. 211 f.) had previously made the suggestion that Vanlandi is to be identified with Vísburr and that the poem should be read as the description of a dead king burned in his ship.

the Latin version of the lost *Skjöldunga Saga*; there are elaborate descriptions of cremation ceremonies in the Edda poems in connection with the funerals of Sigurðr and Brynhildr; and there are casual references to cremation as the accepted custom in the *Hávamál*. These passages are important, and will be examined later because of the evidence for ship-funeral or human sacrifice which most of them contain.

The Norwegian kings in Þjóðólfr's poem are said to be laid in howe. Certainly this custom had made the deepest impression on Old Norse literature, for except for the *Ynglinga Saga* the prose sagas as a whole assume that inhumation is the only method of disposing of the dead and that burial in a howe is the normal practice in pre-Christian times. The memory of cremation seems to linger in them solely as a method of disposing of bodies which will not lie quiet after death, or of someone so troublesome in life that destruction by fire at the funeral seems the only means to prevent the corpse from 'walking' out of its grave-mound. The ceremony of the laying of the dead in howe is often described in the *Íslendinga Sögur*. The dead man or woman is usually provided with grave-goods, and sometimes a man's horse may be killed to bear him company, while sometimes he may be laid in his ship inside the howe. It is the recognised duty of kinsmen and friends to lay the dead man in his grave and to be present at the closing of the howe, and after it is closed they usually return home for the funeral feast, though this may be postponed for a long while after the burial. Occasionally a flat grave instead of a howe is said to be made at the place of death or near the house of the dead man; and a few people, particularly criminals or those who have met with a violent end, are buried under cairns of stones.[1]

If no wealth is buried with the dead, the occasion is represented as an exceptional one. In *Egils Saga* (LVIII) Skallagrímr is laid in howe together with his horse, weapons and smith's tools, and the fact that he received no wealth in addition is noted. The reason for this is clear, because the mercenary disposition of his son Egill who superintends the funeral has been subtly indicated throughout the saga; although even Egill will not let his dearly loved brother be buried without some treasure, and gives up two fine gold bracelets, a king's

1 Stone cairns are found dating from the Viking Age, and have a very long ancestry. Flat graves seem to belong to Christian times, although we have isolated examples which may be earlier. For this see Almgren, 'Vikingatidens grafskick'...(*Nordiska Studier til. A. Noreen*, Uppsala, 1904), p. 334 f.

gift, to rest in the grave with him (LV). In *Laxdœla Saga* (XXVI) it is similarly noted that Höskuldr was buried without any wealth, and here again the meanness of his sons and their reluctance to give their father a splendid funeral has been made abundantly clear. It is thought necessary in one of the *Fornaldar Sögur* (*Friðþjófs Saga*, I) for a king to give a special command to his sons against letting treasure be carried into the grave with him. Grave-goods, too, are only omitted for some good reason, as when in *Njáls Saga* (LXXVIII) Gunnarr's bill is not put into his howe because his mother directs that it is to be used to avenge him. The normal procedure was for the dead man to be laid in the grave with his most cherished possessions and wealth in the form of silver or valuable grave-goods. One instance among many is that of Hrafnkell, said in his saga (XX) to be laid in the grave with much wealth, his war-gear and his spear; Egill himself, who died a little while before the introduction of Christianity, had his weapons and his finest clothes, since he had already disposed of the wealth in his possession a little while before he died;[1] and the grave of a sorceress in *Laxdœla Saga* (LXXVI) was recognisable by the brooch and staff buried with her, the latter the mark of her profession.

A favourite story in the sagas is that of the hero who breaks into a grave-mound to carry off the treasure hidden inside, and if once he can overcome the resistance of the dead guardian the attempt is well worth while. In *Grettis Saga* (XVIII) the mound of Kárr the Old is entered in this way, and the dead man is found seated on a chair with the remains of his horse and much treasure beside him, a description which corresponds with that of the dead man sitting upright in the Vendel graves, and that of King Dan upon his throne in the account in *Skjöldunga Saga*. Even closer to Vendel is the account of the mound of Sóti in *Harðar Saga* (XV), where the dead man, who is robbed of his treasure and a ring, is seated in a ship. In *Landnámabók* (II, 8) we find a verse describing the exploit of a man who robbed the howe of Þorarinn Korni; and there is another story (III, I) of a successful attempt to rob the howe of the famous King Hrólfr and carry off his sword.[2] These grave-robbing exploits almost invariably

1 *Egils Saga*, LXXXV.
2 Skeggi was not so lucky, however, when he tried to add the sword of Hrólfr's follower, Böðvarr Bjarki, to his collection of booty. See *Þórðar Saga Hr.* III, corroborated by one version of *Landnámabók* (*Hauksbók: Landnámabók Íslands*, Copenhagen, 1925, p. 95 (note)).

take place in Norway; and there was of course more likelihood of graves worth robbing there than in Iceland. In the accounts of treasure buried in the howe with the dead, we find that the conception in the sagas is that of the dead man within his grave-mound keeping jealous watch over his possessions.

Besides the howe as a dwelling-place for the dead and his treasures, it is also looked on in the sagas as a sign of honour to the dead, something which perpetuates his memory. This is the idea which we find expressed in Snorri, in his account of cremation; howes as well as memorial stones, he says, were set up in Sweden to the memory of the dead man, if his reputation deserved it. It is also expressed clearly in the Anglo-Saxon poem *Beowulf*, where again the howe is raised after a cremation funeral:

> Bid my renowned warriors raise a noble barrow after the burning, on a headland by the sea. It shall be a memorial to my people, as it towers high upon Whales Ness, so that those who fare across the sea shall in after days name it the mound of Beowulf, when they urge their tall ships far over the misty deep (2802–2808).

Something of the same conception seems to remain in the sagas. Obviously a howe did act as a convenient and unforgettable memorial to the dead; in the *Landnámabók* the position of the howes of the dead settlers is known, and carefully recorded. The obligation on the living to pay this honour to their dead, however, is very strong: 'We are all bound to do honour to the man who is dead, and to make his burial as worthy as possible, and to lay him in howe', says someone in *Gísla Saga* (XIII), and although the words are spoken ironically, the sentiment is clearly a familiar one. Considerable trouble would be taken before this duty to the dead was neglected. After the battle on the heath in *Hrafnkels Saga* (XVIII) Samr returns to raise a howe over his brother and the rest who fell with him. In *Njáls Saga* (LXXVII) the men who have slain Gunnarr actually return to ask his mother for leave to raise a howe on her land over two of their party who have been killed; the request is made formally and humbly, and she accedes to it. In *Svarfdæla Saga* (VI), when the brother of Þorsteinn dies at sea, he puts in immediately to the nearest landing-place and goes to the Jarl who lives there:

> Þorsteinn said 'I want you to lend your hall to me and my men. I want to hold the funeral feast for my brother, and lay him in howe here, with your permission. I will gladly pay money for this, so that you will not suffer.' The Jarl said he would gladly grant this.

This is an extreme case of the importance attributed to the raising of a howe over the dead.

Only murdered men, like the victims of Þjóstólfr and Hrútr in *Njáls Saga* (xvII), are covered with stones and turf in place of a howe; Hrafnkell piles up a cairn over the boy whom he is forced to slay in fulfilment of his vow (vI). Certain men who have been slain in battle are also said in *Landnámabók* to have had cairns piled over them, and so are witches and wizards stoned to death for their crimes, like Kotkell and Gríma in *Laxdæla Saga* (xxxvII), or killed by each other's magic, like the two rival witches in *Harðar Saga* (xL). The sagas and *Landnámabók* give plenty of information as to the places chosen for burial. The howe might be raised in the place where the man met his death. It might be set on a lonely headland overlooking the sea; the usual explanation in the sagas is that in such a position dangerous characters were thought to be less likely to do mischief. In *Eyrbyggia Saga* (xxxIV) the body of Þórólfr Bægifótr is removed to the ness after he has been haunting the countryside, while in *Egils Saga* (LVIII) Egill chooses such a site as a grave for his father, who, from the preparations taken at his death and funeral, was evidently judged to be a character likely to rest unquiet. This custom, however, might be one remembered from earlier times; Beowulf's mound was placed in just such a position, and the explanation given there is that it will be visible to sailors out at sea and so his fame be continually remembered. Again, a number of the kings in *Ynglinga Saga* are cremated and stones raised to their memorial beside a river; whether this was due originally to a belief in the departure of the dead by water is a question to be discussed later, but we may notice in passing that Snorri tells us that the ashes of the dead, according to Othin, might either be buried in the earth or borne out to sea. Many of the settlers in *Landnámabók* are said to be laid in howe close to the place where they had lived; one of them is even said to have been buried in the yard.[1] In *Laxdæla Saga* (xvII) we find Hrappr demanding to be buried after death within the house itself, in the doorway of the living-room. There seems to have been no tendency on the part of the living to shun the howes, and only in the case of dangerous characters who would not rest in the grave was any attempt made to keep them away from human habitation.

The burning of the dead in the sagas was only practised in order to

[1] *Lndn.* I, 17, p. 45; I, 21, p. 51; II, 7, p. 65; IV, 10, p. 188; V, 13, p. 244; II, 14, p. 81.

destroy a dangerous corpse which otherwise would do harm to the living. In *Eyrbyggja Saga* (xxxiv, lxiii) Þórólfr Bægifótr leaves his grave-mound and comes out at night to kill men and animals; his son first tries to quieten him by moving the body to a more lonely grave, and when this proves unavailing it is finally dug up and burnt to ashes, and the ashes thrown out to sea. In *Grettis Saga* (xxxiii) similar trouble is caused by the dead Glamr; he is overcome by Grettir after a terrible wrestling match, and after his head has been cut off the body is burned to cold ashes by Grettir and the householder whom he has been tormenting. Oddr in *Laxdæla Saga* (xvii) treats Hrappr in a similar way, and after his ashes have been thrown out to sea we are told that no one has any further trouble with him. In *Flóamanna Saga* (xiii) the body of a dead woman who had been a witch in her time proves restless on the way to burial, until when the bearers are unable to carry her any farther they build a pyre and burn the remains on the spot. We can be sure that this custom did not die out with heathenism. In the same saga a district in Greenland was haunted by a number of people who had died from a mysterious plague, and Þorgils, although a Christian, resorted to the usual remedy and had the corpses dug up and burned—'and from that time there was no harm done by their walking' (xxii). The same method was used in Europe up to the eighteenth century and probably later to dispose of vampires.[1]

Thus the division of grave-customs made by Snorri, the burning of the dead and the burial in howe, is found also in Old Norse literature. The burning of the dead is found recorded only of certain kings of Sweden, some of the gods, and certain characters in the poems. Burial in howe is the only custom remembered in the sagas of Iceland, and the records of the Norwegian kings seem similarly to be without any memory of cremation of the dead, although we know from archaeological evidence that it was practised until late into heathen times. However, the fact that cremation died out early in the west coastal region of Norway and never reached Iceland at all, according to our present knowledge, may well account for the emphasis on howe-laying in the prose literature which we possess. The speech of the orator at the Frosta Thing in *Hákonar Saga Góða* (xv) admittedly refers to an age of burning before that of burial, but this is probably an interpolation by Snorri himself since it accords so

---

1 E.g. from Greece: de Tournefort, *Relation d'un voyage du Levant* (Lyons, 1717), I, p. 158 f.

neatly with his statements in the Preface. We shall find however that the practice of cremation has been recorded outside the prose literature, and shall meet it when we examine the accounts of ship-funeral and human sacrifice.

## SHIP-FUNERAL

In Iceland, it will be remembered, ship-burials have been found, though they are not numerous or rich; and literary evidence for ship-burial without cremation comes from the *Íslendinga Sögur*. In *Gísla Saga* (xviii) for instance we have an account of the laying of Þorgrímr in his howe. He is buried in his ship, and Gísli lays a great stone upon it just before the howe is closed, with the ironical comment: 'I do not know how to make a ship fast if the wind moves this'—a veiled reference to his own part in Þorgrímr's death.[1] No particular reason why a ship should be used is obvious from this passage; indeed, a little while before we are told that another dead man in the same district is laid in his howe with no ship but with 'hel-shoes' on his feet (xiv), so that if there is any idea of a journey for the dead man the means provided for making it are quite different. There is no special connection apparent between Þorgrímr and the sea, and in any case we find later that the dead man is thought to be still within his burial mound, since we are told that his howe was always clear of snow and frost, and that this was thought to be because 'he was so dear to Freyr on account of his sacrifices that Freyr would have no frost between them' (xviii). Ingimundr, in *Vatnsdæla Saga* (xxiii), was also buried in a ship, or rather a ship's boat, but here there is no indication of any belief in a future existence in the grave or elsewhere. Auðr, in *Laxdæla Saga* (vii), is also said in one account to have been buried in a ship within her howe, with much wealth laid beside her, though *Landnámabók* (ii, 19) contradicts this, and tells us she refused to be buried in unconsecrated ground, and was laid below high-water mark on the seashore. In any case ship-burial has apparently no special significance here, and again we get the impression that while the custom has been remembered

---

1 Compare with this the mooring of the Oseberg ship in its mound, and the stones thrown in above it. For other examples of this see Major, *Folklore*, 1924, p. 146. The parallel with the Iron Age ship found in a bog at Hjortspring (*Nordiske Fortidsminder*, iii, 1, 1927, p. 37 f.), where flints had been piled up on the vessel and apparently thrown in large numbers on the surface of the bog round it, is an interesting one.

by the saga-tellers, they have no recollection of the beliefs that prompted it.

In *Landnámabók* (II, 20) a man called Germund is said to have been buried in his ship in a wood, though no details are given. Elsewhere (II, 6) we have an example of ship-burial with human sacrifice; a certain Ásmundr is laid in his ship, with his thrall to accompany him. According to lines found in some versions [1] the sacrifice in this case is not appreciated, since Ásmundr is heard singing a song in which he complains of the lack of room in his ship, and the thrall has to be removed. Here again we get the notion of the dead man continuing to exist in his ship inside the howe. The same conception is present in the tale of the breaking into the mound of Sóti, in *Hárðar Saga* (xv). The story of the lowering of the hero into the mound and of the struggle with the *draugr* inside is a familiar one; the idea that the dead man is sitting in a ship, however, is, as far as I know, peculiar to this saga. The ship is placed in the side chamber of the howe, and there is much treasure in it, while Sóti sits upright in the prow—a point that reminds us of the dead chief in his ship in the Vendel graves. In *Bárðar Saga* (xv) the viking Raknar is buried with a ship, but he is not in the ship himself, but sits on a chair on the ground beside it. A large number of people—500 men—are said to be laid in the ship itself.

There are other references to a number of people buried in one ship. In *Svarfdæla Saga* Þorgerðr has Karl and the eastmen laid in a ship, 'and much wealth with them' (xxvi). Here there is a fleeting reference to a life elsewhere after death, though the connection with a ship may be an accidental one; before Karl's death his kinsman Klaufi, who 'walks' a good deal after death, appears to him driving a sledge in the air, and finally leaves him with the remark: 'I am expecting you home with me to-night, Karl my kinsman' (xxvi). The other episode comes from one of the *Fornaldar Sögur* (*Áns Saga Bogsveigis*, VI), where Án's brother has been slain by the king, and in revenge he kills a crew of the king's men, and puts them all in their ship inside a howe, 'with Þórir on deck, and the king's men on

---

1 *Hauksbók* has fuller account: 'Ásmundr was laid in howe there in his ship, and with him his thrall, who had slain himself, desiring not to survive Ásmundr. He was placed in the opposite end of the ship. A little later Þóra [his wife, from whom he had parted] dreamed that Ásmundr had told her he was annoyed by the thrall' (c. 60). The verse in which Ásmundr makes his complaint is badly preserved.

either side of the ship, so that it was shown from this that they must all serve him' (VI). In these passages it is clear that no particular belief in a life after death to be reached by ship is connected with the practice of ship-burial in the minds of the saga-tellers; if there had been a tradition of this kind, it had been forgotten by the time the sagas were composed, though the custom was still clearly remembered, and connected in some cases with human sacrifice.

The accounts of ship-cremation, as has been pointed out, are found outside the sagas. Two of the most interesting references come from Saxo and have not been preserved elsewhere. He tells us [1] that the laws of King Frode included the edict that a jarl (*centurio vel satrapa*) [2] must be burnt on a funeral pyre built of his own ship. Every king or general (*dux*) shall have a ship of his own, while the bodies of captains (*gubernati*) shall be burnt in groups of ten to every ship. An instance of such a burning after battle is given when Hotherus lays the King of Saxony on the corpses of his oarsmen and has him burnt on a pyre built of vessels, and his ashes placed in a barrow.[3] It has, however, been suggested that here Saxo has departed from the original, and that the source he has used here is in reality an account of the burning of Balder on a blazing ship.[4]

From a more reliable source however, the *Heimskringla* of Snorri, comes a similar incident, though connected with the burial instead of the burning of the dead; it is related of the Christian king, Hákon the Good (935–960), who lays his faithful old follower Egill Ullserk in a ship after his death in battle:

King Hákon took over the ships which had run aground there, which had belonged to the sons of Eric, and had them drawn ashore. He had Egill Ullserk laid in a ship there, and with him all those who had fallen out of their company, and had earth and stones heaped over them. King Hákon had many other ships brought ashore, and the slain carried into them, and the howes can be seen south of Frædarberg. High memorial stones stand beside the grave of Egill Ullserk (*Hákonar Saga Góða*, XXVII).

The other account of ship-funeral from Snorri is found in quite a different setting, in his picture of the world of the gods given in the

1 Saxo, V, 156, p. 193.
2 Translations of the Latin terms are those suggested by Herrmann in his commentary on the passage (*Dänische Geschichten des Saxo Grammaticus*, II, p. 353).
3 Saxo, III, 74, p. 89.
4 Herrmann, *Dänische Geschichte des Saxo Grammaticus*, p. 211.

*Prose Edda*. There we have a detailed account of a cremation on board ship, when Balder is burned on the pyre built on his ship Hringhorni. It is a strange and puzzling account, full of vividness, movement and detail, and abounding in fantastic pieces of information. The four berserks who guard the horse of the giantess who launches the ship, Thor's sudden vicious attempt to slay her with his hammer, the kicking into the fire of the dwarf Litr by the irritable god, the arrival of Freyja with her cats—these incidents stand out unforgettably, like scenes on a tapestry. We find the funeral treated much earlier by one of the tenth-century skaldic poets, and it is probable that it was from some such source that Snorri's information came. It is to Snorri himself, moreover, that we owe the preservation of such parts of Úlfr Uggason's *Húsdrapa* as we possess, since he has preserved them in his *Skáldskaparmál* as examples of poetic diction.[1] If we piece together the lines which deal with the funeral of Balder, we find some of the information given by Snorri, and also some fresh points about the procession of mourners who rode to the pyre to honour the dead god:

> Battle-wise Freyr rides first on a golden-bristled boar to the hill of Othin's son, and leads the hosts.
> Far-famed Hroptatýr rides towards the exceeding great pyre of his son —but the song of praise glides through my lips—
> I see the valkyries following the wise and victorious one, and the ravens too, for the holy blood of the slain.
> Splendid Heimdallr rides his horse to the pyre which the gods raised for the fallen son of the Friend of ravens, the very wise one.
> Hildr, exceeding powerful, caused the horse of the sea to move slowly forward, but the warrior-champions of Othin felled the steed.[2]

In Snorri's account the pyre is built on the ship after it has been launched. There is still connection between the ship and the shore. Balder's body is carried on to the pyre, and after him the body of his wife, who is said to have broken her heart and died of grief; then Thor hallows the pyre with his hammer; Othin comes with his offering, the magic ring Draupnir, and lays it on the pyre beside his son; and lastly the horse of Balder is led to the pyre in all its trappings. The tradition of Othin approaching the pyre of his dead son is

1 *Gylfaginning*, XLIX.
2 *Norsk-Islandske Skjaldedigtning*, F. Jónsson, 1912, B, I, p. 129. The stanzas, scattered in Snorri, have been taken in the order in which Jónsson arranges them.

evidently well known, since in one of the Eddic poems the giant Vafþrúðnir is defeated in a contest of wit by Othin's question: 'What said Othin into the ear of Balder before he mounted the pyre?' (*Vafþrúðnismál*, 54).

At this point Snorri's account ends, and he changes the scene to that of Hermóðr's ride to Hel. He gives us no indication as to whether when the fire was kindled the ship was allowed to float out to sea. Since we are told of no howe raised for Balder's ashes, this may have been the case, especially since such trouble was taken to launch it. We have two other stories, again apparently old literary traditions, where this is actually said to have been done. One of them is told of one of the earliest of the kings mentioned by Snorri in the *Ynglinga Saga*, the sea-king Haki.[1] He died from wounds in battle, and just before his death, Snorri tells us

he bade them take a warship which he had, and load it with dead men and weapons, and push it out to the open sea. He ordered them to ship the rudder and hoist the sail and set fire to the fuel, making a pyre in the ship. The wind was blowing from the land. Haki was then at the point of death, or even dead, when he was laid on the pyre. Then the ship sailed blazing out to sea. This was famous for a long time afterwards (XXIII).

There is a similar account of a king going to his death in the Latin version of the *Skjöldunga Saga*,[2] of which the original is lost:

He (King Sigurðr Hringr), when Alfsola had been borne to her funeral, went aboard a great ship, laden with corpses, the only living man among them. He placed himself and the dead Alfsola in the stern, and ordered that a fire should be kindled with bitumen and sulphur. Then with full sails set and a strong wind driving from the shore, he guided the rudder and at the same time slew himself with his own hand....For he preferred to go to King Othin in royal pomp in the manner of his ancestors—that is to the underworld—rather than to endure the weakness of a sluggish old age...(XXVI).

Here we have two accounts closely resembling one another. Sigurðr, like Haki, had been seriously wounded in battle, and the loading of the ship with dead men, the kindling of the fire, the wind blowing out to sea, and above all the idea that this death was the deliberate choice of the king, and that the rudder was placed as if for him to steer, are striking features in both accounts. It is quite likely

1 Haki is the brother of Hagbarðr, whose death is discussed on p. 53 below.
2 *Skjöldunga Saga*, A. Jónsson, *A.f.n.O.* 1894, p. 132 f.

that we are dealing indeed with two versions of the same story. It is thought[1] that Snorri obtained the part of *Ynglinga Saga* which includes the story of Haki from the original *Skjöldunga Saga*, which is likely to have been composed about 1200. Arngrimr, who recorded the Latin version, certainly knew this too, as part of his version is taken from it. It seems at least possible that the two stories have been confused, and the tradition transferred from one king to the other. This however need not prevent it from being a genuine tradition all the same, although it might well have resulted from an imaginative account of the cremation of a king in a ship, and not originally have been the record of such a ship being set adrift on the sea. However, we are again reminded of the dead chief sitting upright in his ship in the Vendel grave, and of another account, this time in the Anglo-Saxon poem *Beowulf*, of a dead king floating out to sea. The ship of the dead Scyld is laden with treasures, and then launched on the sea to float to an unknown destination, bearing the mysterious king with it: 'Those who hold office in kings' halls, heroes under the heavens, cannot say in truth who received that burden' (50–52).

There is also a passage in one of the *Íslendinga Sögur* which might well be a confused echo of such a tradition as this. At the end of *Njáls Saga* the valiant old warrior Flosi goes to Norway to buy timber in the last year of his life. He does not begin the return voyage to Iceland until rather late in the summer, and as he is leaving, people tell him that his boat is unseaworthy. But in reply to this

Flosi said it was good enough for a man who was old and had forebodings of death (*feigr*); and he went on board and put out to sea; and that ship was never heard of again (CLIX).

Such traditions might reflect a definite belief in a land of the dead across the sea, originally the inspiration behind ship-funeral and afterwards forgotten, or again they might be literary or religious traditions of a different kind. There are other small pieces of evidence that might be taken into consideration here. Sinfjötli's dead body is carried off by a stranger in a boat, who seems to be Othin, in *Völsunga Saga* (X); on one occasion, though a ship is not used, Othin is said to carry off Hadingus to his house across the sea;[2] and several of the gods are said to have possessed ships: Skíðblaðnir, which could hold all the gods, is connected sometimes with Freyr and sometimes

1 F. Jónsson, *Litt. Hist.* II, p. 659; Introduction to *Skjöldunga Saga, op. cit.* p. 146.
2 Saxo, I, 24, p. 29.

THE EVIDENCE OF LITERATURE

with Othin;[1] Balder has a ship called Hringhorni;[2] and Njörðr is said to rule the winds and the sea, and to dwell in Noatun, the 'enclosure of vessels'.[3] There is also the fact to be taken into consideration that several of the early kings of Sweden were said to have been burnt at the water's edge, and that according to Snorri the ashes of the dead might be thrown out to sea after cremation.[4] Such scraps of evidence are of little value separately, but they are interesting taken together, because they might all fit into place as scattered memories of a home of the gods across the water.

Before discussing this further, there is some evidence outside Scandinavia to be taken into account. A description of a cremation in a ship, which is of great interest because of its late date and the detailed information which it gives, is found in the writings of an Arab traveller, Ahmed ibn Foszlan, who was sent into Russia as an envoy in the year 921, to teach Islamic law to the 'King of the Slavs'. Part of his account of his experiences there has been preserved in Yaqut's *Geographical Dictionary*, and in it he describes the 'Rus', who, if Ahmed is correct, are the descendants of Scandinavians settled on the Volga.[5] Taken as a whole, his account of the Rus has a strangely sensual and fantastic ring, very different from Norse literature, so that one rather wonders how far the teller has read his own interpretation into what he saw; the description of the funeral of a Rus chieftain, however, is very relevant to our study.[6]

---

1 *Gylfaginning*, XLIII: 'Certain dwarfs...made Skíðblaðnir, and gave the ship to Freyr; she was so big that all the Æsir could go aboard her...and as soon as the sail was hoisted she got the breeze that she wanted.' (cf. *Grímnismál*, 43). *Ynglinga Saga* VII: 'Othin...had the ship called Skíðblaðnir, in which he travelled over great oceans, but which could be folded up like a tablecloth.'

2 See p. 42 above.

3 *Gylfaginning*, XXIII; *Grímnismál*, 16. Cf. Olsen, *Revue de l'histoire des religions*, nos. 111–112, 1935, p. 188 f. He points out the number of place-names on the Norwegian coast where the god's name occurs.

4 See p. 32 above.

5 Arguments for identifying the 'Rus' with Scandinavians who settled in Russia are given by V. Thomsen in his lecture on the 'Scandinavian Origin of the Ancient Russ' in *The Relations between Ancient Russia and Scandinavia*, Parker, 1877. See also Braun, 'Das historische Russland im nordischen Schrifttum des X.–XIV. Jahrhunderts', in *Festschrift für Eugen Mogk*, 1924. Archaeological evidence is given by Arne, *La Suède et l'Orient* (Uppsala, 1914).

6 Two accessible versions of this are (a) a translation into German (Arabic text also given) by C. M. Frähn in *Ibn Foszlan's und anderer araber Berichte über die Russen älterer Zeit* and (b) a translation of the account of the funeral, from which the passage quoted is taken, by Miss Waddy in *Antiquity*, 1934, p. 58.

Ahmed describes how the dead chief was first buried for ten days, while the women sewed garments for him. In the case of a man of importance, Ahmed explains, a third of his money will be spent in this way, and another third goes to buy wine for the final ceremony, when one of the chief's slaves gives herself to die with her master. At the ceremony at which Ahmed was present, it was a woman who made the offer—this apparently being the usual custom. He describes at some length the girl's life up to the time of the burning; how she was waited on hand and foot, and was very merry up to the end. Before she was slain by an old woman called the 'Angel of Death', she took part in a strange ceremony:

They brought the girl to something they had made, which resembled the frame of a door. She put her feet on the palms of the men there, and looked over the frame. She said what she had to say, and they lowered her. Then they lifted her up a second time; she did the same and they lowered her. Then they lifted her up a third time, and she did the same again, after which they gave her a hen, and she cut off its head and threw it into the boat [i.e. the ship prepared for the pyre]. I asked the interpreter what she was doing, and he replied: 'The first time she said "Behold, I see my father and mother". The second time she said "Behold, I see all my dead relations seated". The third time she said "Behold I see my master seated in Paradise, and Paradise is green and fair, and with him are men and servants. He is calling me. Send me to him".'

Meanwhile the dead man has been taken out of the earth, dressed in the new garments, and placed on a bed in the tent on the ship. He is supplied with liquor and food, and all his weapons laid beside him. A dog, two oxen, two cows, a cock and a hen are all killed and thrown into the boat. Finally the girl herself is slain within the tent.[1] This is done by the old woman, who stabs her in the ribs with a knife, while two men strangle her; her screams are drowned with the loud beating of shields. Then the ship is set on fire, and burns easily by reason of the wooden piles placed under it beforehand. A gale,

[1] The reliability of Ahmed's statement to the effect that a number of men had intercourse with the girl before death saying that 'she was to tell her master they did this for love of him' is, I think, doubtful. It is very characteristic of Ahmed, who loves to introduce little incidents of this kind whenever possible, and it will be remembered that by his own confession he was obliged to depend on the services of an interpreter, and is here describing something taking place out of sight, within the tent. Parallels from primitive tribes in Australia are however given by Crawley (*The Mystic Rose*, London, 1902), pp. 307 and 347 f., where the ceremony is 'the last detail in the preparation of the bride for her husband'.

says Ahmed, came up just in time to fan the flames, and within an hour the ship and all in it were burnt to ashes. One of the men standing by explained to Ahmed that out of love of their great men '"We burn them with fire in a twinkling, and they enter Paradise that very same hour". Then he laughed heartily and said "Out of love of him his Lord has sent the wind to take him away".'

This funeral must have resembled in many respects the most elaborate ship-burials of the Viking Age in Norway. Again the dead man rests on a bed within the ship, surrounded by all the necessities of life and many choice possessions, with various animals sacrificed to accompany him and the dead slave girl laid in the tent beside him, just as in the Gokstad and Oseberg ships, although there we have no definite evidence for human sacrifice. Here however the ship is burned and not buried; and the attitude to cremation as recorded by Ahmed is more in accordance with the earlier literary traditions, with the stories of Haki and Sigurðr Hringr, and the description of Othin's teaching about cremation given by Snorri; since the wind is sent to fan the flames, as a wind was sent to drive the ships of the dead kings out to sea, and the chief is said to have gone to dwell with his Lord, who loves him, in a green Paradise.

In spite of the resemblances to the story of the dead kings carried out to sea in their ships, we may notice that here we have a boat used without any obvious conception of a journey to the land of the dead by water; it is the flames, and not the ship, which seem to be regarded as the medium by which the dead is to be borne to Paradise.

The question of the origin of ship-funeral has been discussed by Olrik in his *Danmarks Heltedigtning* (I, p. 39) and the view of it which he takes is that the essential feature of such early stories as those which we have examined is the drifting of the boat out to an unknown destination, with no connection with cremation or inhumation of the dead within a ship. The instances he gives to support this, and to show that such a conception is met with to a considerable extent in Western Europe, are not however very conclusive ones. There is the belief that the souls of the dead are carried by boat over the sea to Britain, recorded by Procopius and elsewhere, and the stories of a land of departure over the sea in Irish mythology; otherwise the legends to which he refers are late and doubtful ones. Stjerna,[1] on the other hand, wishes to trace three definite stages in the practice of ship-funeral. The first is that of sending the king in a blazing funeral

1 Stjerna, *Essays on Beowulf* (Viking Club, Coventry, 1912), p. 103.

pyre out to sea, or the setting adrift of a corpse in a boat. The second is the burying of a ship in the ground, or the making of a grave in ship form, and the third, the belief in the journey to a land of the dead without the necessity to provide the corpse with any visible form of transport. Again, however, Stjerna is unable to give any really convincing evidence for the support of this theory, or to show that ship-funeral has developed by these three steps in any part of the world. As an example of the first stage in actual practice, he gives an example from further India of the launching of a blazing funeral pyre; but when the body is committed to fire and water in India, the idea behind it is usually that of purification by a return to the elements—a complex mystical idea which can hardly be regarded as the first stage in the development of ship-funeral. He also instances the sending out to sea of a corpse in a canoe by Australian natives, but gives no authority for this. It is possible, however, to produce evidence from other parts of the world which shows that the setting of a corpse in a boat to drift out to sea can be an actual practice, though this does not prove, of course, that the Norse literary traditions are founded on memories of such a custom. In an account of Sarawak and British North Borneo,[1] Ling Roth gives a number of instances of the custom of setting adrift the property of the dead man in a boat 'in order that the deceased may meet with these necessities in his outward flight'. In particular, he quotes the account of the drowning of a young chief, written by Bishop McDougall, who records that he himself saw an effigy of the corpse with a number of rich possessions —including weapons and gold ornaments—which after three days was launched on the river in a boat made for the purpose; had the body of the dead man been recovered, he says, it would certainly have been launched with the property: 'this is the invariable mode of burial with the Milanows.' On another occasion the bishop met a boat rolling in a heavy sea, with what he first took to be a man sitting paddling in the stern; but when he tried to reach it, he saw that it was only one of their 'death boats'.[2] Again in Polynesia there is a good deal of ship-burial in various forms. Cases are recorded from Samoa of bodies being rudely embalmed, put into a canoe and set adrift on the ocean.[3] There is also some evidence for the practice of laying the

1  H. Ling Roth, *Natives of Sarawak and British North Borneo* (London, 1896), I, 8, p. 144 f.
2  *Ibid.* p. 145.
3  R. W. Williamson, *Religious and Cosmic Beliefs of Central Polynesia*, I, p. 246.

dead man in a boat, and killing his wife—usually with her consent—to accompany him.[1] In the Marquesas Porter records that he once saw four war-canoes, splendidly decorated, loaded with a number of corpses of enemies slain in battle. One of these contained the body of a priest of the district, who had been slain in battle; when they had a full crew for him, they said, he would be able to start on his voyage, and they would see that the boat was well supplied with provisions.[2]

This evidence is particularly interesting for our purpose, since both in North Borneo[3] and Polynesia[4] we have evidence for the belief in a journey to the land of the dead, reached in the first case along a river, and in the second across the sea; so that in either a boat will be needed. This belief is by no means universal or consistent; it exists side by side with ideas about the dead continuing to exist in the grave and so on;[5] however, the very fact that it is found alongside with the practice of ship-burial and with the actual launching of the dead out to sea provides an argument for Stjerna, and at least suggests the possibility that ship-funeral in the North may have originated in the practice of which we read in the literature, and in a belief in the land of the dead across the sea. On the other hand, it proves almost impossible to decide from the mass of evidence from Polynesia which of these beliefs came first; the development may have been in the order suggested by Stjerna, but it might equally well have been in the other direction, or the different practices may have developed in different regions. Probably had we the same amount of evidence from the early days of ship-funeral in Scandinavia, we should find it just as contradictory and confusing.

It is noticeable, however, that in the evidence for ship-funeral elsewhere we do not find it linked with cremation. If we look back on the Norse evidence as a whole, it seems that Olrik is justified in distinguishing two separate ideas—one that of sending the dead man to an unknown destination, whether this is merely a literary tradition or based on early practice to some extent—and the other that of burning the dead man on his ship on a funeral pyre, for which we have evidence from Russia in the tenth century, and which we know

1 Murray, *Missions in Western Polynesia*, p. 50 f.
2 Williamson, *op. cit.* I, p. 274; Porter, *Journal of a Cruise*, II, p. 111.
3 Ling Roth, *op. cit.* I, p. 208; N. K. Chadwick, *Growth of Literature*, III, p. 476 f., esp. p. 490.
4 Williamson, *op. cit.* I, pp. 323 f., 343, 379 f., II, 36 f., etc.
5 Williamson, *op. cit.* I, p. 252. Cf. story recorded by W. W. Gill, *Myths and Songs from South Pacific* (London, 1876), p. 211.

was practised in Scandinavia for a good many centuries before that. There remains the custom of burying the dead in a ship, but before discussing this further it is necessary to turn to another question, that of human sacrifice.

## HUMAN SACRIFICE

We have already noticed a number of cases in Norse literature where ship-funeral is accompanied by human sacrifice, and in the account of the cremation on the Volga in the tenth century we have a vivid and detailed account of suttee. There are some striking resemblances in Ahmed's account to those of suttee carried out in India and the Island of Bali within comparatively recent times. In, for example, the descriptions of suttee given by eyewitnesses from the Island of Bali in 1877,[1] there are a number of points which may be noticed. A considerable time passes between the death of the man and the cremation of the women, since they die at the funeral ceremony held later; the wives and concubines of the dead man are allowed to choose whether they will die with their lord, but once the choice is made they may not draw back; the woman who volunteers to die is treated as a privileged person until the day of the burning; the victim is encouraged by emphasis on her status as the wife of her lord in the next world—and incidentally by the use of intoxicating drugs before death. All these points were also made by Ahmed in his account of the funeral of the Rus chieftain. Even the killing of the hen by the girl in the strange ceremony before death in Ahmed's account reminds us of the releasing of the doves over the heads of the doomed women in the Bali ceremony, when these are said to represent the soul. These features can be traced in other accounts of suttee as practised in the East;[2] modern records can be found in the works of S. C. Bose,[3] who witnessed the burning of a member of his own family when a child, and of J. A. Dubois;[4] Crawfurd[5] gives a most full and interesting account of earlier ceremonies in Bali from the records of the Dutch mission sent there in 1633, from which we learn that it was usual there to have old women attending those who were to die to instruct and encourage them, just as did the 'Angel of

1 Friederich, *Journal of the Royal Asiatic Society* (N.S.), IX, 1877, p. 89 f.
2 For most of the references to suttee in India I am indebted to Mr E. J. Thomas of the Cambridge University Library.
3 S. C. Bose, *The Hindoos as they are*, XXI, p. 272.
4 Abbé J. A. Dubois, *Hindu Manners, Customs and Ceremonies*, 1897, chapter XIX.
5 Crawfurd, *Indian Archipelago*, II, p. 241 f.

'Death' and her daughters in Ahmed's account; and there is a large collection of records of 'suttee' from various parts of India, Bali and Java, ranging in date from 317 B.C. to A.D. 1870, collected under 'suttee' in *Hobson-Jobson*. Nearly all these cases are cremation ceremonies, and the main features on which we have commented are the same throughout. Usually the number of those put to death is small, but a few travellers report cases where hundreds have died. Were such ceremonies as these ever known in Scandinavia? And what is their original significance? It is known from the evidence of archaeology that suttee was practised in Northern Europe by Celtic peoples; we have the undoubted instance from the cemetery at Thuizy already mentioned, and other less extreme examples from cemeteries on the Marne. In Scandinavia we have what appear to be examples from the Bronze Age, and possible examples from the Viking Age also, though these are scarcely conclusive taken alone.[1]

Turning to the evidence of literature, however, we find a passage in *Flateyjarbók* where the practice of suttee is recorded as continuing in Sweden into historic times. We are told of the marriage of Auðr, Hákon's daughter, to King Eric of Sweden in his old age, and the chronicler adds:

> Now at that time Sigríðr the Proud had left King Eric, and people said he felt disgraced by her behaviour: for it was in fact the law in Sweden that if a king died the queen should be laid in the howe beside him, and she knew that the king had vowed himself to Othin for victory when he fought with Styrbjörn his kinsman, and that he had not many years to live (*Flateyjarbók: Óláfs Saga Tryggvasonar*, I, 63, p. 88).

This Sigríðr the Proud is an historical figure; she married Eric Sigrsæll, the king of Sweden mentioned here, whose dates are about 980–995; she intended at one time to marry Olaf Tryggvason, until they quarrelled over religious matters, and as a result of this she married instead his rival, Svein of Denmark (Tjuguskegg). She helped to bring about the death of Olaf, whom she had never forgiven, in A.D. 1000, and may have lived long enough to accompany her husband to England, where he died in 1014 and was succeeded by her stepson, Cnut. The connection of this tradition with so well known a character at such a relatively late date is thus of great interest.

A passage which may be compared with the one from *Flateyjarbók* occurs in the *þáttr Egils Hallssonar ok Tófa Valgautssonar* in the *Forn-*

[1] See p. 15 above.

*manna Sögur*, where the custom of suttee is represented as being still possible in Gautland in the reign of Olaf the Holy. In this case the sacrifice of the wife was not actually carried out, but not because of any rebellion on the woman's part. Jarl Valgautr of Gautland was summoned to the court of the Christian king Olaf, and left his home in no very happy state of mind, since he could anticipate only two possible results of the interview—his conversion to the king's faith or death; and his forebodings, as a matter of fact, proved all too well justified. Before leaving he told his wife

...he would send a gold ring to her as a token, if he were baptised; and then she must do the same, and all those over whom she had control... but if she learned that he had been slain, then she should first hold the funeral feast, and next make a pyre and burn all the wealth that she could, and afterwards herself go into the fire.

(*Fornmanna Sögur* (Copenhagen, 1825–1837), v, p. 327 f.)

It is perhaps significant that in both these passages we find suttee represented as a practice that was rapidly dying out at the close of the Viking Age.

We have a number of other references in Norse literature which do not come from historical sources, but which nevertheless seem as though they may be memories of a tradition such as that described above. In the story of Balder's funeral, quoted earlier, it will be remembered that the wife of Balder breaks her heart with grief, and is burned with her husband.[1] This sounds like a reminiscence of the voluntary death of a wife at her husband's funeral, and the evidence of the *Fornaldar Sögur* strengthens this impression. In *Hervarar Saga* (III) and *Örvar-Odds Saga* (xv) we get two different accounts of the same incident, the death of Ingibjörg on hearing that her betrothed, Hjálmarr, had been slain in battle. The second account is the fuller one; here the girl falls back in her chair dead when Oddr brings her Hjálmarr's ring and his last message, and 'then Oddr burst out laughing and said: "Now they shall enjoy in death what they could not have in life"'. There is the same fierce delight here as we encountered in the story of Ahmed, when the man of the Rus laughed at the sight of the gale that brought his dead chief to Paradise the sooner.[2] One text of *Hervarar Saga* moreover goes further and

[1] See p. 42 above.
[2] Cf. Death-song of Ragnarr Loðbrók, who died with a laugh upon his lips. See p. 74 below.

makes Ingibjörg slay herself.[1] In the same saga we have the incident of King Harald's wife, who, when her husband was killed in battle as a sacrifice to Othin, slew herself in the temple of the Dísir (VII). In *Sörla Saga Sterka* the same motif recurs; here Hálfdan's queen dies of grief at the news of her husband's death, and she is buried with him (XIV). Saxo gives us two more examples; the first is that of Gunnhilda, who after Asmundus was killed 'cut off her own life with the sword, choosing rather to follow her lord in death than to forsake him by living'. Accordingly she is buried with him, but Saxo is not over-impressed by this act of devotion: 'There', he remarks, 'lies Gunnhilda clasping her lord somewhat more beautifully in the tomb than she had ever done in the bed.'[2] The other example is the more moving one of Signe,[3] who slays herself and causes her maids to do the same at the instant that her lover Hagbardus is hanged. Here it is noticeable that the method chosen by the women is that of strangling, while the house is set on fire, and their last action before death is to drink a cup of wine. These are all features of the ceremony witnessed by Ahmed; while the practice of one form of suttee, known as *satia*, on the island of Bali, involves a double suicide as here; the women stab themselves with the 'creese' at the instant that they jump into the fire. Friederich[4] himself did not witness such a ceremony, and was told that it was rarely practised, but was thought to be a much nobler death than that by burning alone. In the passage from Saxo Hagbarðr is not killed until the women have died, because he persuades the executioner to hang his cloak first to test whether his betrothed will be faithful enough to die with him; the sight of flames breaking out in her house tells him that she has not failed to keep her promise, and he utters a song which, muddled though the sense is in Saxo's ponderous Latin, nevertheless seems to contain allusions to some future life when they will be together:

> Unus erit finis, unus post federa nexus,
> Nec passim poterit prima perire Venus.
> Felix, qui tanta merui consorte iuuari,
> Nec male Tartareos solus adire deos.
> Ergo premant medias subiecta tenacula fauces;
> Nil, nisi quod libeat, pena suprema feret,

1 Rafn gives this variant in a note. *Hervarar Saga*, v, p. 429 (*Fornaldar Sögur*, Copenhagen, 1829–30).
2 Saxo, I, 27, p. 33.  3 *Ibid.* VII, 234, p. 281 f.
4 Friederich, *Journal of the Royal Asiatic Society* (N.S.), IX, 1877, p. 89 f.

Cum restaurande Veneris spes certa supersit,
Et mors delicias mox habitura suas.
Axis uterque iuuat; gemino celebrabitur orbe
Vna anima requies, par in amore fides.[1]

(There shall be one end for us both; one bond after our vows; nor
shall our first love aimlessly perish. Happy am I to have won the joy of
such a consort; I shall not go down basely in loneliness to the gods of
Tartarus. So let the encircling bonds grip my throat in the midst; the
final anguish shall bring with it pleasure only, since the certain hope
remains of renewed love, and death shall prove to have its own delights.
Each world holds joy, and in the twin regions shall the repose of our
united souls win fame, our equal faithfulness in love.)

According to Saxo and Snorri,[2] Hagbarðr is the brother of Haki,
the sea-king who met his death on a blazing ship; and in Saxo Haki
avenges the death of his brother on Sigarr. There is also a reference to
the brothers in *Völsunga Saga* (xxv). A resemblance may be noticed
moreover to another story which concerns us in this chapter, that
told in the Helgi poems;[3] there, in addition to the death of the wife
beside her husband, we meet the incident of the hero disguised as a
woman, a feature of the Hagbarðr story; while the conception of the
Valkyrie is introduced into both. Evidently the story of Hagbarðr
was one widely circulated. Herrmann[4] points out that the references
to it are found in the works of Norwegian and Icelandic skalds from
the ninth to the thirteenth century, and a reference in a verse of
Kormákr shows that it was known in Iceland in the mid-tenth
century, and cannot be a late romantic story.

The account which seems to have most in common, however,
with the fierce magnificence of Ahmed's story is the account of the
burning of Sigurðr and Brynhildr, in the Edda poem, *Sigurðarkviða
hin Skamma*, from which the account in *Völsunga Saga* seems to be
copied. Here Brynhildr begs Gunnarr to build so broad a funeral
pyre for the hero's burning that Sigurðr and those who die with him
may lie easily side by side. It shall be adorned, she says, with costly
cloth, and with shields, and with the bodies of many slain; for she
herself will lie beside Sigurðr, with only a sword between them, as

---

1 Saxo Grammaticus (ed. Holder, Strassburg, 1886), VII, 132, p. 237.
2 Saxo, VII, 237, p. 285; Snorri, *Ynglinga Saga*, XXII.
3 Symons, 'Zur Helgisage' (*Beiträge zur Geschichte der deutschen Sprache und
   Literatur*, IV, p. 190 f.).
4 Herrmann, *Dänische Geschichte des Saxo Grammaticus*, II, pp. 490 ff.

once they shared the marriage bed. Their following also shall be no mean one, for five bondwomen and eight menservants, followers of hers who have grown up with her from childhood, shall share the last resting-place of the tragic lovers.

Finally in another poem, *Helgakviða Hundingsbana II*, we have the scene where Sigrún enters the grave-mound of her husband and clasps him once more in death; here, fused by the poet's imagination, many different conceptions seem to have met and mingled, but in the words of Helgi as he welcomes his wife there comes again that familiar ring, the echo of a once fierce and vital belief, which seems to animate so many of these stories:

> Well may we drink a noble draught,
> Though lost to us now are love and lands;
> Sing shall no man a song of sorrow
> Though wide are the wounds upon my breast;
> For now are our maids shut in the mound,
> The brides of the heroes with us, their husbands.
>
> And now you sleep in the arms of the slain
> Within the howe, white daughter of Helgi,
> And yet are alive, young daughter of Kings....

There can be no question in these passages of a mere literary motif, copied from one to another. The majority of the passages referred to in the *Fornaldar Sögur* are irrelevant episodes outside the plot of the story; and the link between the separate accounts is not so much the description of the incident, which differs widely in different cases, but the spirit behind it—such as could not spring from a mere imitation.

There is another side of sacrifice seen in the sagas, that of voluntary burial while alive by others besides the wife of the dead man. The most vivid account of it is the story of the foster-brothers Aran and Ásmundr, in one of the *Fornaldar Sögur*.[1] Here the two make a pact that whichever of them outlives the other shall spend three nights with the dead man in his howe. Aran falls dead one day in the hall, and Ásmundr is forced to keep his promise; the dead man is placed in the burial mound together with his horse, saddled and bridled, his weapons, and a hawk and hound; and his foster-brother has a stool carried in too, and sits beside him. At this point the story takes a

1 *Egils Saga ok Ásmundar*, VII.

gruesome turn, for on the first night the dead man rises and devours the hawk and hound; the second night he 'slew the horse and broke it in pieces and began to devour it vigorously, chewing it up so that the blood ran down his jaws. He invited Ásmundr to eat with him.' On the third night the inevitable happens, and Aran tries to devour his former foster-brother; Ásmundr, however, overcomes him and cuts off his head before he himself has lost more than his ears. Saxo tells us the same story, and here Ásmundr is rescued from the mound by King Eric of Sweden (v, p. 199).

We have also record of several kings burying themselves alive with much treasure, sometimes with a number of followers. In *Heimskringla* King Herlaugr goes into a howe with twelve men rather than be deprived of his kingship by King Harald Hárfagr;[1] in *Bárðar Saga* King Raknar is said to walk alive into his howe after ruling the land for a long time (xvIII). Similarly a certain Agnarr is said to enter a howe with his ship's crew in *Þorskfirðinga Saga* (III). He is probably connected with Agði Jarl who goes alive into a howe specially built for the purpose in *Þorsteins þáttr Bæarmagnis*.[2] In nearly all these cases these men turn into powerful *draugar* after burial, and cannot be vanquished without a struggle; the same is true of another figure, in *Hrómundar Saga Greipssonar*, who 'when he was so old that he could fight no longer, had himself put living into the howe, and much treasure with him' (IV). But these stories seem to be of a different kind from those of human sacrifice; they give no impression of a half-remembered custom, and here the resemblance between them is one of motif rather than of spirit infused into them. We are in any case dealing here with ideas about the vigour of the dead founded on a belief in life continuing in the grave, which will be discussed more fully later on.

Behind the idea of sacrifice as practised at the funeral, we seem to discern two distinct ideas. One is that the possessions given to the dead, the animals and even the human beings slain with him accompany him into the next life; such a belief can be seen, for instance, in the story of the death of the Rus chieftain, in the suicide of Signe, in the suicide of Brynhildr; it is stated in the words of Snorri, who attributes the origin of the belief to the teaching of Othin, and it is neatly illustrated by another story which has not been alluded to

---

1 *Haralds Saga Hárfagra*, vIII.
2 *Þorsteins Þáttr Bæarmagnis: Fornmanna Sögur* (Copenhagen, 1825–1837), III, p. 197 (chapter XII).

before, that of Sigurðr Hringr—the man who is said to have been sent out to meet death in a burning ship—at the death of an honoured enemy, King Harald.[1] He had the body of his vanquished foe drawn to the howe by his own horse; 'afterwards he had the horse killed, and then King Hringr made them take the saddle on which he himself had ridden, and gave it to his kinsman, King Harald, bidding him do which he would, ride or drive to Valhöll'. This last example shows how the idea of possessions and companions given to the dead to be used in another life links up naturally with a belief in a journey to the land of the dead, and the desirability of providing means for the dead man to make that journey.

The second idea which can be seen behind the custom of sacrifice, as described in the literature, is that possessions are given to the dead man for use in the grave-mound, which is visualised as a kind of house; we see this in the picture of the dead Sóti, sitting on his ship in the mound, and brooding over his treasure; in the story of Ásmundr, who insisted on the removal of the thrall who had been sacrificed with him, because he was so pressed for room in his ship— a passage whose unmoved reaction to heroics is typically Norse, and which helps us to understand why a religion of elaborate sacrifice never really established itself in Scandinavia—and in its most crude and gruesome form in the tale of the other Ásmundr, who was buried with his foster-brother. Ship-funeral, it will be seen, can be linked up with either of these conceptions.

As seen in Norse literature, suttee is presented as an act of sacrifice; the woman is slain that she, together with the dead man's other possessions, may be his in another life. Brynhildr and Signe desire death, because only by means of it can they usurp the wife's place which has been denied them in life. Again in the account of suttee among the Rus, it may be noticed that any of the slaves and not only a lawful wife may die, while even the sensually-minded Ahmed puts the emphasis on the death of a *slave*, and tells us that this may be either a man or woman, though in practice it is usually the latter. The idea that by sacrificing herself the woman earns the right to call the dead man her husband is however again marked here. It may be noticed too in Friederich's[2] account of the ceremony on the Island of Bali in the last century; there he tells us how the glory of the next life is described to the slave-women who consent to die, when they are

1 *Sögubrot af Fornkonungum*, IX, p. 134 (*Fornaldar Sögur*, I).
2 *Op. cit.* p. 50 above.

told they will attain to a higher caste and become wives of the deceased, but that the dead man's successor, on the other hand, regards them simply as slaves who will be needed by his father after cremation. Some of the other accounts of suttee in India and Bali already referred to bear out this impression. In particular it may be worth remembering that in the great ceremony which took place in Bali in 1633 [1] at the death of the queen twenty-two female slaves were burnt with her, so that the same ceremonial was evidently observed in the case of women of high rank as with men. Even in India, where the idea of 'the faithful wife' was most firmly established, there is some reason to think that the idea of it being the widow's duty to die with her husband was never taught in Vedic literature, but was only introduced much later, when widows were prohibited by law to re-marry.[2]

It is indeed towards the conception of the slave sent to serve the dead man rather than the more lofty conception of the faithful wife dying with her husband, that the evidence for the origin of suttee in the East seems on the whole to direct us. The same is confirmed by the references to the practice in Norse literature, whether the attendant is to dwell with the dead man inside the tomb or to accompany him through the flames to another world. But the idea that she who gives up her life to follow the dead man has the right to become his wife in the next world is very significant, and we find this emphasised again in Norse literature, since out of the comparatively few examples given there three of the women, Ingibjörg, Signe and Brynhildr, were not married to the men with whom they died, although they desired to be. In short, suttee as presented in Norse literature appears to be the logical extension of the ideas about the future life which Snorri describes to us in *Ynglinga Saga*, and which he states to be part of the teaching brought into Sweden by Othin. The fact that most of our evidence—though not all—is connected with cremation ceremonies, and with the idea of a future life spent with the gods and in particular with Othin, confirms this. It is also significant that the most important piece of evidence relating to suttee, from the *Flateyjarbók*,[3] attributes the custom to the kings of Sweden, and records that it was still practised there in the tenth century.

1 Friederich, *op. cit.* p. 50 above.
2 N. K. Datta, *Indian Historical Quarterly*, XIV, 4, 1938 (Dec.).
3 See p. 51 above.

## THE FUNERAL FEAST

Throughout the sagas it is made clear that an important way of paying honour to the dead was to hold a funeral feast in his memory; and this was important for the living as well as for the dead, since it was at the feast that the son took over the inheritance of his father. Snorri describes the proceedings at such a feast:

It was the custom at that time when a funeral feast should be made in honour of king or jarl that he who held it and who was to succeed to the inheritance should sit on the step before the high-seat up to the time when the cup was borne in which was called Bragi's cup. Then he should stand up with the cup of Bragi and make a vow, and drink off the cup afterwards; then he should proceed to the high-seat which his father had had, and then he succeeded to all the inheritance after him.[1]

It seems probable that there is a connection between this ascent to the high-seat and the descent from the king's seat on top of the mound described in *Heimskringla*, when Hrollaugr 'rolls himself down' into the seat of a jarl;[2] the significance of the seat on the mound will be discussed later.[3] The grandest feasts were of course those of the kings, when the royal title was handed over; but the important men of Iceland could distinguish themselves when they chose; in *Laxdœla Saga* we have a description of the elaborate memorial feast held by the sons of Höskuldr for their father, carried through by the enthusiasm of Olaf, who was determined that his father should be fittingly honoured. All the great men were invited, and the saga records that there were nearly eleven hundred guests, and that no such feast had been held in Iceland since that of the sons of Hjalti (xxvii), on which occasion, *Landnámabók* tells us,[4] there were over fourteen hundred guests. Important guests were always sent away with gifts. The feast might be held immediately after the laying in howe, like the two described in *Gísla Saga*,[5] or, as with Höskuldr's feast, some months might elapse. If there were no children to succeed the dead man, the brother might hold the feast, and it is interesting to find what a sacred duty one brother at least makes of it, in a passage already quoted from *Svarfdœla Saga*.[6]

1 *Ynglinga Saga*, xxxvi.  2 *Heimskringla: Haralds Saga Hárfagra*, viii.
3 See p. 105 below.  4 *Lndn.* iii, 9, p. 145.
5 *Gísla Saga*, xiv, xvii, xviii.  6 See p. 36 above.

What then was the original motive behind this custom? Was there some idea of well-being for the dead dependent on the holding of a feast for them? We know that poems in honour of the dead man were recited, for in the famous scene in *Egils Saga* Egill's daughter proposes that her father shall make a poem to be recited at his son's funeral feast (LXXVIII). The poem that resulted was the *Sonatorrek*, and this contains clear allusions to some kind of future life shared with the gods. It has been suggested that this may be due to the fact that Egill, who must certainly have mixed with Christian people on his travels, was influenced by Christian teaching about immortality,[1] and this may well be the case; on the other hand, it is interesting to notice that in a passage from Snorri's *Hákonar Saga Góða* (XXXII), we find that at the funeral of the king it is said 'men spoke at his burial as was the custom with heathen men, and directed him to Valhöll'. We may note too the subject-matter of the *Hákonarmál* and the *Eiríksmál*, tenth-century skaldic poems describing the entry of the kings into Valhöll; could this be a late development of a once well-established tradition, and if so, is the Christian influence in Egill's poem shown in the reticence he displays on the subject of the future life rather than in the brief allusions to it? We may remember at the same time the belief stated in *Eyrbyggia Saga* (LIV) that it was a lucky omen if drowned men appeared at their own funeral feasts, since it was a sign that they had been well received by Rán.

In the case of important people, the funeral feast does not seem, in later times at any rate, to have been confined to men, for the wedding banquet at Auðr's house in *Laxdæla Saga* (VII) turned into a funeral feast in her honour. It seems to have been a privilege for those who left wealth or a position to be inherited, or for a specially loved son or brother who died and left no succession. It is not recorded in the case of poor and unimportant people with few possessions.

In the accounts of funeral feasts and of honours paid to the dead there is the same contradiction which has already become apparent in the literature. As practised in Iceland the feast was evidently considered to be a last mark of respect paid to those who were to dwell in the tomb, since this was the general conception of the fate of those laid in howe. Such eccentric customs sometimes recorded at funerals as the carrying of the corpse through a hole in the wall instead of a door, as in the funeral of old Skallagrímr in *Egils Saga* (LVIII) or Þórólfr in *Eyrbyggja Saga* (XXXIII), are clearly somewhat crude

1 N. Kershaw, *Anglo-Saxon and Norse Poems* (Cambridge, 1922), p. 133.

methods of ensuring that the corpse shall not find its way back to the house to 'haunt' the living after it has been laid in the grave. Parallels among various peoples in an early stage of civilisation can easily be supplied; there are any amount, for instance, in Frazer's collection of customs concerned with the dead, *Belief in Immortality*. This conception of the dead is quite consistent with the picture of the corpse guarding his treasures within the howe. But when we find it recorded of a tenth-century king of Norway that at his burial he was 'directed to Valhöll' it is clear that here we have a different conception—nearer to the ideas about the future life which we have found to be connected with the worship of Othin in Sweden. Nor can the *Hákonarmál* and the *Eiríksmál*, composed in the tenth century at the death of historic kings of Norway, be easily reconciled with a belief in the continued sojourn of the dead within the tomb. Even if full allowances are made for poetic imagination, and for the framing of an artistic compliment to the dead man, it is hard to comprehend how such a picture of the departure of the dead to another realm, the realm of Othin, could be composed and accepted if no such conception had been a reality to the people for whom the poem was composed, either at that time or within recent memory.

## CONCLUSION

Surveying the evidence as a whole, there is nothing to justify us in connecting any one custom rigidly to any one belief; one cannot say that ship-funeral is evidence of one belief in the future life, cremation another, and so on. It is clear that in Scandinavia different beliefs and customs have intermingled, and it is very unlikely that any consistent and definite body of beliefs was ever held at any one time about the disposal of the dead and the meaning of it. The varying beliefs current simultaneously in other countries where oral tradition prevails and religious dogma is unknown leads us to expect this; the islands of Polynesia, for instance, afford an excellent example.

But it is, I think, possible to distinguish some conceptions which stand out clearly in the evidence which we have examined. One of these is that the dead man continues to exist in his grave-mound as in a house, and that sacrifices may be made to him, and possessions laid in the howe beside him, so that he may have the use of them as he dwells there. Such an idea of the dead is not a frightening one; only if he has been a menace to other men in his life is he likely to interfere with them after death. This is the belief that seems according to the literature to have been supreme in Iceland at the end of the heathen period, when interment in the howe was the normal method of disposing of the dead; and other customs, such as the putting of shoes on the dead man and laying him in a ship, or of cremating those who 'walk' after death, only linger on as reminiscences of former beliefs without any real meaning of their own.

What then of those other beliefs, faintly remembered in Iceland? Out of them we must select the practice of cremation of the dead. If we run briefly over the allusions to it in the literature, the result is interesting. Snorri explains the origin of the practice as a belief that those cremated go to join Othin in Valhöll, and all the possessions burned with them go too. He illustrates this by the traditions of the funeral ceremonies of Othin and Njörðr, and of those of the earliest kings of the Swedes of which he has heard. We know also that Haki and Sigurðr were said to be burned in their ships as they floated out to sea, and in the case of Sigurðr we are told that it is the kingdom of Othin to which the winds and the flames are bearing him. Balder, the son of Othin, is also said to be burned after death. In the accounts of the burning of Brynhildr and Sigurðr, and of Signe, there are references to another life where the lovers will be together. It will be remembered that Lindqvist's interpretation of some of the obscurer verses of the *Ynglingatal* dealing with the Swedish kings fits in perfectly with the conception found in the passages just mentioned; he believes that in several cases the original account deals with a cremation ceremony, and that the flames are described as bearing away the dead man to Othin, although Snorri, and even Þjóðólfr, did not fully realise this. The evidence as a whole seems to suggest then that an earlier conception than that of life continuing in the grave-mound was that of life continuing after the destruction of the body in some other place, when the vital principle—the soul, if you will—has been set free from the body by burning. Such a belief seems to be an integral part of the passages to which we have referred above; and it is borne out by the attitude of the Rus in the tenth century at the cremation of their chieftain, recorded for us by an eyewitness. The two different conceptions which seem to lie behind sacrifice fit in with these two beliefs. Death alone, for those who practised cremation, is not enough to set free the part which survives; there must be the destruction of the material body and the material possessions too; and the fact that in Iceland those who will not rest in the grave are burnt may well be a last echo of this belief.

Literary tradition supports the connection made in the *Ynglinga Saga* between these beliefs about cremation and the worship of Othin. It also suggests that these beliefs were particularly connected with men and women of royal blood, since it is in the traditions dealing with princes and chieftains that it has survived. It is significant that Othin is represented in the literature as the god of kings and chieftains, in contrast to Thor, whose affinities lie rather with the common people. In the skaldic poems he is seen welcoming kings to his side; in *Hárbarðsljóð* (v, 24) we are told that those of noble blood who fall in the fight belong to Othin, while Thor has the race of thralls; and similarly in the strange and vivid account of the assembly of the gods in the *Fornaldar Sögur*[1] a similar distinction is made between them, for besides the gifts of skaldship and victory in battle Othin grants to his protégé Starkaðr that he shall find favour among men of distinction, while Thor, not to be outdone, replies by depriving him of the good-will of the common people. We have also noticed that the kings of the Swedes, according to the source used by Snorri, claim descent from Othin. The impression given by the literature is that this belief in cremation of the dead was never very widespread in Scandinavia, but that it was a vigorous, perhaps fanatical, belief within a restricted circle, and having left its mark on some of the most impressive passages in the literature it passed to leave the other conception, that of life continuing in the grave and the world under the earth, to develop in ways of its own, ways that will need to be discussed further when we reach the question of the cult of the dead and the belief in rebirth.

The practice of ship-funeral, on the other hand, seems never to have represented any one outstanding belief in Scandinavia. It is possible that in the Migration period the idea of travelling by ship to the land of the dead did have some real meaning, and we have seen that archaeological evidence gives us some reason to believe that such a conception did enter the North in much earlier times, at the end of the Bronze Age; such a conception is also hinted at in the literary traditions. But it seems far more likely that ship-funeral came to be adopted as a practice in Scandinavia in the Viking Age because burial or cremation in a ship linked itself so readily to already existing conceptions. A belief in a life elsewhere when the material body and its

1 *Gautreks Saga*, VII. Cf. Chadwick, *Heroic Age* (Cambridge, 1912), p. 395 f.

possessions have been destroyed can, as we saw earlier, be very easily extended to include a belief in the necessity of a journey to the land of the dead. Moreover, when we find the idea of the wind fanning the flames and speeding the dead on his way to another world it is easy to see how this, linked with the practice of using a ship as a coffin, might result in such a tradition as that of the death of Haki finding its way into literature; probably there were others beside Snorri who found these odd ideas about the next world beyond their comprehension when they came to write them down. Again the belief in life continuing in the grave, where possessions are still appreciated by the dead, makes the retention of a ship by a man who had owned one in life a natural conclusion. The idea of the wife of necessity dying when the husband dies, and of the giving of chariot or horses or shoes to the dead, seems likely to have belonged originally to the conception of a life elsewhere and then to have been transferred to the other idea of life continuing in the earth, to which they could easily be adapted. Certainly the practice of putting the queen to death, which is associated with tenth-century kings of Sweden, can hardly be expected to have survived unless a fierce and vital belief in survival apart from the body lingered on too.

But at this point it seems necessary to leave the evidence for funeral customs in order to commence a new study—that of the ideas connected with the future life which are to be found in the literature, particularly those connected with Othin, to which the evidence up to now has perforce directed us.

# Chapter III

# THE CONCEPTION OF THE FUTURE LIFE

And down from thennes faste he gan avyse
This litel spot of erthe, that with the se
Enbraced is, and fully gan despise
This wrecched world, and held al vanite
To respect of the pleyn felicite
That is in hevene above.   CHAUCER, *Troilus and Criseyde.*

A study of the evidence for funeral customs in Scandinavia left us with the impression of two main conceptions preserved in literary tradition, one of another life after the body is destroyed, and the other of a life after death down in the earth where the body lies. From this starting-point then we can approach the evidence for ideas about the future life given in the sagas and poems, to see how far they will bear out this impression. Since the belief in an after-life after the destruction of the body seemed in several of the passages we studied to be connected with the worship of Othin, the first part of the evidence to be examined in detail is the description of Othin's paradise, Valhöll, as given in the poems and in Snorri's *Prose Edda.* The problems to be considered are, first, how far the idea of a warrior's paradise of eternal conflict and feasting is merely an imaginative conception of the poets, without any religious significance, and, secondly, how far it is possible to equate the conception of Valhöll in the literature with that of the other world beyond the grave.

The simplest form of the conception of life continuing down in the earth is that found in the *Íslendinga Sögur*, of the dead man dwelling in the grave-mound as in a house, and still enjoying his possessions there. There are also two more elaborate variations on this idea which must be considered; one is that of a gloomy underworld realm of the dead, and the other that of a kingdom of the dead inside the mountains. To decide on the extent and the consistence of these conceptions in the literature is, I think, of some importance, even though it is impossible to arrive at any conclusions as to whether we are dealing with memories of real beliefs or not from the evidence as it stands, for only in this way can the ground be cleared for further investigation.

THE CONCEPTION OF VALHÖLL IN THE POEMS

For evidence about Othin's dwelling at Valhöll, we must first consult the Eddic poems. The Edda contains a number of poems of the 'question and answer' type, in which one character, god, giant or dwarf, tries to outdo another in his knowledge of cosmology and the future of the human and divine worlds, but these poems contain little information about the fate of mankind after death. In *Vafþrúð-nismál*, a dialogue between Othin and the wise giant, Vafþrúðnir is asked who do battle each day in the courts of Othin. He replies that it is the *einherjar*—that is, single, or out-standing champions—who after choosing the slain and riding home from the battle sit at peace together. It is from *Grímnismál*, a monologue supposed to be spoken by Othin as he sits in torment between the fires in the hall of Geirröðr, that we learn more of these *einherjar*.[1]

Here the word is used more than once to describe the warriors who dwell with Othin, who, we are told, chooses certain of those killed in battle on earth to dwell with him in Valhöll, his bright dwelling in Glaðsheimr. The life they lead there is one of joy and feasting, with no mention of the eternal conflict. However the hall is full of shields and mailcoats, it is haunted by wolf and eagle, the creatures of battle, and is large enough to hold mighty hosts. There are over six hundred doors to the hall, and through each doorway will pour hundreds of warriors when the time comes to fight the wolf. The poet goes on to give an account of the feasting in Valhöll; he tells of the boar Saehrímnir, whose flesh feeds the warriors for ever, and of the bright mead from the goat Heiðrún, which will never give out. Eleven maidens, whose names are given, bear the cups to the warriors, and two more carry the horn to Othin, who himself needs no meat, and lives by wine alone. From verse 21 we assume that the host of the slain reaches Valhöll by wading the strong river Þund, and enters by the gate Valgrind, which is never closed. Lastly we notice the sinister reference to the day which will bring this life of revelry to a close, the day when the heroes will go out to fight the wolf.

This practically ends the information about Valhöll in the poems. There are only brief and cryptic references to be added. *Grímnismál* itself tells us elsewhere (v. 14) that Freyja allots the seats in her hall, Folkvangr, to whom she will, and that she has half the slain that fall each day, while half belong to Othin. In *Hárbarðsljóð* (v. 24) the

1 Vv. 8 ff., 18 ff., 21 ff., 36.

adversary of Thor, about whose identity there is no complete agreement, taunts him by the remark that Othin has the jarls who fall among the slain, but Thor the race of thralls. In *Völuspá* we have only the awakening of the warriors of Othin by the crowing of the cock Gollinkambi mentioned among the signs of the approaching doom at the end of all things.

The poems then do not give us much information, and what they do give comes mostly from one poem, *Grímnismál*. The account is by no means clear. There is apparently some system of choice by which only part of the slain reach Valhöll, but what it is we do not know. There are a number of alternative possibilities suggested; *Grímnismál* tells us that Othin himself (Hroptr) chooses the slain, but also remarks, in verse 14, that Freyja chooses half of them for her own hall. In *Vafþrúðnismál* the choice is said to be the work of the *einherjar*. The eleventh-century poem, *Darraðarljóð*, tells us, on the other hand, that the Valkyries have the power to choose the slain (v. 6). The expression *kjósa val* itself is difficult to interpret since it might mean to decide either (a) who is to fall in battle,[1] or (b) who out of those slain may enter Valhöll.

If we turn from the Edda poems to *Gylfaginning*, the first part of Snorri's *Prose Edda*, the first impression gained is that here we have plenty of evidence about Valhöll. This opening section is a kind of summary of the mythology, in the form of a dialogue between the insatiably curious and refreshingly ignorant Gangleri and three mysterious powers; and Valhöll is one of the subjects in which he is, naturally, very interested. In chapters XX, XXIV, XXXVI, XXXVIII, XXXIX, XL and XLI we find a fairly coherent and consistent account of it, but if this is checked point by point with the evidence of the poems, it will be seen that there is no new information given us—only implications such as could be drawn by an intelligent reader with a little imagination working on the information in the poems which we have already studied.

There is considerable linking up of scattered pieces of information; for example in chapter XL Snorri goes straight on from the account of the number and size of the doors in Valhöll, taken from *Grímnismál*, to the idea of the perpetual fighting found in *Vafþrúðnismál*, but there are no links which we could not have made for ourselves from our knowledge of the poems as we have them. Snorri also enlarges the statements made in the poems, as he has done in the

[1] In this case it might be merely a poetic expression for 'to slay in battle'.

delightful treatment of the eating and drinking of the *einherjar* in chapters xxxviii and xxxix, but there seems to be no additional information which entitles us to conclude that he was using other sources which we do not possess. Only on very minor points does he volunteer statements of his own. The account in *Grímnismál* of the feeding of Gera and Freka by Othin does not tell us who or what these creatures are; Snorri tells us definitely that they are wolves. Again he tells us that the mead drunk by the *einherjar* runs from the horns of the goat Heiðrún (xxxix). This at first sight hardly appears an obvious assumption, but in the next verse of *Grímnismál* to that mentioning Heiðrún we are told that all the rivers of the world flow from the horns of Heiðrún's companion, the hart Eikþyrnir, so that here again Snorri's statement may be based on nothing more than a careful reading of *Grímnismál*. Moreover Snorri does not clear up such problems as the choosing of the slain by Freyja; he merely paraphrases the verse as it stands, and then quotes it (xxiv). Snorri certainly knew how to make the most of what evidence he had at his disposal, but as regards the subject of Valhöll we have reason to believe that we are as well informed as he.

The two skaldic poems which go back to the tenth century, the *Eiríksmál* and the *Hákonarmál*, have both the same theme—the entry of a king into Valhöll after his death in battle. The picture they draw is in accordance with *Grímnismál* and Snorri, though the idea of the last great conflict is more stressed. Valhöll was certainly a familiar poetic theme in the tenth century, that could be used with great dramatic and emotional effect, but this tells us nothing as to how recent or real a belief it had been. But though Snorri and the earlier skaldic poets can be seen using the material at their disposal artistically, so that inconsistencies and problems are no longer visible, this is by no means true of *Grímnismál*. This poem assumes a background of knowledge lost to us, and there is no attempt to make an artistic whole out of the scraps of information vouchsafed in it. It does at least suggest that the Valhöll conception, as seized on with enthusiasm by the court poets and later by Snorri, was only one small part of a much larger conception, which the later writers have forgotten.

## THE VALKYRIES

This is borne out particularly by the strange figures of the Valkyries. In *Grímnismál* (36) we are told of eleven maidens who carry wine to the warriors in Valhöll: Skeggjöld, Skögul, Hildr, Þrúðr, Hlökk, Herfjötur, Göll, Geirönul, Randgríðr, Ráðgríðr and Reginleif. Two more are said to carry the horn to Othin: Hrist and Mist. Snorri tells us, though the poem does not, that these are the Valkyries: 'And these does Othin send to every battle; they ordain which men are doomed to death, and decide the victory' (XXXVI). He adds three more names, saying that 'Guðr and Róta and the youngest Norn, who is called Skuld, ride always to choose the slain and to rule the battle'.

Two of these names are certainly found in the list of Valkyries given in *Völuspá* (30), though there we are told nothing of them except that they are riding to the battle; Skuld, Skögul, Gunnr, Hildr, Göndul and Geirskögul are given here as the names 'of the Valkyries of the Lord of Hosts'. In the *Hákonarmál* Göndul and Skögul reappear as the Valkyries who conduct Hákon to Valhöll. The *Darraðarljóð* gives two more names: Hjörþrimul and Svipul; while Hildr reappears, and Sanngríðr may be the same as Randgríðr in *Grímnismál*.[1]

The most interesting thing about the Valkyries, however, is the different guises in which they appear. In the *Hákonarmál* they are noble and dignified women, sitting high on their horses in full armour; they are depicted as carrying out the commands of Othin and giving victory according to his will. In the *Darraðarljóð* they are very different figures, much fiercer and cruder, who are shown weaving the web of battle and exulting in blood and carnage. They have little in common with the elegant abstractions of the *Hákonarmál*; rather are they akin to the creatures who carry a trough and ride on a wolf,[2] sit in a house drenched with blood,[3] wave blood-stained cloths over those about to fight,[4] or sprinkle blood over a district,[5] in various passages in the sagas; they seem a natural part of the company of strange elemental beings who appear here and there in Norse literature to rejoice in slaughter and the conflicts of men.

1 N. Kershaw, *Anglo-Saxon and Norse Poems* (Cambridge, 1922), p. 193.
2 *Haralds Saga Harðráða: Heimskringla*, LXXX–LXXXI.
3 *Sturlunga Saga (Kongelige nordiske Oldskriftselskab*, 1906), I, p. 285.
4 *Ibid.* p. 494.      5 *Víga-Glúms Saga*, XXII.

Again we have the Valkyrie Sváva, who appears in a company of nine maidens before the youthful Helgi, to grant him his name.[1] She acts thereafter as his supernatural guardian and protector in battle, and he hails her as his 'radiant bride'. She rides over land and sea in shining armour, but here the conception of her is very different from that of the handmaids of Othin, and she is attached to one prince through his life. Sigrún, the betrothed of the later Helgi, said to be Sváva reborn, is also described as a Valkyrie who rides through the air, in the prose links in *Helgakviða Hundingsbana II*. She is at the same time, however, a mortal maiden and the human bride of Helgi. In *Fáfnismál* and *Sigrdrífumál* Sigurðr visits the Valkyrie Sigrdrífa, and finds her asleep in a castle surrounded by flame, because, she says, she has offended Othin by giving victory to a king for whom he had ordained defeat. In *Helreið Brynhildar* and in the *Völsunga Saga* there is again a curious mixture of the human and the supernatural, and Sigrdrífa becomes Brynhildr.[2] Lastly we have the idea of the Valkyrie as a woman who can assume the shape of a swan. This occurs in *Völundarkviða*, where Völundr and his two brothers capture and marry three Valkryies, by stealing their swan-shapes from them so that they cannot fly away, and again in *Hrómundar Saga* (VII), where the warrior is protected by a woman in the shape of a swan, who flies over his head in battle and chants spells so that he cannot be vanquished. Here, it is true, the word *Valkyrja* is not used, but there seems to be a close connection with some of the other passages we have mentioned. We shall have to discuss the Valkyrie conception further in the chapter on *The Conception of the Soul*; it is only necessary here to notice the wide and complex nature of the Valkyries who appear in Norse literature, and how often they exceed the characteristics which skaldic poets and Snorri give to them as the handmaids of Othin. The strange tradition of 'shield-maids' or 'fighting-maids' which reappears continually in the *Fornaldar Sögur* and is also found in Saxo is evidently linked up with the Valkyrie conception, and is one found outside Scandinavia. Saxo, it will be observed, also seems to introduce Valkyries into the legend of Balder and Hotherus, since they claim to take part invisibly in battle, and to decide the fortunes of war.[3] He, however, calls them 'wood-nymphs', and it is in a wood that Hotherus encounters them. They

---

1 *Helgakviða Hjörvarðssonar*, II: prose introduction.
2 The Sigrdrífa-Brynhildr question is discussed in detail on p. 181 below.
3 Saxo, III, 70, p. 84.

like the other Valkyries mentioned above are not the servants of Othin, but act as the supernatural guardians and protectors of those whom they favour.[1]

Supernatural 'choosers of the slain' were known also to the Anglo-Saxons. By the tenth century they have taken their place among the adversaries of the Christian God, and are placed contemptuously by Wulfstan beside witches and criminals;[2] similarly as late as the fourteenth century they are still paired off with witches in the alliterative poem *Cleaness*.[3] But it is more significant to find the 'choosers of the slain' (*walcyrge*, etc.) appearing several times in the early Anglo-Saxon vocabularies and glosses for Latin words. In one word list[4] which may be dated as early as the eighth century *wælcyrge* (*walcyrge*, *walcrigge*) is given as the Anglo-Saxon equivalent for Tisifone, Eurynes and Herines (Erinys); and in another eleventh-century manuscript[5] once for Herinis, once for Allecto and twice for Bellona; while in Ælfric's vocabulary[6] the plural (*wælcyrie*) is given again for Tisifone. Finally in one manuscript of Aldhelm's *De Laude Virginitatis*[7] *wælcyrie* is given as a gloss for *veneris*.

The choice of Bellona, Goddess of War, and of the Furies, Erinys, Tisiphone and Allecto, suggests female beings connected with fate and with slaughter, resembling, in fact, the wilder Valkyries of Norse literature whom we have seen to be distinct from the more conventional figures of fair attendants upon a dignified Othin; this is borne out by a passage in which they appear as a gloss for Gorgons.[8]

---

1 The distinction between fierce elemental beings and protective supernatural women has been noticed by Neckel (*Walhall*, XVI, p. 82 f.). He suggests that the class of Valkyrie delighting in blood and slaughter belongs to an older belief in a kind of battle demon, akin to the giantesses and hostile to the gods, while Freyja is the chief spirit of the other class, helpful and protecting, which he calls *dísir*. The question of the *dísir* will be discussed further in chapter V.

2 *Wulfstan* (ed. Napier, Berlin, 1883), LVII, p. 298.

3 *Early English Alliterative Poems*, E.E.T.S. 1864, *Cleaness*, l. 1577.

4 Corpus Christi MS. CXLIV (ed. T. Wright, *Vocabularies*, 1873): II, 122. 34; 107. 43; 110. 34.

5 MS. Cotton. Cleopatra A III, *ibid.* II, 43. 2; 5. 70; 12. 12; 94. 15.

6 *Ibid.* I, 60. 21; in the following line we have *Parcæ*, *hægtesse*, and since *wælcyrie* is in the plural, it has been suggested that the meanings have been transposed.

7 Aldhelm, *De Laudibus Virginitatis* 4449. (*Old Eng. Glosses*, ed. Napier, Oxford 1900, p. 115.)

8 *Ða deor habbaþ wælkyrian eagan* (hae bestie oculos habent Gorgoneos). *Narratiunculae Anglice conscriptae* (ed. Cockayne, London, 1861), 34. 6.

It seems possible that this was the older conception, bound up with the early worship of Woden in Northern Europe, and that the idea of a supernatural guardian whose province extended to a life in the next world later influenced it in the literature. The connection between *veneris* and the 'choosers of the slain' is both suggestive and puzzling, since it confirms the link between the Valkyries and Freyja which we have seen presented but unexplained in *Grímnismál*.

The idea of the supernatural guardian attending the favoured warrior in the next world is found in most elaborate form in *Gísla Saga*,[1] where a number of verses are quoted in which the hero relates his dreams. Language, vocabulary and style appear to belong to the best period of skaldic verse, and there seems no particular reason to doubt the tradition which ascribes them to Gísli himself.[2] In the first of these 'dream-poems' the poet is taken to visit a hall by someone who, in the prose description, he calls his better dream-woman, and there finds many others who welcome him. There are fires burning in the hall, and his guide tells him that the number of the fires represents the number of years he has left to live. She gives him certain moral counsels, and in particular tells him to avoid magic, not to seek quarrels, or to injure the poor and helpless. Later on we are told that his dreams become worse, and now the verses tell of another woman who comes to him 'covered in men's blood', and washes him in it (XXIV). Then the first woman comes to him again; she is described as the 'bride', which apparently is more than mere poetic diction, since when she carries him away with her on a grey steed, and takes him to a hall in which there is a soft bed and pillows of down, she says: 'Here shall you certainly come when you die...then shall the chieftain possess these riches and the woman also' (XXIX). The other woman is angry at this, and swears it shall not be so; she is the last to visit Gísli before his death, according to the verses, and when she appears finally she covers him in blood and wraps him in blood-stained garments (XXXII). It will be seen that there is a certain resemblance to the Valkyries in the woman who rides on the grey steed and in the other woman with her horrible insistence on blood and slaughter, reminding us of the weavers of the *Darraðarljóð*; while in the conception of a female supernatural guardian who is called the wife of the man she protects there is some

---

1 *Gísla Saga*, XXII f.
2 F. Jónsson, *Gísla Saga* (*Altnord. Saga Bibliotek*, X, 1903), introduction, p. xxi.

likeness to the passages which have been mentioned above. There seems to be some connection here with a story in Saxo, who records that Balder dreamed, on the night before he died, that Proserpine stood beside him, and promised him that 'on the morrow he should have her embrace' (III, 77, p. 93). It is interesting to notice that there are other instances of rivalry between the warrior's Valkyrie guardian and another supernatural being of a grimmer type, who contend for possession of the man they desire; in *Helgakviða Hjörvarðssonar* (24ff.) the giantess Hrimgerðr grumbles because, she says, Helgi prefers 'the gold-adorned maid', Sváva, to her; and Brynhildr, who is often represented as a Valkyrie, is reproached by a giantess because she has caused the death of Sigurðr, whom (in the introduction to the *Helreið Brynhildar* in the *þáttr Norna-Gests*) the giantess says she has herself often favoured. Is it possible that these are echoes of a rivalry between two different schools of thought connected with the after-life, one of which has superseded the other?

## THE REALM OF THE GODS

The description of the Valkyries given by Snorri, in the section dealing with Valhöll, is seen to need considerable enlargement if all the evidence in the literature is taken into consideration, and similarly the conception of Valhöll in the literature as a whole seems to indicate something much wider than a warriors' paradise. Snorri himself, who as we have seen is relying exclusively on *Grímnismál* and *Vafþrúðnismál* in the *Prose Edda*, evidently knew of one other tradition at least, since he tells us in the *Ynglinga Saga* that those whose bodies were burnt went to join Othin in Valhöll after death, and their possessions with them. In one of the later sagas, *Gautreks Saga*, we have a fantastic opening chapter dealing with an absurd family of misers who sacrifice themselves to Othin on the slightest provocation, and their way of reaching Valhöll is to hurl themselves over a cliff. That this was a recognised form of sacrifice seems to be indicated by the words of the missionary Hjalti,[1] while the fact that Bede alludes to parties of men throwing themselves voluntarily over precipices[2] suggests a survival of the same tradition in England. Moreover it is interesting to notice that in the story in *Gautreks Saga* a servant was on one occasion allowed to sacrifice himself with his master as a

1 *Kristnis Saga*, XII (*Altnord. Saga- Bib.* 11, 1905), p. 49.
2 *Historia Ecclesiastica* (ed. Plummer, 1896), IV, 13. 231.

special privilege; of him it is said: 'He is to enjoy happiness in his [i.e. the master's] company. My father is quite sure that Othin will not come out to meet the thrall unless he is in his company.'

This odd story of the family who went in twos and threes 'cheerfully and gladly to Othin' reads like a parody or misunderstood echo of the tradition of dying by fire already discussed, which, as we have seen, appears to be connected with the conception of some kind of future life with Othin in a Valhöll which was not merely a paradise for warriors who fell in battle. We have the same note of fierce joy and certainty in the *Krákumál*,[1] the death-song of Ragnarr Loðbrók:

> It gladdens me ever to know that Balder's father makes ready the benches for a banquet. Soon we shall be drinking the ale from the curved horns. The champion who comes to Fjölnir's dwelling does not lament his death. I shall not come into Viðrir's hall with words of fear on my lips (v, 25).
>
> The Æsir will welcome me; death comes without lamenting....
>
> I am eager to depart. The *dísir* summon me home, they whom Othin has sent to me from the halls of the Lord of hosts. Gladly shall I drink ale in the high-seat with the Æsir. The days of my life are ended. I die with a laugh (v, 29).

Ragnarr, it will be remembered, did not according to tradition die in battle. The poem itself as well as the saga states that he was killed by snakes at the command of Ella of Northumberland. This sounds like some kind of sacrificial death, and if so, this would explain Ragnarr's firm conviction that he would be received by Othin, and would be in accordance with other passages dealing with human sacrifice which we have noticed.

Sometimes, though rarely, we find references to Valhöll in the *Íslendinga Sögur*. There are two examples in *Njáls Saga*. Jarl Guðbrandr exclaims after his shrine of the gods has been destroyed:

> A man must have burned the house and carried the gods out. But the gods do not revenge everything at once. The man who has done this will be driven out of Valhöll and will never enter there (LXXXVIII).

Again, when Högni is taking down his dead father's weapon to avenge him, he says: 'I mean to bear it to my father, and he shall carry it with him to Valhöll and bear it out to the meeting of the

---

1 *Ragnars Saga Loðbrókar* (*F.A.S.* 1), p. 56. F. Jónsson believes the poem to be earlier than 1200 in date, but not earlier than 1100 in its present form (*Litt. Hist.* II, p. 153 f.).

warriors' (LXXIX). Possibly Högni's statement is a merely ironical one; possibly, however, it is significant in the light of the fact that we know Gunnarr to be thought of as resting within his grave-mound; to this we shall return later. In *Gísla Saga* we are told that 'hel-shoes' are bound 'on to men that they may walk to Valhöll' (XIV); while in *Egils Saga* there are the puzzling words of Þorgerðr, who implies that she intends to starve herself to death by the words 'I will have nothing, till I sup with Freyja' (LXXVIII).[1] In *Grímnismál* (14), indeed, we are told that Freyja shares with Othin the power to 'choose' the slain, and that they share with her her hall, *Folkvangr*. Neckel[2] argues that this is merely a synonym, like *Valhöll*, for the field of battle, but he also suggests that Freyja is the true Valkyrie, welcoming the dead with wine within the house of the gods.

It would certainly seem that we have a persistent tradition for a goddess of the dead; since not only Hel, who will be discussed later, and Freyja, but also Gefion and Rán are connected with death. Snorri[3] tells us that Gefion is attended by all those women who die unmarried; apart from this she is chiefly connected with the land, and her name appears in many place-names. Attempts have been made to identify her with Frigg,[4] and also with Freyja, who is some-times called *Gefn*.[5] One rather slender piece of evidence which seems to agree with Snorri's representation of her as the goddess of chastity is the fact that she is invoked by the girl in *Völsaþáttr*[6] who opposes the phallic cult practised by the rest of her family. In some of the later sagas in the *Hauksbók* she is also identified with the virgin goddesses of the ancient world, in the stories of Paris and Brutus.[7] This is certainly an argument against identifying her with either Frigg or Freyja, who were not exactly renowned for their chastity. Moreover the use of her name in place-names suggests that at one time she had a local cult of her own.

The third goddess to be connected with the dead is Rán, the wife of Ægir, the god of the sea. *Eyrbyggja Saga* (LIV) tells us that if drowned

1 Cf. Danish charm recorded by Grimm from Jutland (*Teutonic Mythology*, trans. Stallybrass, IV, Appendix, p. 1867):

> A ligger mä paa mi hyver ley
> Saa souer a paa vor frou Frey.

2 Neckel, *Walhall*, pp. 17 and 87 f. (Dortmund, 1913).
3 *Gylfaginning*, XXXV.
4 F. Jónsson, *Lexicon Poeticum* (1913–6).
5 Müllenhof, *Deut. Altertumskunde*, II, p. 362.   6 See p. 157 below.
7 *Hauksbók: Trojonararsaga*, VII, p. 199; *Breta Sögur*, VII, p. 241.

men attended their own funerals it was looked on as a sign that Rán had received them well. We obtain little information about Rán from other sources. The most detailed allusion to her reception of the drowned comes from the late *Fridþjófs Saga* (VI) where, when the hero and his companions seem doomed to perish in a storm, he divides all the gold he has between them, saying that it will be better if they have some gold to show when they come to the hall of Rán. The verse that follows contains the same sentiment:

> So shall the guests be seen
> gold-adorned, if we need lodging
> such as befits brave warriors
> within the halls of Rán. (Altnord. Saga-Bib. p. 25).

A variant of the shorter version from *Landbókasafn* (used by Ásmundarson in his edition) has another verse on the same theme:

> Now has the sea
> destroyed the lives
> of our comrades,
> who should have lived;
> but Rán,
> that ill-bred woman,
> offers brave warriors
> seats and benches.[1]

In the *Sonatorrek* (7) Egill seems to be using Rán for nothing more than a mere personification of the destroying sea. What picture lies behind the widespread use of her name by the skaldic poets it is hard to say, but at least in the *Edda* it would seem that no distinction can be made between the halls of Rán and the assembly of the gods in Ásgarðr under the leadership of Othin. In *Grímnismál* XLV Othin declares that

> All the Æsir shall enter in
> To the benches of Ægir
> To drink with Ægir.

*Hymiskviða* ends with a promise that the Holy Ones shall drink together in Ægir's halls, while in *Lokasenna*[2] it is in the halls of Ægir, again, that the famous 'flyting' takes place, although it is noticeable

1 Although the saga as we have it is late, the verses are likely to be older than 1300, and F. Jónsson is inclined to accept the whole as one of the earliest of the *Fornaldar Sögur*, although it has undergone much editing (*Litt. Hist.* II, p. 812).
2 E.g. vv. 3, 4, 10, 14, 16.

that neither Ægir nor Rán take any part in the discussion. Whatever early cults may have been connected with the name of Rán, it certainly seems in these poems as if personification of the sea, at once destroyer and welcomer of the seaman, which has been visualised as a woman by poets of all time, has merged with the idea of a home of the gods to which the dead may come and in which certain supernatural women receive them.

The distinction which must be drawn between the 'house of the gods' and the 'hall of the slain' in the literature dealing with Valhöll has already been pointed out by Chadwick in *The Cult of Othin*, and by Neckel in *Walhall*. The former suggests that there has been confusion between *Valhöll* and *Ásgarðr*, the court of the Æsir. Neckel emphasises the heavenly house of Othin, which he believes to be a conception originally separate from that of *Valhöll*. Both have noticed, too, the distinction between two different kinds of Valkyries; Chadwick emphasises the implications of the Anglo-Saxon word *walcyrge*, that of a creature of the werwolf class rather than of the heavens, while Neckel argues that the idea of a valkyrie possessing werwolf characteristics is found in certain Norse passages where the word is used also. The conception of the Valkyries has already been discussed in some detail, and will be treated further in chapter v, where the subject of the *dísir* will be considered. The chief difficulty seems to be that the idea of the Valkyries as the servants of Othin, welcoming the souls of the slain into his halls, does not seem to fit in easily either with the conception of the fierce creature delighting in blood and slaughter, or with that of the supernatural guardian who attaches herself to certain warriors. But a great deal obviously depends on our knowledge of Othin himself. As the ruler of the heavenly halls, dwelling in the midst of the gods, it is hard to reconcile him with his Valkyrie attendants; to a god of the dead in earlier belief, however, to whom the bodies of the slain were offered, the bloodthirsty women may well have formed a fitting following.

These two different conceptions of Valhöll discernible in the literature are reminiscent of the two contradictory conceptions of the life after death, suggested by a study of both archaeological and literary evidence: the departure to the home of the gods, and the sojourn within the howe. Valhöll as the realm of the gods is in keeping with the ideas associated with cremation, human sacrifice and the worship of Othin; and it is to Valhöll, according to the

account used by Snorri in the *Ynglinga Saga*, that the Swedish wor-
shippers of Othin believed they would journey when their bodies
were burned on the pyre, together with all possessions burned with
them or buried in the earth. Moreover the idea of the Valkyries in
the role of the bearers of the dead to Othin is suggested by the
language of Þjóðólfr's poem, although the sense is obscure.[1] Whether
the other conception, with its emphasis on life within the howe,
should be associated with the god Freyr, who according to Snorri
was the first in Sweden to be laid in howe without burning, is a
question which will be considered later.

## THE EVERLASTING BATTLE

It will be remembered that the characteristic of Valhöll emphasised
in *Vafþrúðnismál* is the battle between the dead warriors which is
renewed every day. None of the other sources mention this, though
Snorri has made a paragraph out of it. There is however a certain
amount of evidence given to us on this theme elsewhere in Norse
literature.

The most detailed account of the raising of dead men on a battlefield is that given in one of the *Fornaldar Sögur*, in *Hrólfs Saga Kraka*
(LI). Here Skuld, the evil daughter born to King Helgi of an elf-
woman, raises a mighty army against her half-brother Hrólfr. Her
men cannot be slain, and though hundreds of them are cut down by
Hrólfr's men they are on their feet again immediately, fighting with
more strength and vigour than before. Böðvarr Bjarki, Hrólfr's
great champion, finally declares in desperation:

Skuld's force is an ample one, and I suspect that their dead roam at large
here, and rise up again to do battle with us; difficult indeed it must prove
to fight against *draugar* [i.e. the animated dead]. Here many a limb is cut
asunder, many a shield riven, helm and mailcoat cut into small pieces, and
many a chief hewed in twain, but they are grimmest to deal with after
they are dead, and against this we have no power.

We are then told how Hjörvarðr, Skuld's husband, meets Böðvarr in
single combat, when the great champion cuts off hand and foot from
his enemy and cleaves his body from the shoulder down with a
mighty blow; and yet in spite of this Hjörvarðr, no whit perturbed
by the missing limbs, is found shortly after fighting as boldly as before.

Skuld is said to have raised such a force as this by the working of

1 See p. 33 above. Also Lindqvist, *Fornvännen*, 1921, p. 138 f.

magic; and the raising of the slain is said to be among the powers of a wizard in another of the *Fornaldar Sögur, Göngu-Hrólfs Saga* (xxxiii). Here Grímr the wizard goes on the field at the end of a day's fighting, turns over the slain, and tries to raise them. However on this occasion he does not succeed, because a rival practitioner in magic, Möndull the dwarf, has been there before him, as we learn from the previous chapter:

Möndull went twice widdersins round the slain; he blew and whistled in all directions, and recited ancient charms over them; then he said that these slain would do no harm (xxxii).

Here the raising of the dead is carried out by night, in readiness for the renewed fighting the next day. In the case of Skuld, the resurrection is more mysterious, for it is practically instantaneous, and much closer to the picture of the fighting within Valhöll; apart from the information that she used magic and was assisted by evil powers we are not told by what means she pressed the dead into her service. It is, in fact, a more illogical, fairy-tale—or mythological—kind of magic; the other kind is described rather as a practical exercise in necromancy, and seems to have been attributed to the Bjarmians, since when Örvar Oddr is fleeing from them, he tells his men to throw any who fall from their own side into the river, 'for they will be able to do magic at once against our forces if they get hold of any of them who are dead'.[1]

Another tale which is connected in several versions with the raising of the dead is that of Hildr, who is said to have raised those who fell in the battle between her father and her lover so that it might never come to an end. The story is known in a number of sources; it is begun in the *Ragnarsdrápa*,[2] but the verse leaves off at a point where the battle is about to begin; it is told briefly in Saxo,[3] who tells us that Hildr conjured up the spirits of the combatants by her spells, because she longed so ardently for her husband; and more fully in Snorri's *Skáldskaparmál* (L), where the scene is laid in the Orkneys, and Hildr is said to go every night to the battlefield, where all the slain and their weapons are turned into stone, and arouse the fallen men by witchcraft. The fullest account, however, is that given in the *Flateyjarbók*, in the *Sörla þáttr*. In this version a number of other

1 *Örvar-Odds Saga* (*F.A.S.* iii), v, p. 190.
2 *Skaldedigtning*, F. Jónsson (Copenhagen, Christiania, 1912), A i, p. 3, v. 10.
3 Saxo, v, 160, p. 198.

characters are introduced into the tale, and the responsibility for the conflict is placed not on Hildr but on a mysterious woman called Göndul, who gives Heðinn a magic draught which forces him to carry off Hildr and provoke her father to fight him. Ultimately, however, the work is clearly that of Freyja, and to her also the perpetual battle is due, since the task of creating this situation has been laid upon her by Othin at the beginning of the story in return for the delivery of her necklace. In this account of the everlasting battle, the raising of the slain is not done by night, but the situation is parallel to that in *Hrólfs Saga Kraka*; for we read: 'though they were cleft down between the shoulders, still they sprang up as before, and went on fighting' (VIII). Here, however, the fight does not go on for ever, but is brought to an end by a follower of the Christian king Olaf Tryggvason, who alone has the power to deal blows which will strike home and quieten the dead for ever.

In these stories it is not only the idea of the everlasting battle which recalls the Valhöll tradition. We may notice too that three of the women concerned, Hildr, Göndul and Skuld, bear the names of Valkyries, while in the *Sörla þáttr* Freyja herself is introduced and she is connected by *Grímnismál* with Valhöll, and is there said to have the power to choose half the slain each day. The clue to such raising of the dead as this seems to be given in the word *draugar* in the speech of Böðvarr quoted from the *Hrólfs Saga Kraka*. *Draugr* is the word used for the animated corpse that comes forth from its grave-mound, or shows restlessness on the road to burial. These slain corpses in the stories we have just examined are endowed by malignant magic with a hideous strength which enables them to rise and fight with the power of the *draugr*, which exceeds that of living men. There is no suggestion that the spirits of the dead are recalled into their bodies. The full horror of the dead raised on the battlefield is that expressed by Hrólfr's warrior—the idea of the spiritless corpse, maimed and wounded, showing nevertheless inextinguishable vigour; a descendant of the same family may be seen in Banquo's ghost in *Macbeth*, who enters the hall with his ghastly head wounds still gaping and glaring eyes from which all 'speculation' is banished.

In these tales the raising of the dead takes place on the field of battle, where the slain are lying. We may remember that in the earlier part of his work on *Walhall* Neckel insists that it is essentially the place of conflict where the dead men rest after the battle is over; [1]

1 Especially p. 19.

but he reminds us that neither Valhöll nor the slain must be thought of as belonging to this world. Where, then, is this field on which the slain are called up to fight with ever renewed vigour? In the story of Hadingus' visit to the Underworld, given in Saxo,[1] the eternal conflict is actually placed below the ground, in what is clearly the realm of the dead. He is taken below the earth by a mysterious woman who guides him, and one of the sights he sees is an army fighting; his guide tells him that these are men who have been slain in battle, and that their conflict goes on for ever. Nor is this the only case in which this kind of conflict is represented as continuing beneath the earth. Continually in Norse literature we meet with the idea of the grave itself being the scene of conflict between warriors who, being already dead, are impervious to wounds.

The most striking example of this comes from the story of Þorsteinn Uxafótr in the *Flateyjarbók*.[2] Here the hero is persuaded by a dweller in a burial mound to enter his house. He goes inside, and finds the howe arranged within like a hall, with seats down each side; it is occupied by a company of men, twelve of whom are dressed in black and are hideous and evil to look upon, while the other twelve, of which his guide is the leader, are clothed in red and are fair and handsome. Although they sit on the benches in apparent peace, there is clearly hostility between the two companies, and when Þorsteinn, the visitor from the outside world, refuses to give the leader of the black men any tribute, a battle immediately breaks out in the howe. Þorsteinn soon discovers that the black and red men may give each other great wounds, but they do not have the least effect, for they can spring up and fight again after the worst of them, even as do the men in Skuld's army or those who fight for Heðinn and Högni. The blows Þorsteinn himself deals, however, take effect, just as in the *Sörla þáttr* the follower of Olaf Tryggvason is the only one able to cut down the dead warriors. There is a certain resemblance here to the situation in *Þorsteins þáttr Bæarmagnis*,[3] where another hero of the same name assists the white-skinned, noble Guðmundr against the black, troll-like Agði and his kin, in the halls of King Geirröðr; again Þorsteinn is a man of the Christian king Olaf, while Agði is later represented as a howe-dweller. The story of a third follower of Olaf Tryggvason who fought with the dead is told in *Bárðar Saga Snæfellsáss* (xx), and here again the conflict takes place in the howe

1 Saxo, I, 31, p. 38.     2 *Flateyjarbók: Óláfs Saga Tryg.* I, 206, p. 253 f.
3 *Fornmanna Sögur*, III, p. 181 f.

itself, though in this case the living has not power to quell the dead. The howe into which Gestr, who has been converted to Christianity by King Olaf, makes his way contains five hundred dead men sitting each in his place in a mighty ship. He cuts off the heads of all the crew; but nevertheless, when he seizes the sword of their leader Raknar, the latter springs up and grapples with him, and all the mutilated dead rise too. Only the intervention of Olaf himself at this moment causes them to sink down again.

This story belongs to a series of tales, which will be examined more fully in the chapter on *The Journey to the Land of the Dead*, and which are variations on the theme of the man who breaks into the mound and finds the seemingly dead inmate or inmates suddenly endowed with strength and vigour, so that he only wins his way out into the upper world after a fearful battle. The difference is that this usually ends by the living man cutting off the head of his adversary, while here the sword of Gestr is powerless to quieten his enemies without supernatural help. The majority of these battles take place in the burial mound itself, when the living man has broken his way in to take possession of the treasures in the guardianship of the dead; there is another story in Saxo,[1] however, which seems as though it should belong to the same class on account of the close correspondence of all the details, where the battle is said to take place in the dwelling-place of Geirröðr, and we are only led to conclude from the description that this is a tomb. This gloomy, tomb-like dwelling where a host of the dead appear to lie seems, from Saxo's description, to be closely connected with Valhöll. Neckel has pointed out the close similarity between this hall of the slain, with its roof of spears, and the description of Valhöll given in *Grímnismál*, where the roof of spears is again a noticeable feature.[2]

Thus the picture of Valhöll given us in the poems seems to have a number of links with the idea of the dwelling within the burial mound which is so important in Norse literature. The emphasis on the dead body, which Neckel has brought out in his book on *Walhall*, the idea of the everlasting battle of those who, being dead, cannot be slain, and lastly the roof of spears in the dwelling of Geirröðr, which is itself closely connected with the tomb and the dead, all point in this direction. The idea of the continual rivalry between two sets of warriors, the light and the dark, the good and the

1 Saxo, VIII, 289, p. 348 f.
2 Neckel, *Walhall*, VIII, p. 28.

evil, seen in the story of Þorsteinn Uxafótr and in a more rationa-
lised form in that of Þorsteinn Bæarmagn, is likely to be of some
importance here for the further elucidation of this tradition. The
origin of the tradition of the everlasting battle is not likely to be
Norse. Panzer suggests it may be Celtic;[1] and it is certainly found
in both Welsh and Irish stories. We find what seem to be brief
references to it in the *Mabinogion*: *Kulhwch and Olwen*[2] contains a
reference to the maiden Greiddylad, for whom two heroes fight
every first of May until the day of doom; while in *Branwen the
daughter of Llyr*[3] the bodies of fighting men flung into the magic
cauldron of the Irish come out next day able to do battle as before,
save that they have lost the power of speech. In an Irish story also,
that of the death of Muircertach Mac Erca,[4] the woman Sin, who is
closely connected with a fairy mound, calls up two battalions of
fighting men to prove her magic powers to the king; she creates for
them wine out of water and swine from fern leaves, and though they
have previously been 'slaughtering and maiming and swiftly killing
each other in the presence of everyone' they partake of this food, and
she promises 'that she will give them forever and forever the same
amount'. Here the wine and the swine's flesh that never give out, as
in *Grímnismál*, are found in conjunction with what seems to be another
variant of the everlasting battle. The examples of the tradition of the
everlasting battle given by Panzer, however, are widespread.

## THE UNDERWORLD REALM OF THE DEAD

If we examine the evidence given us for an underworld realm of
the dead in Norse literature, it will soon be seen that it is far less full
and vivid than that relating to the dwelling within the grave-mound.
There are a few puzzling allusions to some kind of kingdom beneath
the earth, but they are vague and inconsistent, and it is scarcely
possible to build up any coherent picture from them.

In *Vafþrúðnismál* (v. 43) the wise giant claims to have gained his
wisdom by a descent into the underworld. 'Of the runes of the
giants and all the gods', he declares, 'I can tell with truth. I have
been into nine worlds below, to Niflhel; there die men out of Hel.'

1 Panzer, *Hilde-Gudrun* (Halle, 1901), p. 330.
2 Loth, *Les Mabinogion* (Paris, 1913), I, p. 284.    3 *Ibid.* I, p. 143.
4 *The Death of Muircertach Mac Erca*, translated by T. P. Cross and C. H. Slover
  from the *Otia Merseiana* (*Ancient Irish Tales*, Chicago, 1935), p. 523.

Snorri refers to these nine worlds in *Gylfaginning* (xxxiv) when he tells us that the goddess Hel was cast into Niflheim, and given power over nine worlds, 'so that she should find places in her abodes for those who were sent to her'. It seems likely, however, that Snorri's account of the queen of the Underworld is chiefly his own work. The idea that those who enter her realm have died of sickness and old age sounds like an attempt to reconcile the tradition with the description he has given of Valhöll, especially since the one detailed picture which he himself gives us of Hel consists of the entry of Balder within her gates, who died neither of old age nor sickness. When he goes on to tell us that Hunger is the name of her dish, Famine her knife, Bed of Sickness her resting-place and so on, he is in another realm from that of eschatology and mythology, one of literary personification; and it is to this realm that Hel as a goddess in the literature we possess seems to belong.

Most frequently we find the word *hel* used simply to signify death or the grave. *Fara til heljar, drepa mann til heljar* are common phrases for 'to die', 'to slay'. In phrases like *biðja heljar*, 'to await death', *þykkir eigi betra lif en hel*, 'life seemed no better than death', the word is equivalent to the English 'death', and like the English word would naturally lend itself to personification by the poets. It is as such a personification, for instance, that Hel appears in the poems of Egill, and is said in the *Höfuðlausn* [1] to trample upon corpses in battle, and in the *Sonatorrek* [2] to stand on the headland where the poet's son has been buried. Whether this personification has originally been based on a belief in a goddess of death called Hel is another question, but I do not think that the literature we possess gives us any reason to assume so. On the other hand, we have seen that certain supernatural women seem to have been closely connected with the world of death, and were pictured as welcoming dead warriors, so that Snorri's picture of Hel as a goddess might well owe something to these.

Turning from Hel as a mythological figure in Snorri to Hel as a kingdom of the dead, we find that the word is certainly used frequently to denote the place where the dead are, but it may be noticed that the use of it is vague, and it seems to signify the place of the dead in general rather than any one place of the dead in particular. A comparison might be made with the use of *Sheol* in the Hebrew poets, which is usually rendered vaguely by English trans-

1 V. 10 (*Egils Saga*, LX).    2 V. 25 (*ibid.* LXXVIII), p. 256.

lators as 'the grave'. In most of the passages where Hel is introduced as the realm of the dead, it may be noticed that the emphasis is on the journey there made by the dead or the living, whether from the world of men or from that of the gods, and this is, I think, of some importance for the understanding of the tradition. In *Baldrs Draumar*, for instance, the descent is made by Othin, who rides down on Sleipnir to summon the *völva* from her grave, which is said to lie beside the hall of Hel itself. Snorri gives us the longest account of the journey to Hel in his magnificent description of the ride of Hermóðr to bring back Balder.[1] Mounted on Othin's horse, Sleipnir, he traverses the road by which the dead have passed, and finally leaps over Hel-gate to find Balder sitting on the high-seat within the hall. Evidently Snorri is here using some rich source which we do not know, but even this apparently told him nothing about Hel once it was reached, except that it was a hall, and all the descriptive power is expended on the journey thither. It will be remembered too that certain passages discussed in the previous chapter contained references to a journey made by dead men to Valhöll, and shoes and a horse and wagon are said in the sagas to be given to the dead to help them on this journey. The poems also sometimes allude to *Helveg*, the path of the slain, and it is here that Brynhildr is said to encounter the hostile giantess, in *Helreið Brynhildar*,[2] though it may be noticed that when the tale is told in *Norna-Gests þáttr* (IX) this is interpreted simply as the road leading to the funeral pyre.

Another account of the visit to the Underworld is given in the story of Hadingus; this however is only given in Saxo,[3] so that the word Hel is not used. During Hadingus' visit there he sees the everlasting battle taking place, a fair land where green herbs grow when it is winter on earth, and finally a wall which shuts in a strange land, about which no more is told us than that the woman herself could not pass the barrier into it, and that when she cut off the head of a cock she had with her and flung it over the wall it came to life again immediately, and could be heard to crow. It seems clear that this passage is linked up with beliefs in the next world; the idea of the everlasting battle is, as we have seen, connected in some way with Valhöll, and also with life within the grave, while the incident of the cock is very similar to the action of the slave-girl who beheaded a cock in the cremation ceremony on the Volga,[4] and flung it into the

1 *Gylfaginning*, XLVIII.                    2 Prose note at beginning of poem.
3 Saxo, I, 31, p. 37.                         4 See p. 46 above.

boat, in the highly symbolic ceremony which must have been concerned with a life after death.

We find Othin depicted as the ruler of the Underworld in a strange story in one of the *Fornaldar Sögur*, which seems to contain a number of elements from other tales of visits there. He is said to guard a mystical cloak in the *ündirdjup*, which appears to be the lowest region of the Underworld, guarded by a ring of fire.[1]

In none of these stories is there any attempt made to present the Underworld as a place of retribution and punishment. Snorri, it is true, attempts to make Hel such a place, but his interpretation is likely to be chiefly due to Christian teaching about the after-life. In *Völuspá* (v. 38), we certainly get a somewhat similar picture, not indeed connected with Hel, but with a mysterious hall called *Náströndr*, 'the shore of corpses', whose doors face northwards, and whose roof is formed of serpents dropping poison. It is said to be prepared for perjured men, murderers and those who beguile the wives of others, and a grim dragon, *Niðhoggr*, bears away the corpses of the wicked on his pinions. It is probable, as Olrik[2] believes, that this part of the poem, and especially the companion hall of Gimli for righteous folk, is influenced by Christian teaching, but the picture of the dark, loathsome dwelling-place inhabited by snakes is one that is found elsewhere in Norse literature. The serpents that drop poison are one of the unpleasant features of the realm of Geirröðr and Útgarðar-Loki, visited by Thorkillus, and the picture of Náströndr is very like those descriptions of the gruesome interior of the tomb that are found many times in the sagas, and which seem to be related to the Valhöll tradition itself. The idea of the evil men in their dark dwelling-place, and of the pleasant fair people in their realm of gold and brightness, may also owe something to that dualistic conception which has already been noticed in certain passages of the literature, like that telling of the two dream-women of Gísli. It is therefore possibly older than Christian eschatology and linked up with the two conceptions discernible behind Valhöll—the dark house of the slain and the bright home of the gods.

In examining the evidence for the Underworld realm of the dead in Norse literature, we seem to be driven inevitably to the conclusion that we are given no justification for assuming a belief in a concrete, simple world of the dead stretching below the earth. Snorri alone

1 *Egils Saga ok Ásmundar (F.A.S.* III), XIII.
2 Olrik, 'Om Ragnarok', *A.f.n.O.* 1902, p. 281 f.

has tried to present something of the kind, but he is not convincing. What we do seem to find, however, in the passages we have examined are indications of what may prove to be more mystical and subtle mantic beliefs. This is particularly suggested by the story of the journey of Hadingus, where the allusions to the everlasting battle, the fair fields, and the resurrection of the dead bird behind the high wall seem more likely to have been originally interpretations of certain ideas about life beyond the grave and the fate of the soul than a piece of straightforward cosmography to be accepted as it stands. The possibility of the numerous tales of journeys to a supernatural land in Norse literature being originally accounts of mantic experiences, adventures of the soul rather than of certain mythological personages, is one at least worth considering, and it will be discussed further in the chapter on *The Journey to the Land of the Dead*.

Only investigation of the traditions connected with the Underworld on such lines as these can, I believe, throw light on the mysterious 'nine worlds' of *Vafþrúðnismál*, or the placing of Hel (in *Grímnismál*) under the third root of the ash Yggdrasil, beside the home of the frost-giants and the dwelling of mankind.

## THE DEAD IN THE MOUNTAINS

One of the presentations of life after death which remain to be considered in Norse literature is that of the dead residing within the mountains. Here the picture given is far more definite than that for a world under the earth. *Landnámabók* gives a number of references to certain Icelandic families who believed that after death they would pass into some particular hill or mountain near their home, showing that this belief, if it really flourished in late heathen times, was closely bound up with special localities, and with the unity of the kindred.

The most detailed account of an entry into the mountains by the dead is that given in *Eyrbyggja Saga*. Þórólfr Mostrarskegg, enthusiastic follower of Thor, is said to have held one particular mountain near his house in great reverence from the time when he entered Iceland, 'and he believed that thither he would go when he died, and all his kindred in the Ness' (IV). After Þórólfr's death his son Þorsteinn Þorskabítr inherited the property, and not long afterwards he went out on a fishing expedition and he and all his crew were drowned. Before the news of the calamity could reach home, says the saga, his shepherd was out on the mountains and chanced to look

over in the direction of Helgafell, the holy hill of Þórólfr. He was
facing the northern side of it, and as he looked it seemed to him that
the mountain stood open and sounds of merriment and feasting
could be heard coming from within. As he listened, he caught something of what was being said, and realised that the company inside
were welcoming young Þorsteinn and his crew, and that Þorsteinn
was being invited to sit in the high-seat opposite to his father (xi).
*Landnámabók* does not give us this story, but agrees that 'it was the
belief of the kinsmen of Þórólfr that they would all die into the fell'.[1]

*Njáls Saga* (xiv) has a shorter account of a story told by certain
fishermen, who claimed that they saw Svanr the wizard (a historical
personage, whose pedigree is well known) receiving a good welcome
as he entered Kaldbak, the great mountain in the district where he
lived, after he too had been drowned on a fishing expedition. The
saga-teller professes some doubt as to the truth of this, but adds that
Svanr was never seen again, alive or dead.

The references in *Landnámabók* on this subject are the more convincing in that they are very brief and unvarnished. We are told of
Auðr, the famous descendant of Ketill Flatnefr, who was converted
before she came to Iceland, that she had a cross put up in the hills to
mark the spot where she used to pray and that this place was afterwards held in great reverence by her kinsmen after they reverted to
heathen beliefs: 'they believed that they would die into these hills',
the account goes on, and adds that a shrine was built there, and that
Þorðr Gellir was led there, before he attained manhood.[2] If this
tradition is reliable, it seems to indicate that the belief in the dead
entering the mountains is part of some kind of cult connected with
high places, and there is a certain amount of evidence in the *Fornaldar Sögur* and *Flateyjarbók*, and in *Bárðar Saga Snæfellsáss*, which
seems to be based on memories of such a cult, and which I have
examined elsewhere.[3] From *Landnámabók* again we learn that similar
beliefs were connected with Þorisbjorg and Melifell into which 'the
kinsmen of Selþorir, who were heathen',[4] and Hreiðarr[5] respectively
'chose to die'.

The belief that the souls of the dead pass into certain holy mountains is one that has continued among the Lapps up to very recent

1 *Lndn.* II, 12, p. 74.    2 *Ibid.* II, 16, p. 83.
3 H. R. Ellis, 'Fostering by Giants in Saga Literature', *Medium Ævum*, June 1941,
   p. 70 f.
4 *Lndn.* II, 5, p. 62.    5 *Ibid.* III, 7, p. 141.

*Genealogical Table, showing relationship of those whose names are mentioned in connection with the belief of the dead entering the mountains. Those concerned are printed in capitals, and underlined.*

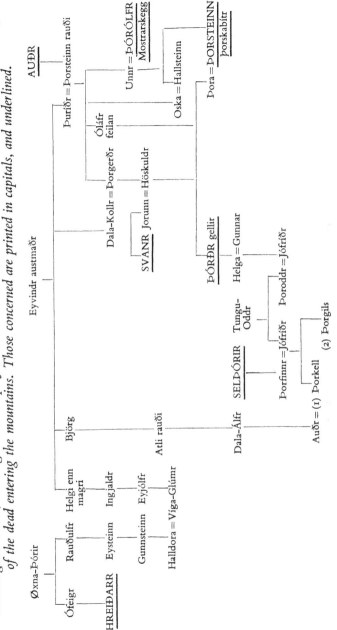

times.[1] It was to these mountains that their shamans were believed to journey during their trances, when they went to commune with the dead, or to fetch back a soul to the world of the living. In the account in *Eyrbyggja Saga* the mountain, like the burial mound, is represented inside like a hall, and there is probably some connection between the mound and the hill in which the dead dwell.[2]

The importance of locality for such a belief is obvious, and it seems likely that here we have a local—perhaps even a family—cult, brought to Iceland in the early tenth century. It may be noticed that all those whose names are connected in *Landnámabók* and the sagas with this belief are related to each other. The relationship is worked out on the table on p. 89, from information given in *Landnámabók* and some of the *Íslendinga Sögur*, particularly the beginning of *Laxdæla Saga*, *Eyrbyggja Saga*, and *Hænsa-Þóris Saga*. It will be seen that there is a good deal of intermarriage between the various branches of the family.

The connecting links between the people whose names are associated with the belief in 'dying into' the hills were evidently for the most part formed after they settled in Iceland, although Þórólfr Mostrarskegg befriended Auðr's brother Björn before he left Norway. Whether the cult of the holy mountains was due to the influence of one person and spread to several of his kindred afterwards cannot be decided for certain, but if it were so, the most probable candidate seems to be Þórólfr himself, since tradition says that he chose Helgafell as his holy hill as soon as he arrived in Iceland. It seems likely in any case that the fact that Thor was worshipped by Þórólfr is of importance; we are also told that Hreiðarr was an ardent worshipper of the god, and Helgi the Lean never gave him up entirely, even after a nominal conversion to Christianity.

## THE GRAVE-MOUND

Already we have seen that the idea of life continuing within the burial mound is of great importance in Norse literature. Some of the evidence for this, for the conception of the dead man dwelling in his howe as in an earthly house watching jealously over his possessions, has been discussed in the last chapter, and the idea of the dead men

1 Unwerth, 'Untersuchungen *ii*. Totenkult und Óðinnverehrung bei Nordgermanen und Lappen' (*Weinhold. Germ. Abhand.* 37, 1911), p. 7 f.
2 Note that Þórólfr is not actually buried on Helgafell; Haugsness is a short distance away.

continuing to battle inside their burial mound has been mentioned because it seems to have some relationship with the Valhöll conception.

In looking over the evidence as a whole which has to do with continued life within the grave, we see that the picture given is not always one of jealous guardianship or violent conflict. The sagas sometimes give us a brief picture of the good and influential man resting at peace in his grave, and still retaining an interest in the affairs of the living. There is a striking example of this in *Njáls Saga*, where we have the wonderfully restrained and effective picture of Gunnarr resting in his howe, which spurs Skarpheðinn on to avenge him:

There was a bright moon, with clouds driving over it from time to time. It seemed to them that the howe was open, and that Gunnarr had turned himself in the howe and looked up at the moon. They thought they saw four lights burning in the howe, but no shadow anywhere. They saw that Gunnarr was merry, with a joyful face... (LXXVIII).

Undoubtedly here the author is fully alive to the imaginative possibilities and the beauty of the idea; elsewhere however we find it in a much simpler and cruder form, as in *Hœnsa-Þóris Saga*, where we are told that Oddr at the point of death insisted that he should be buried up on Skáneyjarfjall—'he said that he wanted to look out from there over the whole district' (XVII).

It will be remembered that Hrappr, a more unpleasant character from *Laxdæla Saga*, insisted that he should be buried inside the doorway of the living-room for a similar reason—'then I can keep a more particular eye on my household' (XVII). In the same saga we have an incident recorded after the time when Iceland became Christian, when the two men concerned lay after death in a Christian church. Gestr, who was famous for his gift of foresight, prophesies one day that 'It will come about that there will be a shorter distance between Osvífr's dwelling and mine, and then we will talk comfortably, if it is allowed us to talk then' (XXXIII); and these words are fulfilled much later on in the saga when he and Osvífr are laid in the same grave (LXVI). This might be nothing more than a mere figure of speech, but it is found elsewhere in the sagas, in *Friðþjófs Saga*, for example, when a dying king declares: 'My howe shall stand beside the firth. And there shall be but a short distance between mine and Þorsteinn's, for it is well that we should call to one another' (I).

The idea of the grave as a house was evidently not incongruous in a Christian setting. *Landnámabók* has preserved a little story of Ásólfr, a Celtic Christian, who lived as a hermit, and who after death appeared in a dream to the girl who herded cattle on the land where he was buried and rebuked her because, he said, she was in the habit of wiping her muddy feet on the mound that covered his grave— 'she dreamed that Ásólfr rated her for this, for cleansing her dirty feet on his house' (I, 16, p. 42). *Landnámabók* goes on to record, without any sense of incongruity, that Ásólfr's bones were afterwards removed to a shrine inside a church.

The peaceful rest of the dead within the grave, however, is frequently interrupted, either because the grave has more than one occupant, or because there is interference from the living. The story of Ásmundr, who protested because a servant was buried with him in his ship, has already been referred to, and so also has the tale of the two companies of red and black men who dwelt within a grave-mound as in a hall, and fought continuously.[1] In many cases a king or leader is said to enter his howe at the head of a large company, and in one story in *Flateyjarbók*[2] a king of Norway is said to have had a great howe specially built in his lifetime, so that he and all his followers could be carried there after death. A number of stories in which a living man is said to break into a burial mound, usually for the sake of the treasure it contains, and to have a terrible struggle with the dead but still very active occupant before he can get away, have also been mentioned before, and will be further discussed in the chapter on *The Journey to the Land of the Dead*. In these tales the corpse within the grave is always represented with vampire-like propensities, superhuman strength, and a fierce desire to destroy any living creature which ventures to enter the mound. In the *Íslendinga Sögur* this idea is further developed, and in the case of particularly strong and troublesome personalities the body will no longer consent to confine its energies inside the grave-mound, but takes the offensive and leaves it to cause trouble farther afield. This has resulted in a number of magnificent tales of haunting by a series of *draugar* who are as individual after death as they have been in life. It is evident here that we are dealing with no stereotyped literary motif, but that what in itself is a somewhat crude and unattractive conception of the dead has fired the imagination of the saga-tellers, and been

1 See pp. 40, 81 above.
2 *Flateyjarbók: Óláfs Saga Helga*, II, 6, p. 7.

worked upon by their superb narrative power and skill in depicting character to create a group of unforgettable 'ghosts'.

The unpopular Hrappr, in *Laxdœla Saga*,[1] who insisted on being buried in the doorway of his own living-room, caused a great deal of trouble after death, since, as the saga puts it, 'unpleasant as he was to deal with while he lived, the more so did he become after he was dead'. At first he hung about the farm, frightening the servants and molesting people in the neighbourhood until the house was left empty. Then a courageous person nearby dug up his body, and Hrappr was somewhat less of a nuisance after this, but still did some damage. At last he lay in wait for a cow-herd of Olaf Pái, and Olaf proved himself more strong-minded than Hrappr's other neighbours, and put an end to his tricks for good. This he did by attacking Hrappr and wrestling with him until the *draugr* took refuge in the ground, after which he dug up the body—still undecayed and with the spearhead he had lost in the previous fight beside it—and burnt it on a pyre; and from that time 'no one had any trouble from Hrappr's walking'.

The son of the wizard Kotkell, in the same saga, also walks after death, but proves a relatively ineffectual ghost, since he is frightened away by the first signs of hostility from the living (xxxviii). More vivid and terrible are the figures of Þórólfr Bægifótr and Glamr.[2] Þórólfr, like Hrappr, was a strong and unlovable personality in life, and died in a fit of rage at being worsted by his son in one of his evil designs. The amount of damage he caused after death was terrific; he killed both men and cattle, and battered the roof of his former home by 'riding' upon it, until the people there were driven to the verge of madness, and abandoned the farm. After a while his body was dug up by his son Arnkell, the only person Þórólfr had ever feared in life, and reburied on a lonely headland; and then there was peace for a while until after Arnkell's death. After that the haunting began again, and men and cattle were killed in the neighbourhood of his new grave, until another man was found who ventured to dig him up once more. His body was still undecayed, and was 'as black as Hel and as huge as an ox', and only after it was burned was there rest from Þórólfr, although the man responsible for the burning paid for it by his own death.

The other outstanding *draugr* is the stranger Glamr, of *Grettis Saga*.

---

1 *Laxdœla Saga*, xvii and xxiv. See p. 37 above.
2 *Eyrbyggja Saga*, xxxiv, lxiii; *Grettis Saga*, xxxii, xxxv.

He was engaged as a shepherd, and showed himself unsociable, un-couth and unpleasant to deal with during his short time of service, which ended when he was killed by some unknown evil creature and buried where he fell because it was impossible to remove his body. Like Þórólfr, he caused terrible damage in the neighbourhood of his grave, and killed men and beasts and ruined buildings by 'riding' on them, until the farm where he had once worked became a ruin. The struggle which Grettir had with him is an epic one, as related in the saga, and only after his head was finally cut off was the horrible creature at last incapable of doing further harm.

There are similar figures, less impressively drawn, in other sagas. Þormóðr in *Hávarðs Saga Ísfirðings* (II, III) and Björn's old father in *Flóamanna Saga* (XIII) return to haunt the living until their bodies are destroyed. In *Svarfdæla Saga*[1] the returning dead is not wholly malicious; Klaufi is killed treacherously, in the period of weakness following a fit of berserk rage, and he comes back to haunt the woman who has caused his death until her brothers cut off his head. This however is not enough to stop Klaufi, who appears several times with his head under his arm and speaks a number of lively verses. He urges on his friends to fight, and takes part in the battle himself when necessary, until none are able to withstand them, and finally he appears riding in a sledge in the air to tell his favourite kinsman Karl that he is to be 'home with him to-night'. A descendant of this Karl, however, finds it advisable later to burn the body, as it continues to walk after this.

In all these cases, with the possible exception of the appearance of Klaufi in his sledge, it is clear that the haunting is done by the actual dead body itself, which leaves its grave-mound and is possessed of superhuman strength and unlimited malice. When the body is des-troyed, the power of the *draugr* is at an end. The same seems to be true of the companies of the dead which sometimes haunt their former homes after death, for example the two companies of the drowned and the plague-stricken who banish the living from their own fireside in *Eyrbyggja Saga* (LIV), the drowned Þóroddr and his crew who appear, dripping wet, to Guðrún in *Laxdæla Saga* (LXXVI) and the victims of the plague who torment the next-door household, until their bodies are dug up and burnt, in *Flóamanna Saga* (XXII). It is evident in the story in *Fóstbræðra Saga* (XIX), where the men who have fallen in battle appear as they fell, covered in blood, and the

[1] *Svarfdæla Saga*, XXII, XXIII, XXVI, XXXII.

sight is so horrible that those who see it are near to fainting—an unusual admission of weakness from characters in the sagas. Sometimes, indeed, there is trouble with the body even before burial; Þorgunna in *Eyrbyggja Saga* (LI) walks on her way to her burial to obtain proper treatment for her bearers, but Víga-Styrr, the father-in-law of Snorri the priest,[1] and Gyða in *Flóamanna Saga* (XIII) are less amiable persons, and are unquiet on the way to the funeral for more sinister reasons.

From a wide range of stories, then, we find that the activity of the body is pictured as going on within the grave, in many cases until the body is utterly destroyed by fire. These stories are so well told that it is evident the story-teller, fully alive to the possibilities for humour and terror in such an idea, has developed it for his own purpose. Nevertheless the picture of the animated corpse, recurring so persistently in stories which differ widely in form, seems to indicate that this conception was one very familiar at the time when the sagas were told. The widespread belief in vampires, which lingered on in Europe for many centuries, is of the same nature, and shows that such a belief in the animated corpse was strong enough to exist side by side with Christianity up to comparatively recent times. There is no case to my knowledge in the sagas of any spirit or 'ghost' returning from a realm of the dead to visit the living. It is from the mound that these *draugar* come, whether they walk forth at night to do damage, or whether they visit men, as they sometimes do in dreams,[2] just as it is from the howe that Gróa answers her son in the Edda poem.[3] In the *Helgakviða*[4] the two conceptions appear to meet for a moment, when the dead Helgi returns from Valhöll to lie in the arms of his wife, but if, as has been suggested, Valhöll itself is closely connected with the grave-mound there may be no such contradiction as appears at first sight. Certainly it is the cold body with its gaping wounds and ice-cold hands which Sigrún grasps, and no ghostly warrior from another world, and Helgi tells her her tears have fallen in burning drops on his breast just as in *Laxdæla Saga* the dead witch complains that Guðrún has dropped burning tears over her as she

1 *Víga-Styrs Saga ok Heiðarvíga*, LX.
2 A good example is the dream of the shepherd in *Flateyjarbók* who thought the dead poet came out of his burial mound to speak with him. As he awoke he caught sight of his visitor disappearing into the howe again (*Óláfs Saga Tryg.*: see p. 108 below).
3 *Grógaldr*, I–III.
4 See p. 55 above.

knelt and wept above her grave (LXXVI). The inhabitant of the grave-mound in Norse literature is clearly none other than the natural one—the dead body buried there, which is believed to be animated with a strange life and power. The burial mound is looked upon as the house, or hall, of the dead, whether they rest there singly or in companies.

## CONCLUSION

In examining the evidence for the conception of the future life in Norse literature, we find that the conclusions which we reach are essentially the same as those forced on us by a study of funeral customs. There still appear to be two main conceptions about the fate of the dead; either they enter the realm of the gods, or they continue to dwell within the earth itself.

The conception of Valhöll which we find in the literature seems to have been built up of these two distinct beliefs, for the picture of the warriors' paradise seems to have resulted from the idea that chosen princes and mighty men of valour had the right to enter the abode of the gods, mingled with the separate conception of an everlasting battle continuing among the dead in the grave. The realm of the gods still appears to be closely bound up with the worship of Othin. The problem is considerably complicated by the fact that both conceptions of life after death seem to include the figures of a number of supernatural women, whose relationship to the gods and whose exact function in the world of the dead is difficult to determine. The idea of an underworld realm does not stand out in the passages we have examined as an alternative to the realm of the gods and the grave-mound; the references to an underworld are vague, and there are no descriptions of such a realm, although on the other hand a wealth of detail is lavished on the journey downwards to a realm of the dead. The home of the dead within the mountains however demands consideration; it is probably connected with the idea of life in the howe in some way, but it gives the impression of having originated in a separate cult held by a few families only.

The impression given by the evidence as a whole is that the subject of the future life in heathen belief was not so unimportant as a cursory examination of Norse literature might indicate, nor was it of so childish and 'primitive' a nature as the account of life in Valhöll might sound on a first reading. But the beliefs were not remembered with sufficient clearness at the time when the literature which we possess came to be written down for a full and clear account of the conceptions of the life after death to be left for us. We are dependent on memories of lost beliefs, half understood traditions, meaningless repetitions of what was once significant, and garbled rendering of what once may have been pregnant symbolism. Moreover it is not likely that all the conflicting evidence could ever be reduced into a consistent whole; behind the two main conceptions which seem to be discernible from the mass of evidence and mixed with them, a number of separate traditions are no doubt involved, and to over-simplify the position would be to falsify it.

One major problem connected with Valhöll which has not been dealt with here is that of Ragnarrökr, the doom of the gods. Most of our information about this last great battle between gods and giants, in which Othin and the great gods perish, is contained in *Völuspá*, of which Snorri has made extensive use for his magnificent account in the *Prose Edda*. In this description, however, little attention is paid to the fate of mankind; and indeed the connection between Ragnarrökr and the future life of man is only touched on in the skaldic poem *Eiríksmál*, where it is implied that Othin's reason for summoning the king to his halls is in order to have the assistance of so valiant a warrior in the battle against the wolf, generally assumed to be the last conflict depicted in *Völuspá*. This reads like a fine imaginative fiction in compliment to the dead king; and we are faced with the problem of exactly how much Valhöll and Ragnarrökr meant to the tenth-century poet of the Norwegian court. A detailed study of skaldic verse would probably go a considerable way to solve this problem; but this can hardly be attempted here. Moreover it seems clear that the cult of the gods and ideas about the life after death in Scandinavia did not include teaching about the final battle; the traditions still discernible in the literature, at least, give us no reason to assume so, and Othin, as we have seen, is said in the *Ynglinga Saga* to die in his bed and to be burned on the funeral pyre. This is one reason why it does not seem advisable to include a discussion on Ragnarrökr at this point.

A second reason is that the picture of Ragnarrökr given in *Völuspá* has strange and varied affinities. Olrik's detailed investigation of the traditions contained in the poem [1] makes it clear that further work on Ragnarrökr will have to take into consideration Celtic traditions

1 Olrik, 'Om Ragnarok' (*A.f.n.O.* 1902): 'Ragnarokforestillingernes Udspring' (*Danske Studier*, 1913).

about the battle of the gods, Tartar traditions about the bound monster, and teaching in the religious books of the East about the end of the world and the fight between the forces of light and darkness, to mention only the most outstanding headings of the evidence he has collected. The comparative method of investigation is clearly of great importance here, and is essential if the obscurities of *Völuspá* are ever to be understood, but any such lengthy survey would be out of place in the present study of the conceptions of life after death in Norse literature; and since it must necessitate a study of theological and poetic speculation rather than of cults, practices and beliefs about the dead, such as concern us here, it would be largely irrelevant.

# Chapter IV

## THE CULT OF THE DEAD

Earth feet, loam feet, lifted in country mirth
Mirth of those long since under earth
Nourishing the corn. Keeping time,
Keeping the rhythm in their dancing
As in their living in the living seasons
The time of the seasons and the constellations
The time of milking and the time of harvest.

T. S. ELIOT, *East Coker.*

The evidence in Norse literature for a cult of the dead is concerned with burial in the earth and not with cremation. It is important to notice, also, that most of it is drawn, not from the *Íslendinga Sögur*, but from the *Fornaldar Sögur*, the sagas of the kings in the *Heimskringla*, *Fornmanna Sögur* and *Flateyjarbók*, and the Edda poems. On the whole, these are the sources connected with Norway and Sweden rather than with Iceland, and it is of course on the mainland rather than in a relatively new colony that we should expect to find evidence for ancestor worship and a cult of the dead, though memories of such a cult might be carried by settlers into Iceland. For such a subject as this, we can hardly expect the evidence to be full, clear and conclusive. Between the practices inspired by a belief in the nearness and power of the dead and those of the Christian religion at the times when the sagas of the kings were being committed to writing by monks and scholars, there is the same gulf in time and culture as rendered the heathen conceptions of the future life so obscure in the literature; while this belief in particular is one with which Christian writers could have little sympathy. But such evidence as can be found is of importance for our study, since it serves to indicate the way in which the conception of life continuing in the grave-mound developed in Scandinavia in heathen times, and so adds to our knowledge of the Norse attitude to the future life and to the relationship between the living and the dead.

## WORSHIP OF THE DEAD AND OF THE GRAVE-MOUND

Direct statements recording the worship of men after death are naturally not very plentiful. However they do exist. One version of *Landnámabók*[1] tells us that sacrifices were made to a man called Grímr (grandfather of a certain Þórólfr Smjor and great-great-grandfather of one of the early Icelandic settlers) 'on account of his popularity,[2] and he was called Kamban'.

Professor Chadwick[3] compares with this a statement made by Adam of Bremen about the Swedes, who, he says, make gods out of men and worship them (*colunt et deos ex hominibus*); it seems as though Adam must be thinking of the worship of men after death, since he instances the story of the deification of a king Ericus told in the *Life of St Anskar*. There are also mentions of family cults among the Prussians, which may be of the same kind as these Swedish ones; and it is indeed possible that some cult on the lines of those of the dead ancestors in the mountains is meant. However as it stands the brief comment from *Landnámabók* does little but arouse our curiosity. Then there is the well-known passage from the *Hálfdanar Saga Svarta* in *Heimskringla* (IX), telling of the burial of King Hálfdan:

> His reign had been more fortunate in the seasons and crops than those of all other kings. So much trust was placed in him that, when they learned he was dead and his body carried to Hringaríki to be buried, there came influential men from Raumaríki and Vestfold and Heiðmörk, all begging to have the body and to bury it in their own district; for they thought it would ensure prosperous seasons if they could obtain it. So it was decided that they should divide the body between four places; the head was laid in a howe at Stein in Hringaríki, and each man bore home a part of the body and laid it in howe; these howes are called 'the howes of Hálfdan'.

It is possible that this passage owes something to antiquarian speculation and the desire to find an explanation of the number of burial places bearing the name of one king; but in any case the direct con-

---

1 *Hauksbók*, chapter 19.
2 *fyrir þockasæld*. Vigfusson translates this by 'popularity', but *sæll* is the word commonly used of the early saints—'blessed'—and seems to have the idea of beneficence, and even the power of giving good fortune; the quality is probably much the same as that ascribed to the body of King Hálfdan in the passage quoted below.
3 Chadwick, *Origin of English Nation* (Cambridge, 1907), p. 321.

THE CULT OF THE DEAD

nection made between the body of the dead man [1] and the fertility of the earth is significant; so also is the additional remark found in the account in *Flateyjarbók*: 'And many people sacrificed and believed in them until it was forbidden by his kinsmen' (I, 456).

A more convincing piece of evidence for the worship of the dead however is found elsewhere in *Flateyjarbók*, in the story of Olaf Geirstaðaálfr.[2] This Olaf, it may be noticed, is the brother of Hálfdan the Black. King Olaf has a dream which foretells a terrible plague, and his own death from it. He directs his people therefore to build a great howe on a headland, into which every important man shall carry half a mark of silver. Into this howe, he tells them, he himself will be carried when he dies:

> ...And I give this warning to you all: there must be no following the example of those who sacrifice to dead men in whom they put their trust while they were alive, because I do not believe that the dead have any power to help.

He goes on to explain, rather ponderously, the results of such an evil practice; and here we evidently have the Christian compiler perplexed and worried by traces of inexplicable heathen thought, for he informs them that those who have been irreproachable characters in life turn into fiends, and in that shape can give help ( !) or do harm. He then continues:

> ...I am much afraid that a famine will come in the land after we are laid in howe. And thereupon sacrifices will be made to us, and we shall be turned into trolls; and it will be through no fault of ours....

This fear of the king was justified, for when the next famine came 'they resorted to the plan of sacrificing to King Olaf for plenty, and they called him *Geirstaðaálfr*'.

Seen through the somewhat unsympathetic eyes of a later writer though it is, this story does, I think, establish an active cult of the dead in Scandinavia beyond question. The very fact that as it stands it is so illogical and so obviously misunderstood makes it the more convincing. We shall return to this interesting character Olaf when discussing the question of elves and rebirth.

---

1 Cf. tradition about heroes among post-Homeric Greeks, who held that 'possession of the corporeal remains of the hero secured the possession of the hero himself', even if only 'single parts of the body'. Rohde, *Psyche* (trans. Hillis, 1925), p. 115 f. and note on p. 144.

2 *Flateyjarbók: Óláfs Saga Helga*, II, 5, p. 6 f.

Two other allusions which seem to deserve mention here, but which have been discussed more fully elsewhere,[1] are first, the statement in *Hervarar Saga* (I) that King Guðmundr was worshipped by men after death and called their god, and that in *Bárðar Saga Snæfellsáss* (VI) to the effect that when Bárðr, who is represented at the opening of the saga as an ordinary settler in Iceland, disappeared, men believed that he had vanished into the mountains and accordingly 'had him for their god to whom they made their vows' (*heitguð*). It will be remembered that the sagas and *Landnámabók* contain the tradition that the dead pass into the mountains. The stories of Guðmundr and Bárðr open up questions which are too complex to be discussed here; it only suffices to quote them as additional indication that the worship of men after death was a notion by no means unfamiliar to the Norse mind. Finally, it is interesting to note that in Saxo some kind of cult of the dead seems to be connected with Uppsala; since when the wife of a certain Halfdanus bore him no children he inquired of the oracle there, and was told that he 'must make atonement to the shades of his brother if he would raise up children'.[2] Here once more we see that birth is closely connected with the dead. This Hálfdan is the father of the famous Haraldr Hilditönn, the ardent worshipper of Othin who fell in battle before King Hringr, and Saxo attributes the fulfilment of the oracle's promise to Othin.

In many cases worship is stated to be given not specifically to a dead man, as in the instances above, but to a burial mound. It has been shown that the howe plays an important part in the worship of Hálfdan the Black and Olaf Geirstaðaálfr, so that *Flateyjarbók* indeed goes so far as to say 'men sacrificed and believed in *them*'—that is in the howes of Hálfdan.[3] Another story which shows the transition from the worship of a howe-dweller to that of the howe itself is that of Freyr. In *Ynglinga Saga* (X) we read that Freyr was buried secretly in a great howe, while the Swedes were told he lived; and they continued to pay tax money to him, pouring in gold, silver and copper through three openings in the howe. *Flateyjarbók*, as usual, gives us a more detailed account, in the *Óláfs Saga Tryggvasonar*;[4] Olaf tells the people of Þrandheim, without unfortunately troubling

1 H. R. Ellis, 'Fostering by Giants in Saga Literature', *Medium Ævum*, June 1941, p. 70 f.
2 Saxo, VII, 247, p. 296.                              3 See p. 100 above.
4 *Flateyjarbók: Óláfs Saga Tryggvasonar*, I, 322, p. 403.

to state his authority, that Freyr was a king in Sweden who was buried in a mighty howe, to whom, because no living man would consent to share his dwelling-place, two wooden men were given for his amusement. To comfort him further, the Swedes made a door and two windows in the howe, and poured in gold, silver and copper, and continued to do so for three years. After this they realised that he must be dead, but continued to sacrifice to him and called him a god. It might be mentioned in passing that in *Grímnismál* (5) we have Freyr described as lord of Álfheim,[1] while Saxo consistently connects his worship with Uppsala.[2] It is interesting to note that the cult of the howe connected with Freyr, like the cult of cremation connected with Othin, is consistently placed in Sweden.

This is not the only case in which we find silver and treasure in general connected with a burial mound. In the *Fornmanna Sögur* we have an episode in the *Saga Óláfs ens Helga* (XXXVI)—omitted by Snorri, who disliked such fantastic tales in his histories—in which the practices of the people of Karlsám are described. In one version we read that Olaf and his men

went up inland and carried away much treasure from a sacrificial mound (*blóthaugr*). There had been a bad storm, and the turf had been stripped off the howe, leaving silver lying exposed; and they got a good deal of wealth from it.

In the other version[3] we are told in addition:

He commanded them to break into a sacrificial mound of these heathen folk; it is so called because whenever they made a great sacrifice for the season or for prosperity they had all to go to this howe and sacrifice...and they carried much treasure there and laid it in the howe before they went away.

The compiler connects this practice with the worship of a mermaid and a sacred boar, to whom he says the sacrifices were made. The basic idea behind such a custom is clearly however similar to that in the story of Freyr we have just quoted, and we can, I think, dismiss the mermaid as superfluous, although the fact that the boar is closely

---

1 *Álfheim Frey*  2 III, 74, p. 90.
*gófu í árdága*
*tívar at tannféi.*
3 *Fornmanna Sögur: Óláfs Saga Helga*, Appendix A, p. 164 (Copenhagen, 1825–1837).

connected with Freyr [1] should perhaps make us hesitate before we banish him and his sacred herd from the tale. The allusion to the 'seasons and prosperity' is interesting, because it echoes the phrase in the incidents of Hálfdan and of Freyr himself, who after death were associated with just these blessings.

The word *ár*, which I have translated 'plenty' or 'season' according to the context, is again connected with the worship of a howe in the *Fornaldar Sögur*, in *Ketils Saga Hœngs* (v). Here we are introduced in a puzzling and rather irrelevant episode to a king called Framarr, who, we are told, 'worshipped Ár-haugr; no snow ever settled on it'. His son Boðmóðr lived near the 'howe of plenty' and on the eve of Yule 'Framarr and all the people of the land sacrificed to it for plenty'. Here we are also told that Framarr was a worshipper of Othin.

To return however to the silver which was offered to certain of these howes, to Freyr's howe, that of Karlsám and that of Olaf Geirstaðaálfr, we find a further allusion to this practice in the *Örvar-Odds Saga*, where it is attributed to the Bjarmians, a curious race of which strange things are related. Oddr is told:

...A howe stands beside the river Vína. It is made of two things, silver and earth; a double handful of silver is carried into it for every man who goes out of the world, and likewise when he comes into the world; and the same amount of earth. You will have done something the Bjarmians will mind more than anything else if you go to the howe and carry away the treasure from inside it (IV).

This practice of the Bjarmians is borne out by the detailed account of the journey of Karli and Þórir Hundr to Bjarmaland, given in the *Heimskringla*, in the *Saga Óláfs ens Helga* (CXXXIII). Again the place mentioned is close to the river Vína. Þórir urges his companions to risk an expedition inland, for he says:

...It was the custom in that country when a rich man died that such of his possessions as were moveable should be divided between the rich man and his heirs; he should have a half or a third or rather less; this wealth should be taken out into the woods and sometimes put into howes and covered with earth; and sometimes houses were built to hold it.

They attempt to carry off some of this wealth, and reach a high fence which surrounds a howe 'in which', explains Þórir, 'gold and silver

---

1 For connection between Freyr and the boar, see Chadwick, *Origin of English Nation*, p. 249.

are mixed together'. They take much treasure from it, although this is found to be mixed with earth. The howe is evidently near the shrine of the god of the Bjarmians (*Jómali*), for some confusion is caused and the adventurers are nearly caught because Karli insists on stealing the god's necklace. This rational and business-like tale of Snorri's can hardly be interpreted otherwise than as evidence for a cult òf the dead on a large scale continuing in Bjarmaland until a fairly late date, and continuing alongside worship of the gods, though of what god the *Jómali*[1] in the story represents Snorri gives no indication here.

In the *Prose Edda* however there is a connection between the offerings made to a burial mound and a particular deity, though the passage where it occurs is vague and puzzling:

> That king who is called Helgi, after whom Halogaland is named, was the father of Þorgerðr Hölgabrúðr; they were both worshipped with sacrifice, and a mound was reared for Helgi, one layer being of gold and silver—that was the sacrificial wealth—and the other of earth and stones
> (*Skáldskaparmál*, XLII).

Here then we have that most tantalising of goddesses, Þorgerðr Hölgabrúðr, who received such devoted worship from Jarl Hákon, associated with the cult of the dead, and this is in accordance with the fact that she alludes to the *draugr* Sóti as her 'brother' in *Harðar Saga* (VIII).

### THE CUSTOM OF SITTING ON A HOWE

It is necessary at this point to consider the numerous allusions to the custom of sitting on a howe which we find in the sagas and poems, and which are perhaps more varied in their nature than Olrik admitted in his article 'At sidde paa Hoj' in the *Danske Studier* for the year 1909.

In this article he argues that all the examples except the story of Þorleifr Spaki in *Hallfreðar Saga* reveal the custom of sitting on a mound to be restricted to kings in their official capacity. He refuses to include allusions to shepherds who sit on a howe, since this, he argues, can be given a purely rational interpretation and the shepherd sits higher than his flock in order to watch over it. He suggests that this practice of the king is dependent on the conception of his person as sacred and something to be kept inaccessible, a belief derived from

---

1 Finnish word for 'god'. A recent survey of information about the Bjarmians is *The* Terfuinas *and* Beormas *of Ohthere*, A. S. C. Ross (Leeds Monographs VII, 1940).

the priestly origin of the kingship in Scandinavia, and connected with the custom of prophesying from a high platform which we find in accounts of the *völva* (seeress). Without attempting to disprove Olrik's main thesis—the peaceful and mantic origin of the kingship in early times—I would suggest that the fact that it was undoubtedly a burial mound on which the king chose to sit deserves greater emphasis. It will be worth while, I think, to examine the evidence for the custom in some detail.

Olrik in his article refers to the passage in Saxo where Hotherus is said to have made it his custom to give out decrees to the people from the top of a high hill;[1] to the story of King Hrollaugr, who rolled himself down from the king's seat on top of the mound as a symbol of his vassalage to Harald Hárfagr;[2] to the dog-king Eysteinn imposed on the Thronds, that 'sat on a howe like a king';[3] and to a fourteenth-century Icelandic tale, 'The Dream of Stjærne-Oddr', in which a place is prepared on a howe for the king to sit on a stool. These, he points out, show that it is from a mound that the king displays his power. The description of Þrymr, king of the giants, sitting on a mound in Jotunheim,[4] of King Rerir who receives Frigg's apple while sitting on a howe,[5] and the incident of King Gautrekr who flies his hawk from the mound of his queen in *Gautreks Saga*[6] are also quoted; but the statement in the last passage that the king sat on the howe out of sorrow for his queen's death is dismissed by him as an imaginary reason introduced to explain so widespread a custom.

This passage does not, however, stand alone; we may also notice that in *Hjálmðérs Saga ok Ölvérs* we are told that Hjálmðer's father Yngi 'had his throne placed on the howe of the queen; there he sat night and day enduring sorrow and grief for her loss' (II). Again in *Göngu-Hrólfs Saga*, though there is no idea of excessive grief, we read:

...Jarl Þorgnýr had loved his queen dearly, and her howe was near the palace. The Jarl often sat there in fine weather, or when he held conferences or had games played before him (v),

and further on in the saga the Jarl is said to be watching sports one day in autumn from his queen's howe (x). While it is fairly certain

1 Saxo, III, 76, p. 91.  2 *Heimskringla: Haralds Saga Hárfagra*, VIII.
3 *Ibid. Hákons Saga Goða*, XII.  4 *Þrymskviða*, 5.
5 *Völsunga Saga*, II.  6 *Gautreks Saga*, VIII.

that the idea of King Gautrekr's and King Yngi's grief is something supplied by the saga-teller to explain a prevalent custom—for indeed hunting and sports hardly accord with inconsolable sorrow—the tradition as we have it in the third extract that the Jarl or King made a practice of sitting on the burial mound of his queen, either in private or for public sports, deserves further consideration.

We may notice that it is not always the queen's howe on which the king is said to sit, but that it may also be the howe of his father, the former king. In *Friðþjófs Saga* the hero finds the two brother kings, Helgi and Hálfdan, sitting on the mound of their father, King Beli (II). Even more significant are passages in which the practice is directly connected with succession. In *Flateyjarbók* we read of a boy of twelve, Björn, the son of a king Olaf, who was brought up by his father's brother, Eric, after his father had been slain. Eric had no intention of letting his young nephew take over his father's kingdom, and Björn makes his first protest in a peculiar way:

When Björn was twelve years old, he sat on the howe of his father and did not come to table with the king. Then for the first time he claimed the kingdom. This was repeated the following spring and the third.

(Flateyjarbók: Óláfs Saga Helga, II, 9, p. 70).

Another example of a dispossessed heir who considered he had full claim to half his father's kingdom is found in the poem on *The Battle of the Goths and Huns*[1] from *Hervarars Saga*, when Gizurr, foster-father of Heiðrekr, remarks of the illegitimate son Hlöðr: 'While the prince (Angantýr) divided the inheritance, the base-born son sat on the howe' (v. 13).

In view of these passages, there may be special significance in two allusions which Olrik dismisses rather summarily. Is it accidental that the apple sent by Frigg, the eating of which by his queen brings them a child, drops into the king's lap while he sits on a howe?[2] And again, that it is while sitting on a howe that the young Helgi, for whom no name can be found, receives one at last?[3] The importance attributed to the choosing of the right name is closely connected with rebirth, as we shall see later.

It is perhaps worth noticing that two pieces of evidence for a similar custom connected with inheritance outside Scandinavia are found in the *Book of Llandaff*.[4] In two separate records of grants of

1 Kershaw, *Anglo-Saxon and Norse Poems* (Cambridge, 1922), p. 152.
2 *Völsunga Saga*, II.                              3 See p. 140 below.
4 For these references I am indebted to Professor Chadwick.

land made over to the church by Welsh kings, it is there recorded
that the king in question chose to make his gift while he either sat or
lay upon a tomb, in one case that of his father and in the other his
grandfather. King Gurcant did so *sedens super sepulchrum patris sui et
pro anima illius,*[1] and King Morcant similarly *super sepulchrum
Mourici regis jacentis coram idoneis testibus.*[2] This seems to indicate that
the same custom lingered on in Wales into Christian times, and that
here too the sitting on the tomb of the former ruler is closely connected with the possession of the kingdom, so that the ceremony has
to be repeated if part of the land is given up. It will be remembered
that the Norse king who gave up his realm to Harald Hárfagr sat on
top of a mound and then 'rolled himself down' from it.[3]

But while the idea of succession is one that seems apparent in
examining the evidence for this practice, the idea of inspiration which
Olrik emphasises is certainly present too; only I would suggest, and
intend to give more reasons for doing so in chapter VI, that here the
connection with the dead is at least as important as the connection
with a high place. Nor do I see any reason why the evidence re-
stricts us entirely to kings, though the fact that the practice is so
widely prevalent among them is undoubtedly of importance in
considering the origin of the kingship. There is a story in *Flateyjarbók* from the *þáttr þorleifs Jarlaskálds*[4] that is perhaps relevant here.
A shepherd named Hallbjörn used to make it his habit to sit on the
howe of the poet þorleifr, and sometimes he would sleep on it at
night: 'It often occurred to him that he would like to make a poem
in praise of the howe-dweller, and recite it whenever he lay on the
howe.' But since he had no skill as a poet, he did not get very far with
his attempts. One night, after an unavailing struggle at poetic composition, he fell asleep, and dreamed that the howe opened, and a man
of great size stepped out and climbed up beside him. He thanked
Hallbjörn for his efforts on his behalf, and told him that he should not
find poetry hard to compose any longer: 'Now I will recite a verse
to you, and if you learn the verse by heart, and can say it when you
wake, you will become a great poet.' We are told that Hallbjörn
woke up, and thought he caught sight of his visitor disappearing into
the howe. He remembered the verse, and found no more difficulty

1 *Liber Landavensis* (W. J. Rhys, Llandovery, 1840), p. 156.
2 *Ibid.* p. 141.
3 *Heimskringla: Háralds Saga Hárfagra*, VIII.
4 *Óláfs Saga Tryggvasonar*, I, 174, p. 214.

in composing his poem, and subsequently, as Þorleifr had promised, he became a great poet. This story forms a striking contrast with Bede's tale of Caedmon;[1] now the gift of poetry, still thought of as something bestowed on the fortunate from outside, comes not from a dweller in heaven, but from a dweller in the earth. Viewed from this angle, it seems altogether natural that in *Hallfreðar Saga* (VI) we should find Þorleifr Spaki, renowned for his wisdom, sitting on a mound.

It is perhaps worth noticing at this point that several of the Irish stories contain allusions to sitting on an eminence of some kind, occasionally specified as a mound, as a means of entering into communication with the supernatural world. For instance, Muircertach is said to be sitting alone on his hunting mound when the supernatural woman Sin appears beside him.[2] It is while he is on Mur Tea in Tara that Cormac is joined by a warrior from the Land of Promise,[3] while his father Art is sitting on Ben Etair, bewailing his dead wife —here the likeness to the Norse accounts may be noticed—when a woman from the Land of Promise joins him;[4] and all who journey to and fro from that land throughout the story, it may be noticed, begin by going to Ben Etair. It is on the hill of Usnech, also, that Art's brother Connla is sitting with his father when a woman from the Land of the Living, who is said at the same time to dwell in a fairy mound, arrives to summon him to Mag Mell.[5] From Wales, also, we have the tale of Pwyll Prince of Dyved, from the *Mabinogion*,[6] in which there is mention of a mound on which whosoever sits must either receive blows or behold a wonder; and it is while sitting on this mound that the king perceives his future wife, Rhiannon. It seems likely that these allusions point to a Celtic variant of the Norse traditions we have been studying. An eighteenth-century antiquary, writing on 'The Ancient Topography of Ireland',[7] also refers to 'the cairns and tumuli' where 'those slept who consulted the manes of their ancestors who were supposed to inform them either by dreams

1 *Historia Ecclesiastica Gentis Anglorum* (Plummer, Oxford, 1896); IV, 22, p. 259.
2 *The Death of Muircertach Mac Erca*, translated by T. P. Cross and C. H. Slover from the *Otia Merseiana* (*Ancient Irish Tales*, Chicago, 1935), p. 518.
3 *Ibid. Cormac's Adventures in the Land of Promise*, p. 503.
4 *Ibid. Adventures of Art Son of Conn*, p. 492.
5 *Ibid. Adventures of Connla the Fair*, p. 488.
6 Loth, *Les Mabinogion* (Paris, 1913), I, pp. 92–97.
7 *Collectanea de Rebus Hibernicis*, Vol. 3, XI: The Ancient Topography of Ireland, W. Beauford, p. 395.

or visions of circumstances relative to the future events of their life',
although unfortunately he does not say where he obtained this information.

The two allusions in Norse which I find most difficult to comprehend, and which are ignored by Olrik, come from the Edda. When
Skírnir arrives at the palace of Gerðr,[1] there is a 'shepherd watchman'
sitting on a howe outside. The verse which he speaks is incomplete,
but it is a threatening one, defying Skírnir to reach Gerðr through
the wall of fire which protects her. He seems to be the 'loathsome
giant' to whom Skírnir referred before he began his journey, with
whom he was to compete in wisdom, and in that case we are faced
with the question of the exact connection between him and the other
sinister figure in Völuspá (41), again a 'herdsman of the giantess',
who sits on a mound and strikes his harp, exulting in the ruin of the
worlds of gods and men. These figures will be further discussed in
the chapter on *The Journey to the Land of the Dead*, when it will be
seen that there are a number of parallels to them elsewhere. Again,
are we to attach any deep significance to Ketill's action in sitting
through a wintry storm on the sacred howe of King Framarr, and
interpret it as an attempt to tap a rival source of power, or is it
merely a typical gesture, like that made by the brothers in *Vatnsdœla
Saga* (xxxiv), of a man who will not be kept back from a duel by
such a trifle as bad weather? It is impossible to answer these questions without more information than we at present possess about the
significance of this custom.

It is worth noticing, however, that there is archaeological corro-
boration for the practice of sitting on a howe. A number of Swedish
howes of the Migration period are not rounded at the top but
flattened to give them an appearance of platforms. This is true for
instance of 'Ingjald's howe' at Husby, and of the howes called after
Ottar and Thor at Old Uppsala. The platform tops of the two first
sloped slightly downwards, like a stage at a theatre. Lindqvist, who
has commented on this feature in his article on *Ynglingättens Grav-
skick*,[2] believes that in some cases stones were set on the tops of the
howes, and suggests that these may have been used for seats; he also
notes the fact that in many cases howes in Scandinavia and Scandinavian colonies were situated on the sites of the local assemblies or
Things, and that flattened howes are among these, although they are
not confined to Thing-places. It seems clear from the evidence that

1 *Skírnismál*, 11.                    2 *Fornvännen*, 1921, p. 92 f.

the flat tops of these howes were intended for some public ceremony; for when the howe was particularly high and steep, as in the case of 'Frey's howe' at Old Uppsala, there was no flat place on top, but one made at the foot of the howe of about the same size; and sometimes this is marked by a ship formed of stones.

This evidence, taken in conjunction with that given in the literature, is significant, for it shows us that the practice of sitting on a howe was almost certainly known in the Migration period in Sweden. 'Ingjald's howe' is thought to belong to the seventh century, and some of the other cases are probably of still earlier date. The exact nature of the ceremonies connected with these howes is unknown, although we have obtained certain indications from the literature; but it is clear in any case that the cult of the dead must have been of importance, and that the howe played its part in ceremonies in some cases held in the place of local assembly. It also seems that the practice is not, as might have been expected, confined necessarily to inhumation burials; in the cases mentioned at Old Uppsala and Husby the howes held burnt remains. We do not know whether the custom originated with cremation or inhumation graves; certainly from the rich literary traditions it would seem that it was at one time familiar in Norway, and connected there with burial of the dead. The fact that ship-forms in stone are found associated with certain of these howes is extremely interesting, although its significance is not clear from the limited evidence we possess.

## ELVES AND LAND-SPIRITS

It is increasingly apparent that it is impossible to consider this subject of the cult of the dead as an isolated one, so closely is it linked up with other Norse beliefs. It seems necessary, for instance, to touch the subject of elves, since without it the survey would be obviously incomplete; but we shall have to return to this in greater detail when discussing the evidence for a belief in rebirth.

In Scandinavian folklore, particularly Swedish, elves are connected with mounds. Such a belief is also found in the sagas, since in one passage in *Kormáks Saga* (XXII) a witch, Þórdís, directs a man who desires to be healed from a serious wound to go to

a mound (*hóll*) not far from here, in which dwell elves; take the bull which Kormákr slew, and redden the outside of the hill with bull's blood, and make the elves a feast with the flesh; and you will be healed.

The tempting assumption to be made from this is that the elves are the dwellers in the grave-mound; although *hóll* actually is an ambiguous word and may signify only a natural hillock. The argument for the grave-mound is strengthened by the story of Olaf Geirstaðaálfr, since we are told that it was only after the king was laid in howe and sacrifices were made to him for plenty that the name *álfr* was given to him. Unfortunately the rest of our evidence does not carry us any further.[1] There is an allusion to *álfa-blót* in *Heimskringla*, when Sigvat the poet is refused admittance to a farm in Sweden because the farmer's wife declares they are holding a sacrifice to the elves; and he comments on this in one of his verses.[2] There is the association of Freyr with Álfheim in the Edda. In the *Fornaldar Sögur* (*Hrólfs Saga Kraka*, XLVIII) we find elves and norns mentioned together as the supporters of the witch Skuld against King Hrólfr 'so that mortals could avail nothing against such a company'.

The chief difficulty with regard to the elves is to decide how accurately the term is used in these passages, in, for example, *Hrólfs Saga Kraka*, where Skuld herself is said to be the child of an elf-woman who visits King Helgi by night (xv). The use of the word in the *Fornaldar Sögur* is evidently different from that in the Edda poems, where continually the elves seem to be regarded as equivalent to the Æsir; in *Lokasenna*[3] for instance, where the gods are represented as drinking together in the hall of Ægir, an appeal is made three times to 'Æsir and elves who are here within'. In *Skírnismál*[4] the messenger of Freyr is asked whether he is of the Æsir, the Vanir or the elves; and it would seem on the whole that the affinities of these mysterious creatures are with the gods of Ásgarðr rather than with giants or dwarfs, just as the Vanir, although clearly of different race, are represented as mingling freely with the gods.

As for the inhabitant of the grave-mound, the usual word for him is *draugr*—that is, the animated corpse which dwells within the howe, brooding over its treasures and occasionally leaving it to trouble the world of men; and there seems to be no example of such a creature

1 Mogk (*Grundr. Germ. Philologie*, Paul, III, 11, p. 287) suggests that the passage about the holy mountain in *Eyrbyggja Saga* (IV), where we are told that no *álfrekr* (excrement) was allowed to defile it, is evidence for the dead dwelling within the mountain being equated with the elves. This however seems doubtful, and probably the use of that particular word is mere coincidence.
2 See p. 114 below.
3 *Lokasenna*, 2, 13, 30; cf. *Grímnismál*, 4; *Þrymskviða*, 7, 8; *Skírnismál*, 7.
4 *Skírnismál*, 17, 18.

being described as an elf. On the other hand, it may be remembered that Olaf Geirstaðaálfr did not merely remain in his howe in this way; he is represented as being born again into the world of the living as Olaf the Holy, so that possibly we should seek the meaning of his name in the belief that he was reborn; in that case the connection of elves with mounds may depend on the connection of mounds—that is, howes—with rebirth; this is a subject to be discussed further in the following chapter.

The position is further complicated by the fact that in the Viking Age there was a district in Scandinavia called Álfheim. It lay in the extreme south-east of Norway, between the rivers Gota and Glommen, just below the Oslo Fjord, and now belongs mainly to Sweden. Snorri[1] records the struggles of Hálfdan the Black and Harald Hárfagr with King Gandálfr of Álfheim and his sons, which did not end finally until Harald slew Gandálfr in battle. The account given by Snorri contains no allusions to supernatural powers of any kind possessed by Gandálfr and his men. By the time of the *Fornaldar Sögur* however Álfheim has become a country on the border-line of mythology, as when for example we are told in *Þorsteins Saga Víkingssonar* (1):

Álfr the Old...ruled over the kingdom which lies between two rivers; these took their names from him, and each was called *elfr*; the one called Gautelfr [i.e. the Gota] ran to the south, by the land of the king of the Gauta, and divided the land from Gautland; the other was called Raumelfr [i.e. the Glommen] and lay to the north, and was called after King Raum; the kingdom there was called Raumaríki. The land over which King Álfr ruled was called Álfheim, and the people who sprang from him were all of elfin race; they were fairer than all other peoples except the *rísir*.

In this passage the saga-teller is trying to fit together place-names and mythology; and a land called Álfheim lying between the rivers Gautelfr and Raumelfr was obviously just the place in which to put his elves. This however does not help us to discover any more about the nature of these puzzling beings, and only shows how easily misunderstandings and additional complications could spring up in the interpretation of old beliefs and traditions.

To return again to the vexed subject of elf-worship: the most valuable and definite evidence about the elves seems to be their association with Freyr. In the passage in *Óláfs Saga Helga* referred to

1 *Heimskringla: Hálfdans Saga Svarta*, I, IV; *Haralds Saga Hárfagra*, I, II.

above we have evidence for their worship in Sweden during the early part of the eleventh century; Sigvat the Skald recorded his visit to a farm where *álfa-blót* was said to be in progress while on an errand for Olaf the Holy:

> 'Go thou in no further,
> Base wretch', the lady said;
> 'I fear the wrath of Othin,
> For we are heathen people.'
> That unattractive lady,
> Who drove me from her dwelling,
> Curtly, like a wolf, declared she
> Held elf-sacrifice within.[1]

Is the connection between Othin and the elves here to be taken seriously? It may merely be used by the Christian poet as typical of the heathenism to which he was now opposed; it is also possible to interpret the phrase in such a way as to see worship of the elves (and Freyr) in opposition to that of Othin.

The connection with Freyr, however, suggested in *Grímnismál* might also help to explain the references to elves and howes. What we know of Freyr's cult suggests associations with both fertility and the dead, and it is perhaps significant that the evidence for the meaning of the cup-markings on rocks, traditionally associated with elves in Sweden, points in the same directions. These marks are found together with the rock-engravings discussed earlier, and also on tombs from the time of the Stone Age to the Iron Age. In Sweden offerings have been made by pouring milk and other drink-offerings into them up to recent times. Are these originally intended for the dead, or for the earth? The question has been discussed by Hammerstedt, and later by Almgren.[2] The former believes that when the markings are away from graves the offerings must be intended for the earth, and Almgren, after an extensive review of the evidence, also decides in favour of a fertility cult rather than a cult of the dead. He is influenced by the fact that recent researches on

1 *Ibid. Óláfs Saga Helga*, XCI:

| | |
|---|---|
| Gakkat inn, kvað ekkja, | rýgr kvazk inni eiga |
| armi drengr, in lengra; | ópekk, sús mér hnekði, |
| hræðumk ek við Óðins | álfa-blót, sem ulfi |
| (erum heiðnir vér) reiði; | ótvín ór bœ sínum. |

(Ed. F. Jónsson, *Heimskringla*, Copenhagen, 1911, p. 254.)
2 Almgren, *Nordische Felszeichnungen als religiöse Urkunden*, p. 237 f.

similar markings in Palestine seem to establish clearly that they were originally associated with the earth, though afterwards extended to include the dead within the earth, and also that the cup-markings have a resemblance to certain Indian cult-symbols representing generation and fertility. He suggests that while such markings— found in Sweden in close connection with the sun-wheel—were in early times associated with the worship of the sun and the cult of fertility in nature, they were afterwards introduced into the grave and perhaps signify the rebirth of the dead.

It is interesting to find that Almgren, working quite independently on cup-markings in the Bronze Age and later, comes to conclusions very similar to those suggested by literary evidence about the cult of Freyr, with whom the elves are associated. Both Freyr and the elves are also connected with the sun, it may be noticed; Freyr is said in *Gylfaginning* (xxiv) to control 'rain, sunshine and the fruitfulness of the earth', while the sun is several times called *álfröðull*, 'glory of the elves',[1] and in *Alvíssmál* (16) they are said to name it *fagrahvél*, 'fair wheel'. This last is particularly interesting in view of the connection between the cup-marking and the sun-wheel mentioned by Almgren. If Almgren is right, the association of the elves with fertility is the essential one, and it is through their relation with fertility cults that they have allied themselves with the dead; this alliance, however, clearly goes back very far in time, and by the period with which we are chiefly concerned, that of heathenism a mere century or two before the coming of Christianity, it must have been an accomplished fact. The suggestion made much earlier in this chapter, that it is rebirth out of the grave rather than existence within the grave on which the emphasis should be placed, is if anything strengthened by the work of scholars like Almgren, working on signs of religion in Scandinavia much earlier than this; but as yet the evidence is insufficient to declare on this with certainty.

There is, I think, no doubt that the conception of elves in the literature has been influenced by ideas about another class of supernatural beings, which I group under the general heading of 'land-spirits'. Various attempts have been made by earlier scholars to convert these creatures into 'ancestral spirits', but this tendency has lately fallen into disrepute, and, as we shall see, the literature does not really provide very much ground for doing so. One of the most vivid accounts of a solitary spirit of this kind comes from the story of

1 E.g. *Vafþrúðnismál*, 47; *Skírnismál*, 4.

Þorvaldr enn Víðförli.¹ Þorvaldr's father is unable to accept the
Christian bishop's teaching, good though his credentials are, because,
he says, he has a *spámaðr* of his own already. (The word is used for
someone with powers of second sight.) Kóðran says:

...He tells me many things beforehand that are to happen in the future;
he guards my cattle, and gives me warning of what I must do and what I
ought to beware of; and so I have much faith in him, and I have worshipped him for a long time. But you he mistrusts greatly, and also your
*spámaðr*....'Where does he live?' asked Þorvaldr [who had been brought
up away from home]. 'He dwells here,' replied Kóðran, 'not far from
my house, in a big and splendid stone.' Þorvaldr asked how long he had
dwelt there. Kóðran said for a long time.

Þorvaldr and the bishop, of course, disapprove of this; and holy
water is dropped on the stone, with lamentable results to the *spámaðr*. He appears to Kóðran in a dream, in accordance apparently
with his usual custom, but now, 'shivering as if in terror', he reproaches
him bitterly:

You have done ill in bringing these men here, who plot against you in
that they seek to drive me away from my dwelling—for they have poured
boiling water over my house, and my children suffer no little pain from
the burning drops that run in through the roof; and though this does not
hurt me much, it is hard indeed to hear the wail of little children, as they
cry out from the burning.

Þorvaldr and the bishop, however, continue their campaign, and
next night the *spámaðr* appears a second time; he is now in a miserable
cloak of skin, and again protests against the treatment he is receiving.
The third night the spirit—rather unfairly described as 'malicious'—
appears for the last time. The bishop, he says, has 'spoilt his home,
poured boiling water over him, soaked his clothes and torn them and
made them useless', so that he and his children are forced to leave.

This story gives us no grounds for classifying the *spámaðr* as an
ancestor spirit. It is of course possible that this was the origin of such
a conception, but we should need more evidence before we could
conclude as much. The story must be taken together with certain
others. In the *Flateyjarbók*,² for instance, we get a rather similar
picture of the spirits fleeing before the approach of Christianity,

1 *Þáttr Þorvalds ens Víðförla* (*Altnordische Saga-Bibliotek*, XI), chapter 2, p. 65;
cf. *Kristnisaga*, II.
2 *Flateyjarbók: Óláfs Saga Tryggvasonar*, I, 335, p. 421 f.

when Þorhallr, a man of second sight, sees many hills opening and every living creature getting his baggage ready, both great and small, and making it a day for moving. Reading the story in the light of the one immediately before it, that of the slaying of Þiðrandi, the impression given is that the protective spirits of the new faith have come in advance of it, even though it has not yet been preached, and that before their superior might the spirits of the old religion are forced to flee—strikingly like Milton's vision in the Nativity Ode. It is with such protective spirits that we must rank the land-spirits, who haunt mountain, river, tree and valley. There is a tale in the *Ólafs Saga Helga*[1] of one such spirit haunting a mountain pasture high up above the scree on a hillside, and far from any human habitation. The expulsion of this creature bears a close resemblance to that of the *spámaðr* from his stone:

> At mid-night...there was a hideous cry outside the milking-pen, and a voice spoke: 'The prayers of King Olaf so burn me', said the creature, 'that no longer can I abide in my home, and now I must flee.'

It will be remembered that *Landnámabók*[2] records the statement at the beginning of the heathen laws that men must not sail to land with grinning and gaping figureheads on their ships, but must remove them while some distance from Iceland, so that the land-spirits may not be frightened by them. The idea of the land-spirits as protective beings, whose friendship is a valuable one, is brought out again by the little incident in *Landnámabók*, of the lucky man called Björn who was assisted by the land-spirits so that his herds increased and he prospered greatly:

> ...Men with the gift of second-sight watched all the land-spirits following Hafr-Björn to the Þing, and Þorsteinn and Þórðr [his brothers] hunting and fishing (IV, 12, p. 194).

The best revenge Egill can take on King Eric and Queen Gunnhildr is to set up a horse's head on a pole, so that the spirits of the land, he says, may be driven astray, and will in turn drive the king and queen out of the country.[3] Finally we have the story in *Heimskringla*[4] of how King Harald Gormson of Denmark, after a quarrel with the men of Iceland, sends a man to their country in the shape of a whale to act as a spy for him. The whale swims round the south-west corner of

1 *Heimskringla: Ólafs Saga Helga*, CLXXIX.
2 *Lndn.* IV, 7, p. 183.                         3 *Egils Saga*, LVII.
4 *Heimskringla: Ólafs Saga Tryggvasonar*, XXXIII.

Iceland and up the north coast: 'He saw that all the mountains and hillocks (*hólar*) were full of land-spirits, some great and some small.' These spirits come down to the shore and bar his way whenever he tries to come inland up one of the fjords, taking sometimes the form of serpents, sometimes of adders or toads; once a bull and once a bird intercepts him, and finally he is encountered by an enormous cliff-giant, at which his nerve fails him and he returns to Harald.

One would hardly expect Iceland, a colony founded only a short time before, to be equipped with ancestor spirits in as extensive a number as is indicated by this story. In the same way one might instance the story of one of the early settlers in Iceland, who, according to *Landnámabók*,[1] began practically as soon as he arrived to sacrifice to a waterfall. On the other hand one cannot demand too much logic from traditions of beliefs preserved so long after Christianity had entered the North. The points that stand out from the references to land-spirits which we possess in the literature are, first, their close identification with the world of nature; secondly, their association with particular localities, and, to a lesser degree, with certain people living in these localities; and thirdly, the marked hostility between them and the preachers of Christianity. The idea of fertility is obviously of importance throughout, for since they are linked to the earth, its fruitfulness must be to a large extent attributed to them, and the passage in *Landnámabók* where the friendship of the land-spirits results in good luck in hunting and fishing and rearing animals for the family which they take under their protection is significant. If they are associated with the dead in the earth, it is likely to be through this idea of fertility, which, as we have seen, was connected also with the dead in the grave; this also must prove the link between them and the elves. In *Ynglinga Saga* (VII) the spirits in mountains and stones are placed alongside those within the howe, and Othin is said to have power over all alike. But the link between the spirits of the earth which help to render it fruitful and the spirits of the dead must, as we have seen, go back very far in time, so that we can hardly expect that in the late heathen period it will remain clear-cut and distinct in the minds of the saga-tellers. These land-spirits, it may be noticed, seem to belong to the world of popular belief rather than to the world of imaginative mythology. They are not mentioned in the Edda or discussed by Snorri, and have, as far as we can tell, no entry into the world of the gods. In this they are distinct

1 *Lndn.* v, 5, p. 207.

from the elves; probably later conceptions of these, and the position they occupy in folklore, are largely due to confusion with land-spirits. The enmity expressed on the part of the Church is probably due to the fact that these popular beliefs about spirits controlling the fertility of the soil and the health of human beings proved harder to eradicate than all the mythological concepts of the heathen gods; we find the same story in converted Anglo-Saxon England, in the threatening list of penalties for those who 'bring gifts to any spring or stone or tree' or 'worship springs or stones or wooden trees of any kind', which it was thought necessary to repeat in the Penitentials and Laws up to the time of Cnut.[1]

## CONCLUSION

The evidence for a cult of the dead in Norse literature, although at first sight scanty, proves on closer examination to be rich in sugges-tion and not inconsistent. Even though we are dealing only with memories, misunderstood by later compilers of the sagas as we have them, enough remains to demand our attention. It is clear that the cult of the dead was no mere vague sense of their influence over fertility in the natural world; in the evidence for sitting on the howe, for worship of the howe in Bjarmaland, and in traditions connected with certain of the early kings of Scandinavia, we find signs of a definite cult, and of organised rites associated with the worship of the dead in the earth.

The practice of sitting on the howe seems, as far as one can tell from the sketchy nature of the information and from the corrobora-ting evidence of archaeology, to go back into the Migration period, but to continue into the Viking Age; and it has left unmistakable marks on the literature. The indications are that the significance of this custom was bound up partly with ideas about mantic inspiration from the dead, and partly with ideas about rebirth. We have not yet followed up these lines of thought in detail, but they should become clearer as we proceed. It would seem from the marked interest shown in the howe-worship of Bjarmaland as though the cult continued there late in the heathen period, after Christian kings ruled in Norway.

1 E.g. B. Thorpe, 'Ancient Laws and Institutes of England', *Poenitentiale Ecgberti*, *Arch. Ebor.* II, 22, p. 371; Liebermann, 'Die Gesetze der Angelsachsen', I, *Cnut*, II, 5, p. 312.

We can see that there are deities concerned with this cult, but it is difficult to determine their exact relationship with it. It would be enlightening to discover the identity of the god of the Bjarmians, whose image, wearing the great necklace, stood near to the sacred howe. In Sweden we have seen reason to believe that Freyr, with whom the elves are associated, was of great importance, owing to the connection with howes, and with fertility in the natural and the human world; one is even tempted to suggest that the Vanir as a whole may have had specially strong links with this cult, which carries the conception of fertility in nature into the world of the dead also. Were indeed the elves themselves originally the Vanir, although later they forsook their high calling and became little creatures of the earth, akin to the land-spirits of popular belief? But a great deal more evidence is necessary before such a suggestion can be accepted seriously.

Þorgerðr Hölgabrúðr, the strange goddess worshipped by Jarl Hákon in the north of Norway, is also likely to be of importance because of her close association with howes; but of her we know sufficient only to perplex us. Lastly Othin must not be forgotten, since not only is he connected with cremation of the dead, but also in several passages with the dead in the earth. But it is clearly necessary to examine the evidence for the belief in rebirth before attempting any further conclusions.

# Chapter V

## THE CONCEPTION OF THE SOUL

*Yea, man giveth up the ghost, and where is he?*
                              JOB, Authorised Version.

The problem of the nature of man's inner self is one that seems to have had great interest for the Norse writers. The emphasis and value placed on personality and the individual throughout the prose sagas, and the widespread interest in the powers which certain persons could obtain by sorcery over the minds of others perhaps tended to give the question a practical interest which ideas of the future life never possessed. Moreover the dramatic possibilities of abnormal states of mind—madness, trance, dreams, hallucinations and so on—were bound to occur to such creative artists as the Norse saga-writers proved themselves to be. It would seem as though the problem as to what part of man gives him consciousness and individuality had been answered somehow to the satisfaction of the Norse mind in heathen times, for in the literature we can discern traces of vivid conceptions of man's inner self, strikingly different from later Christian teaching. It is difficult however to trace out this conception sufficiently clearly to receive any impression of a consistent whole, since as usual we are limited to isolated fragments here and there, often misunderstood and imperfectly remembered.

It will be necessary to approach the subject from a number of different starting-points in order to discover whether there is any trace of a conception of the 'soul' comparable to that of later times. The connection between man and the animal world as brought out in the sagas is one that is very relevant to our subject, and this emerges first in the idea of shape-changing, and secondly in the conception of an invisible animal form accompanying the human one. Then it is impossible to study this animal form in Norse literature without being led on to discuss the guardian spirit in human form also, and the connection between this and divine beings independent of man. The meanings of the different terms *fylgja, hamingja, dís* and so on must each be examined in some detail, in order to see what bearing the ideas behind them may have on the Norse conception of the soul. One particular aspect of this subject which is an essential corollary to the study of the future life and the cult of the dead is that of the survival of the personality after death; so that it will be necessary to pass on to the question, first, of the belief in rebirth which is found in the literature, and secondly, to that of human survival as a whole. This will give a convenient opportunity for a survey of the evidence so far, and the conclusions reached in this study of Norse eschatology.

### SHAPE-CHANGING

The practice of shape-changing is one that enters a good deal into the sagas, as indeed into most literature which deals with magic at all. A very cursory examination of the activities of witches and wizards in this direction will make it clear that we have more than one type of shape-changing involved. In Snorri's description of the magic powers of Othin,[1] we can see one distinction made. After Snorri has explained how differently Othin appears to his friends and his enemies, he goes on:

...It so happened that he knew those arts by which he could change his appearance and his shape in whatever way he chose.

Then a little later he continues:

...Othin could change himself; his body then lay as if sleeping or dead, but he became a bird or a wild beast, a fish or a dragon, and journeyed in the twinkling of an eye to far-off lands, on his own errands or those of other men.

Here we have on the one hand the power to disguise the outward appearance, so that spectators are deceived, and on the other the capacity to lie as if in a trance, while some part of the consciousness leaves the body and travels vast distances in animal shape to do its owner's errands. The *sjónhverfing* or practice of 'deceiving the eyes', akin to hypnotic suggestion, need not concern us here; the other form of shape-changing however, for which there is no specific name given in the literature, is one that is very relevant to a discussion on the soul. There are some striking accounts of it, perhaps the most interesting of which is found in the *Fornaldar Sögur*, in the *Saga Hjálmðérs ok Ölvérs* (xx).

Here the foster-brothers Hjálmðér and Ölvér are fleeing from

1 *Ynglinga Saga*, VII.

King Hundingr, an unpleasant monarch with supernatural powers; and with them are Hörðr, a prince with some knowledge of magic, and King Hundingr's daughter Hervör. King Hundingr pursues their ship in the form of a walrus:

...A little while after, they saw a great walrus making for them, angry and frightful to behold. 'There', said Hörðr, 'is a creature very ill-disposed towards me, that I may not look upon...you must not name my name while he is here, for if you do I shall die.' And he lay down in the hold, and they covered him with clothes. Then they saw a sword-fish (?) dart out from under their ship, and make for the walrus at great speed, and he attacked him straightway; the two moved out into deep water. Soon after they saw dart out from under Hervör's ship a fair and shapely porpoise; she turned immediately on the walrus and there was a fierce combat....

For a while the walrus gets the better of it, until Hjálmðér calls upon two women who have promised to help him and they arrive in the form of vultures and join in the combat, with the result that the walrus is finally defeated:

...and the vultures flew off, very exhausted, so that blood ran down from under every feather, and they flew slowly and low. Then Hjálmðér went to where Hörðr lay, and saw that he was wet. 'Is the walrus dead now?' asked Hörðr. Hjálmðér said he had disappeared 'and I have lost my sword and Ölvér his knife'. [They had joined in the fight when the walrus drew near the ship.] 'Here are both of them,' said Hörðr, 'and now that King Hundingr is put to death, we have achieved a good deal.' They thanked him for saving their lives and helping them out of such deadly peril as had threatened them. 'Go to Hervör,' answered Hörðr, 'for she will soon need your help.' So Hjálmðér leaped up on to her ship. She lay unconscious and very weak. Hjálmðér dropped some wine into her mouth, and she soon recovered.

Here the state of trance in which the body remains while the conscious mind is elsewhere is vividly described in the case of Hörðr and Hervör, who are clearly represented as taking on the shapes of fish and porpoise while their bodies remain on board ship. The physical weakness after such an effort, and the necessity not to mention the name of the person concerned as long as the trance continued, are points which are noticeable elsewhere. They recur, for instance, in the story of the three Lapps in *Vatnsdæla Saga* (xii) who are employed by Ingimundr to go to Iceland for him and discover what has become of his lost image of Freyr. This they do for him, but their bodies never leave Norway meanwhile. They ask to be shut up in a hut while none name their names, for three days. Then Ingimundr is allowed to visit them, and finds they are able to describe minutely the part of Iceland they have visited and to tell him the position of the image; he himself verifies this description later on. They emphasise how difficult it has been to do this: 'it has been a hard task for your servants, and much labour have we had.'

In this example there is no indication given that the spirits of the Lapps, while absent from their bodies, took on animal shapes. Another story from one of the *Fornaldar Sögur*, *Friðþjófs Saga* (VI), describes a similar experience. Here two witches remain on an 'incantation platform' (*seiðhjallr*) while at the same time they are able to appear on the sea a great distance away, riding on a whale. They do this in order to wreck the hero's ship, but he succeeds in breaking the backs of them both, and at the instant he does so, we learn later in the saga, the witches fall from their platform in the middle of their spell-working and break their backs.

There are other examples of shape-changing in the sagas which seem to belong to the same category. In the *Íslendinga Sögur* we have the incident of Þuríðr Drikinn in *Þorskfirðinga Saga* who lies down at night on a bed set up at the door and says that 'very little can come without her knowing about it'. When a rival witch, Kerling, leads a party of men to attack the house, she is met outside by a great boar, which leaps at her, 'and at the same moment up sprang Þuríðr Drikinn...saying there was an attack on the house' (XVII). Another clear example is the well-known story of Böðvarr Bjarki in *Hrólfs Saga Kraka* (L) who goes out to fight as a great bear in the battle against Skuld. The bear does havoc amongst King Hrólfr's enemies, but Hjalti misses Böðvarr in the battle and goes to his tent to find him sitting there motionless. He accuses him of cowardice, and at last Böðvarr gets up reluctantly, saying he could help the king the more by remaining as he is, and goes to fight; by this time the bear has disappeared.[1] When the witch Þórdís assumes the shape of a walrus in *Kormáks Saga*, and is only recognisable by her eyes (XVIII); when in *Egils Saga* the hero is infuriated by a swallow twittering at the window while he tries to compose a poem, and 'some shape-changer' is said to be responsible, presumably the malicious queen

---

1 Compare with this the incident in *Hrólfs Saga Gautrekssonar* (XX), which appears to have been originally a story of the same kind. Here the man who does not fight sits in the high-seat, muttering and covering his face (*F.A.S.* III, p. 98).

(LIX); and when Harald Gormson dispatches a messenger to Iceland in the shape of a whale to spy out the land, it seems probable that the change here is the same kind of transformation, though full details are not given. The difference between this form of shape-changing and the *sjónhverfing* is shown by a story in *Þorskfirðinga Saga* (x), when Askmaðr and his wife escape from a burning house in the forms of a pig and a sow, and the pig is brought down by a burning brand, leaving Askmaðr himself visible, dead on the spot. Here it is the body itself which is disguised in animal shape, instead of being in a trance while the spirit is elsewhere, so that there is only one death to describe, not two as in the case of the witches in *Friðþjófs Saga*.

This distinction is not, of course, confined to Norse sources, and in his article on *Lycanthropy* in Hastings' *Encyclopedia of Religion and Ethics* J. M. MacCulloch has collected examples of beliefs in shape-changing from all over the world and has noticed the two types which he defines by the terms 'wer-animal'—that is transformation of the man himself as in the case of Askmaðr above—and 'external soul'. The latter type he finds rare in comparison with the former, and in his examples there is nothing which bears so close a resemblance to those in Norse literature as do some of the accounts of shamanism in North Europe and Asia.

In Holmberg's account of Finno-Ugric Mythology,[1] for instance, he records the belief among the Lapps that the soul of the shaman can leave his body and act as 'a tutelary spirit'; he says too that it can be used against his enemies, and quotes a statement of Kildal to the effect that two shamans will fight against one another in the form of reindeer bulls, until 'the shamans owning the "reindeer" become as tired and exhausted as their "reindeer"'. We may here recall an instance of shape-changing given in *Landnámabók*, when two neighbours who disagree over grazing rights are reported to have been seen by a man with the gift of second sight fighting in the forms of a bear and a bull, and 'in the morning both of them were tired out'.[2] The idea of the spirits of the shamans fighting in animal form is also found in Siberia. Miss Czaplicka[3] notices that this is a familiar conception:

...A typical case is that of a contest between a Samoyed and a Yakut shaman, continued for years, in which the scene of strife was transferred first from the earth to the sky and then to the water and below it.

1 U. Holmberg, *Mythology of all Races: Finno-Ugric, Siberian* (Boston, 1927), XVIII, p. 284 f.
2 *Lndn.* v, 5.                     3 *My Siberian Year* (London, 1916), p. 212.

Again we can parallel this from Norse sources. In the *Saga Stur-laugs Starfsama* (XII) a young man who has been taught magic has a contest with a Finn:

...They set on each other, and fought fiercely, so swiftly that they could not be followed with the eye; but neither of them managed to wound the other. When men looked again they had disappeared, but two dogs were in their place and bit at each other furiously; and when they least expected it, the dogs vanished too, and they heard a noise going on up in the air; they looked up and saw two eagles flying there and each tore out the other's feathers with claws and beak so that blood fell to the earth. The end of it was that one fell dead to the ground, but the other flew away, and they did not know which it was.

The spirit of the shaman, says Holmberg,[1] is called *sueje* (originally 'shadow') among the Scandinavian Lapps. This is believed to take on the shape of various animals, and in particular reindeer, fish, bird or snake, at will. These animals are the means by which a shaman succeeds in winning back the souls of the dead from the Underworld. Among the Siberian tribes too he tells us that the special bird-costume worn by the shaman is said to be his 'shadow' or shape in which the spirit travels.[2] Holmberg is of the opinion that this costume originally represented his soul animal. It is very important not to rouse the shaman from his trance by touching him,[3] just as in the Norse accounts there are warnings against uttering the names of those whose spirits have left their bodies. The *Chronicon Norwegiae*[4] contains a story which is very like some of the Norse instances. A shaman who was seeking to rescue the soul of a woman who had died suddenly dropped dead himself, with a terrible wound in the stomach. A second shaman was more successful, and recalled the woman back to life, and she then related how the spirit of the first shaman in the shape of a whale was pierced by an enemy with a sharp weapon while he was crossing a lake, and the results of the blow were seen by those present on the shaman's own body.

In spite of close resemblances, however, the essential function of the spirit 'sent out' by the shaman, to get into contact with the souls of the dead and possibly to recall them to life, is missing in the saga evidence. Has the real significance of the journey of the soul been forgotten in the Norse traditions, or is this a later conception which

1 Holmberg, *op. cit.* p. 285.        2 *Ibid.* p. 519.        3 *Ibid.* pp. 291, 292.
4 Munch, *Symbolae ad Hist. antiq. rerum Norvegicarum* (Christiania, 1850), *Chron. Norveg.* pp. 4-5.

has come in from Asia and become connected with the conception of the soul in animal form? This is a question to which we must return later in the section on the *Journey to the Land of the Dead*. For the present it is sufficient to notice that the idea of the 'spirit' or 'external soul' leaving the body, either in human or animal form, to travel vast distances or to fight the spirits of others in similar form, is one that occurs frequently in Norse tradition. Many more such stories have probably been misunderstood by later writers and converted into 'shape-changing' stories of the more crude and childish type. A good example of the Norse tendency to convert such stories as these into concrete form is seen in the ravens of Othin. As described by Snorri they seem solid enough, but when we remember their names, *Huginn* and *Muninn*, or 'Thought' and 'Memory', given in the Edda poem, it seems evident that here we have a symbolic description of the sending out of the spirit through the universe, corresponding to the account of Othin given in the *Ynglinga Saga*. This example suggests the possibility of similar conceptions in Norse thought now lost because we have no longer the key which would open the symbolism of the mythology to us.

## THE ANIMAL *FYLGJA*

There are several instances in the sagas where we find the conception of an animal form closely connected with an individual which is visible to others in dreams, and, to those who have the power of second sight, in waking life also. One of the most vivid descriptions comes from the *þáttr þorsteins Uxafóts* in the *Flateyjarbók*:[1]

It happened one day that Þorsteinn came to Krossavík as he often did. The householder's father, Geitir, sat on the dais and muttered into his cloak. Now when the boy entered the hall, he came in with a great rush, as children usually do. He slipped on the floor of the hall, and when Geitir saw this, he burst out laughing....The boy went up to Geitir and said: 'Why did it seem funny to you when I fell just now?' Geitir answered: 'Because in truth I could see what you did not.' 'What was that?' asked Þorsteinn. 'I will tell you. When you came into the hall a white bear-cub followed you, and ran along the floor in front of you. Now when he saw me, he stood still; but you were going rather fast, and you fell over him— and it is my belief that you are not the son of Krumr and Þorgunna, but must be of greater family.'

1 *Flateyjarbók: Óláfs Saga Tryggvasonar*, I, 205, p. 252.

Here we have the attendant animal pictured as sufficiently solid to trip the boy up—characteristic of the vivid and concrete character of Norse narrative. Geitir, the man with powers of second sight, is able to see the animal which is invisible to ordinary men. He is also able to deduce from the fact that Þorsteinn is accompanied by a white bear that he is of better parentage than was generally thought. The bear then is a symbol of high birth, and the animal who attends a human being has come to have a partly symbolic function. The other instance of an animal form seen in waking life is found in *Njáls Saga*:

It happened one day that Njáll and Þórðr were out of doors. A he-goat used to walk round the yard, and no one was allowed to drive it away. Suddenly Þórðr spoke: 'That is a queer thing', said he. 'What do you see that you think queer?' asked Njáll. 'It seems to me that the goat lies here in the hollow and is all covered with blood.' Njáll said that there was no goat there nor anything else. 'What is it then?' said Þórðr. 'You must be a "fey" man', said Njáll, 'and have seen your *fylgja*, so take care of yourself.' 'That will be no help to me', replied Þórðr, 'if things are doomed for me' (XLI).

From this story we get the impression that the life of the animal form depends on the life of the man it accompanies—or possibly this should be put in the reverse order and we should say that the human life is dependent on the well-being of the animal *fylgja*, just as when the animal form in the shape-changing stories we have examined is mortally injured the human body must perish also.

It is usually in dreams that the animal *fylgja* is visible. In a number of cases a person is represented by a particular animal; in *Njáls Saga* (XXIII) Höskuldr has a dream in which a white bear stands for Gunnarr, which tells him that the latter is approaching the house; in *Ljósvetninga Saga* (XXI) Guðmundr is symbolised by a splendid ox, and the dream foretells his death; in *Þorsteins Saga Víkingssonar* (XII) Jökull, the leader of a hostile expedition, appears as a great bear, and two unpleasant wizards who have joined him as vixens. It is interesting to find that in the last case the *fylgja* of Ógautan the wizard is the same animal as that which Ógautan sends out to obtain information; for when he is tracking the heroes, he takes the shape of a little vixen. Here we have the unusual case of a female animal chosen to represent a man.

In all these cases, the animal form seems to depend on the character and the standing of the man in question, those of high birth and outstanding character being represented by dignified and noble animals. When the people concerned are unimportant, they are usually represented by animals which symbolise their activity at the time; an attacking party, for example, being almost invariably represented as wolves if they are not singled out individually. As Þorsteinn puts it in the passage alluded to above: 'The number of wolves I saw must be the number of men with them, for they must have wolfish intentions towards us.' In such cases the wolves seem symbolic merely in the way that the hood and the ring in Guðrún's dreams in *Laxdæla Saga* (XXXIII) are symbolic; the conception of the particular animal form that is attached to an individual, however, seems to be closely akin to the animal form in the shape-changing examples we have studied. Like it, the *fylgja* can apparently wage battle with that of another man; in *Ljósvetninga Saga* Finn the wizard attributes the misfortunes of Eyjólfr to the fact that the *fylgjur* of their enemies are more powerful than those of his own party (XXX); it is not certain from the context here that the animal form is referred to, since the word is not always used with the same meaning, as we shall see later, though on the other hand the animal form accompanying a man is never described by any other term.

The distinction between the animal *fylgia* and the animal form assumed by the spirit of the shape-changer lies of course in the fact that in the second case the animal form is only active while the body of the owner lies in a state of unconsciousness; it is informed, apparently, by the whole conscious mind of the human owner. The *fylgja* however is the active, invisible companion which attends the owner in his waking state; it would usually appear, in spite of its name, to precede him. As in dreams, so those with the gift of second sight can in waking hours tell of the approach of outstanding people by the *fylgjur* that go before them; in a story in *Haralds Saga* when an old woman with second sight is told by her foster-son that no strangers have arrived that day, she replies:

I did not expect you would lie to me, for I recognise the *fylgjur* of Auðun illskáld your kinsman here, and they arrived early in the day.[1]

Similarly the coming of Olaf Tryggvason is known to those with second sight, because of the bright *fylgjur* before him.[2] The fact that here and elsewhere the word is used in the plural does not seem to

1 *Fornmanna Sögur* (Copenhagen, 1825), III, p. 71: *Saga Skálda Haralds Konungs Hárfagra.*          2 *Ibid. Óláfs Saga Tryggvasonar*, I, LVII, p. 96.

alter the conception; we are still dealing with something which precedes a man, to announce his coming and to tell those who have the power to see it what kind of person he is. The Norse evidence gives us no ground for assuming that it is the *fylgja* which can be dismissed by its owner while he is unconscious to carry out various errands for him. It is quite likely that one conception has influenced the other, and that later the two ideas tended to become confused. The *fylgja* however seems to be a conception akin not so much to the soul as to the shadowy double or 'fetch' which is a widespread belief in various European countries, and which has continued into modern times. The idea of a double in human form is not found in Norse literature; the nearest to it is the story of the mysterious woman with large eyes who encountered Guðríðr in Greenland, and told her her name was Guðríðr too.[1] If we are to look for evidence for a conception of the soul in Norse literature, it is, I think, to the animal or human form endued with the spirit of the owner and not to the *fylgja* that we must turn.

## THE GUARDIAN *HAMINGJA* AND *DÍS*

The word *fylgja* is clearly used very loosely in Norse literature. In *Hallfreðar Saga* we find it attached to a new conception, that of a guardian spirit in the form of a woman, called the *fylgjukona:*[2]

... They saw a woman walking after the ship; she was tall and clad in a coat of mail; she walked over the waves as if she were on land. Hallfreðr gazed at her, and saw she was his *fylgjukona.* 'I declare all between me and thee at an end', he said. 'Will you receive me, Þorvaldr?' she asked. He said he would not. Then Hallfreðr the younger said 'I will receive you'. After this she vanished. Then Hallfreðr said 'To you, my son, will I give the sword, the king's gift; but the other treasures you shall lay beside me in my coffin, if I die here in the ship' (XI).

This spirit, unlike the animal *fylgja*, lives on after the death of the man whom she has attended, and must then pass on to someone else. How far young Hallfreðr's acceptance of her is free choice on his part, or due to the fact that she is intimately bound up with the fortunes of one particular family, is not quite clear, but at least it does

1 *Grœnlendinga Saga,* VII.
2 This idea could be easily reconciled with Christian teaching. This is shown from the story in *Njáls Saga* when Hallr consents to be baptized on condition that St Michael will become his *fylgjuengill* (C).

appear that she is not necessarily attached to a man from birth, as the *fylgja* seems to be. In *Vatnsdæla Saga*[1] we read that the woman 'who had attended him and his family' (*er fylgt hafði þeim frændum*) came to Þorsteinn in a dream and warned him not to leave. In *Völsunga Saga*, Signý is warned against her approaching marriage by her *kynfylgja* (IV). Þorsteinn, the son of Síðu-Hallr,[2] is also visited in a dream by three women, who warn him that his thrall is plotting his death. They come to him three times, and the third time they are weeping. One of them asks: 'Where shall we turn after your day, Þorsteinn?' and he replies: 'To my son Magnus.' 'We may not abide there long', she answers, and utters a verse in which she prophesies his son's death also.

In another story of this kind, in *Víga-Glúms Saga*, we find that the word *hamingja* is used:

It is told that one night Glúmr had a dream. He thought he was standing outside the house, and looking towards the firth. He thought he saw a woman walking across the country, and coming towards Þverá. She was so huge that her shoulders touched the mountains on each side. He thought he went out of the homestead to meet her, and asked her to his house. And after that he awoke. All thought this dream strange, but he said 'This is a great and remarkable dream, and I would read it thus: Vigfúss my grandfather must be dead, and the woman who was higher than the mountains as she walked must be his *hamingja*, for he was nearly always above other men in honour; his *hamingja* now must be seeking an abode where I am' (IX).

In all these passages we have a picture of a supernatural woman guardian, attached to one particular family, who at the death of the man she attends passes on to one of his descendants. The woman in *Hallfreðar Saga* seems, as Miss Phillpotts points out,[3] to bring ill-luck to the man she follows, while she in *Víga-Glúms Saga* on the other hand brings honour and distinction with her. In both cases the *hamingja* is described as a huge woman in armour (Glúmr so speaks of her in a verse) and it would seem as if here we have some connection with the Valkyrie conception which was discussed in chapter III. The resemblance is more marked when we remember that in the Helgi poems the Valkyrie is said to be reborn, and to attend the second

---

1 *Vatnsdæla Saga*, XXXVI.
2 *Draumr Þorsteins Síðu-Hallssonar*: published together with *Þorsteins Saga Síðu-Hallssonar*, Ásmundarson, p. 25.
3 *Camb. Med. Hist.* II, p. 486.

Helgi, presumably a descendant, as she did the first, and that on the day she comes to him for the first time she gives him a name.[1] There is no doubt that the word *hamingja* in the sagas is often used also with the abstract meaning of 'luck', and is believed to pass with the name of someone who has once possessed it. In *Vatnsdæla Saga* we find this idea expressed: '...The boy shall be called Ingimundr after his mother's father, and I hope for luck (*hamingja*) for him on account of the name' (VII). Again in *Finnboga Saga* a dying man begs his son to call a child after him: 'he said he was sure that *hamingja* would follow' (XXXVI).

These instances will have to be discussed further when we are concerned with the subject of rebirth, as the relationship between the conception of *hamingja* being passed on with a name to a descendant and that of the soul of the dead being reborn in that descendant is an important one. The *hamingja* was not invariably connected with a name in the sagas; Glúmr claims to have obtained that of his grandfather Vigfúss, and in the *Fornaldar Sögur* the dead king Hreggviðr who comes out of his howe and meets his son-in-law tells him he wishes to 'turn towards you all the valour and the *hamingja* which formerly followed me'.[2]

The *hamingja* of a man may be proved by his success in battle. In *Vatnsdæla Saga* Ketill tells his son that he intends to teach him the laws of warriors—'you are now at an age to prove what *hamingja* will be granted to you' (II). 'Now it is *hamingja* which will decide' (*mun nu hamingja ráða*) exclaims Gestr before a battle in *Bárðar Saga* (XVI), and King Harald Harðraði undertakes to attack a serpent because he says he has the best trust in his luck (*gæfa*) and *hamingja*.[3] The *hamingja* is not something which depends on personal courage, however; Þórir says of one man in *Þorskfirðinga Saga* that 'he has shown himself possessed of more valour than *hamingja*' (XVI); while Grettir and his brother are said by a witch to be 'brave but without *hamingja*' (*Grettis Saga*, LXXVIII).

The *hamingja* of a man, which can pass on to someone else when he is dead, can also apparently be lent during his lifetime, if it is sufficiently powerful. King Mottull of Finmark, in *Flateyjarbók*, offers to let his *hamingja* go with Þórir against King Olaf, 'and my mind tells me', he says, 'that in the end you will be victorious over

1 *Helgakviða Hjörvarðssonar*, II.
2 *Göngu-Hrólfs Saga*, XXXII.
3 *Fornmanna Sögur*, VI: *Haralds Saga Harðráða*, XIII, p. 165.

him'.[1] The *hamingja* of the great kings of Norway was of tremen-
dous power; it could be supplied to their warriors going out on
dangerous enterprises as though it were something concrete they
could carry with them. In the *Fornmanna Sögur*[2] we are told that
when King Harald was angry with his poets and was sending them on
an expedition which would probably mean their deaths, they went
before him on their departure to salute him, and begged that he
would 'grant his *hamingja* for their journey' (*leggja sina hamingja á
ferð þessa*). 'Although the king was angry', we are told, 'he did as
they asked.' Similarly Olaf Tryggvason is told by some of his men
who are leaving on a difficult quest:[3] 'It is certain that this will not be
managed easily unless your *hamingja* helps us', while Olaf the Holy
tells one of his followers on another such occasion:[4] 'It will help this
journey if you go with them, for your *hamingja* has been well proved'
and goes on to promise on his own behalf: 'Know for certain that I
will grant my *hamingja* to you, and to all the party.' He helped
other followers of his in the same way, for elsewhere[5] we read: 'They
had unfavourable weather, so that they lost many men; but because
they had a large force and the king's *hamingja*, all was well.'

It is said even of a Christian, Bishop Jón, 'for a long time men will
profit by his *hamingja*;'[6] and in late Christian times the word was
still used, according to Vigfusson, to mean 'luck' or 'providence'.
In the sagas it is sometimes a power which can prevail against magic;
in the *Flateyjarbók*, for instance, Menglöð wonders whether the
*trollskap* of the giant Brusi or the *hamingia* of Ormr will prevail.[7]
Brynhildr, we may notice, is deceived by the change of shapes
between Sigurðr and Gunnarr because, she says later, her *hamingja*
was veiled.[8]

As used in the sagas then, the *hamingja* stands for an abstract conception, that of something belonging to an outstanding person which
is partly a matter of character and partly of personality, and partly
something more than either—that strange quality of 'luck' or 'luck-
lessness' which attaches itself to certain individuals more than others.

1 *Flateyjarbók*, III; *Óláfs Saga Helga;* Viðbætir, p. 245.
2 *Fornmanna Sögur*, III: *Saga Skálda Haralds Konungs Hárfagra*, II, p. 69.
3 *Flateyjarbók: Óláfs Saga Tryggvasonar*, I, 113, p. 145.
4 *Heimskringla: Óláfs Saga Helga*, LXIX.
5 *Fornmanna Sögur*, IV: *Óláfs Saga Helga*, XLII, p. 66.
6 *Jóns Saga, Biskupa Sögur* I (Copenhagen, 1858), XVI, p. 229.
7 *Flateyjarbók: Óláfs Saga Tryggvasonar: Þáttr Orms Stórolfssonar*, I, 417, p. 529.
8 *Völsunga Saga*, XXIX.

It is something which can be handed on after death, and it usually remains within one family; it is usually connected with the name, so that if a child is called after a father or grandfather it is hoped he will inherit it automatically. Now in one case we get a personification of *hamingja* as a gigantic woman in armour, and in several other passages, although the term is not used, it seems as though we are dealing with the same conception. The difficulty is to decide whether here we have something which has arisen from the abstract term *hamingja* and is a literary personification of it, or whether the abstract term is something which has come into being because of an older belief in a supernatural guardian woman attached to certain families, who later became identified with the *hamingja* or luck of the individual. In either case it is, I think, clear that there is a close connection between the supernatural woman and the guardian Valkyrie discussed earlier.

At this point it is necessary to take into consideration the fact that another term is frequently used for a supernatural guardian woman, that is *dís*. The word is usually found in the plural. In the story of the death of Þiðrandi, told so graphically in the *Flateyjarbók*,[1] Þórir speaks of nine women in black clothes who ride down upon Þiðrandi with drawn swords as the *dísir* of Hallr's family, who are angry, he says, because they realise that he and his kin are about to adopt Christianity and break off connections with them. The white *dísir* who try unsuccessfully to defend Þiðrandi are, he suggests, the *dísir* of the new faith, who prove less efficient than their rivals. Þorhallr also refers to the women in black as the *fylgjur* of Hallr's family (CCXV). In *Njáls Saga* (XLVI) there is a reference to this story, and here again it is said to be the *dísir* who slew Þiðrandi. Another reference to *dísir* comes in the *Fornaldar Sögur* in two verses of poetry in *Hálfs Saga* (XV). In the first of these Útsteinn claims that his *dísir* will help him in battle, but his opponent replies:

> Dead must be
> All your *dísir*;
> Luck is gone, I say,
> From Hálfr's warriors.
> I dreamed this morning
> That our powers
> Vanquished yours
> When they met together.

1 *Flateyjarbók: Óláfs Saga Tryggvasonar*, I, 335, p. 419 f.

Again in a dream of Ásmundr in *Ásmundr Saga Kappabana* armed women appear to him before a combat, tell him they are his *spádísir* and promise to help him (VIII). The *dísir*, like the *hamingja*, can apparently be borrowed, since in *Þorsteins Saga Víkingssonar* (XXII) Sindri the dwarf bids farewell to Þorsteinn and promises that his own *dísir* shall follow and protect him.

In these instances we have the conception of a guardian spirit, usually armed, who will support those with whom she is connected in battle, and in general bring them 'luck'—something which has no essential difference from that of the guardian woman *hamingja* we have already dealt with, except that in these cases we have a number of women and not one alone. The evidence certainly seems to suggest that the guardian Valkyries, the guardian *hamingjur* of the family and the guardian *dísir* are one and the same conception. Moreover in the story of Þiðrandi we get the same dualism—the dark and bright women battling over the hero—which we noticed before in some of the Valkyrie stories,[1] only given a Christian setting. The connection with the future life, which we noticed also, comes out again in the verse spoken by Glaumvör when she describes the dream betokening her husband's death in *Atlamál*:

> I dreamed dead women came here in the night;
> They were poorly clad; they were seeking you;
> They bade you swiftly come to their benches;
> Thy *dísir*, I deem, were parted from thee        (v. 25).

In the *Völsunga Saga* this is paraphrased: 'Then I thought dead women came in here; they were gloomy, and they chose you for husband; it may be that it was your *dísir*' (XXXV).

In this picture we have a very close parallel to the dream-women of Gísli. The invitation to the benches in their hall and the word 'husband' introduced into *Völsunga Saga* are ideas which we found there also. It seems very probable that we are throughout dealing with one conception, and that these huge supernatural women who give help and support to certain men in life, and welcome them to their abodes as husbands after death, are the same, whether they bear the name of *fylgjukona, valkyrja, hamingja* or *dís*. It seems possible that in this conception, which is so widespread in Norse literature, we have memories of a definite cult. We know from the evidence of the sagas that there were cults connected with supernatural women.

---

1 See p. 72 above.

There is one connected with Halogaland, and practised by Jarl Hákon, where a supernatural being acts as guardian to the man who worships her; she appears to aid him in battle, and shoots arrows at his enemies, accompanied by at least one other similar being; and the Jarl is on one occasion called her husband.[1] This being is Þorgerðr Hölgabrúðr; and the similarity of her worship as described in the sagas with that of those supernatural women who occur so frequently suggests the possibility of a cult lingering on in Halogaland after it had been displaced elsewhere by worship of the gods. There seems according to our literary sources however to have been some connection between this and the gods, for it enters into the picture of a future life in the halls of Othin, while in some places worship of the *dísir* is recorded as if it accompanied that of the gods. In *Víga-Glúms Saga*[2] sacrifice to the *dísir* is said to have been made at the beginning of winter at Vors, the residence of Vigfúss, at which Glúmr was present. Miss Phillpotts dates this at about 950. King Eric and Queen Gunnhildr are said in *Egils Saga* (XLIII) to attend a feast at Atley, where there was sacrifice to the *dísir*, and this also was in the autumn; the exact dating of events in *Egils Saga* is a controversial subject, but this can safely be placed in the first quarter of the tenth century. Another account of a sacrifice to the *dísir* is found in the *Fornaldar Sögur* in *Friðþjófs Saga* (IX). Here the hall of the *dísir* is said to be inside the enclosure at 'Balder's Meadows', and the kings Hálfdan and Helgi hold a sacrifice there on their return. The account of the sacrifice is a puzzling one. The kings are said to be sacrificing to the *dísir* as they sit drinking, and their wives meanwhile are said to sit by the fire and warm the figures of the gods. These wives do not come into the saga elsewhere, and one wonders if there can be any connection between the so-called wife of Helgi, whom Friðþjófr drags across the room in an attempt to pull off the gold ring from her arm, and Þorgerðr—Helgi's bride, as she is usually called—whose image in Jarl Hákon's temple is distinguished by just such a ring. The account certainly reads more like an attempt to despoil an image than to rob a woman. Another reference to the hall of the *dís* (here the singular is used) comes from *Ynglinga Saga* (XXIX), where Snorri tells us that King Aðils met his death as he rode round the hall while he was at the sacrifice. In *Hervarar Saga* (VII) the wife of King

---

1 *Flateyjarbók: Óláfs Saga Tryggvasonar*, I, 114f., 154f., 173f., 326f.; also *Njáls Saga*, LXXXVIII.
2 *Víga-Glúms Saga*, VI.

Harald is said to slay herself in the hall of the *dísir* after her husband
has been killed in battle; while in the paper manuscript of the same
saga used by Rafn there is another reference to *dísar blót* (1), the
sacrifice this time being done out of doors by night, and consisting of
a ceremony in which the *hörgr* is reddened with blood—reminding us
of the reddening of the howe in sacrifice to the elves in *Kormáks
Saga*.[1] It is interesting to compare this with what Olsen has to say
about the meaning of *hörgr* in Norwegian place-names.[2] He came to
the conclusion that the word represents an early type of sanctuary,
smaller than the public temple, the *hof* (p. 284). However he points
out that originally the word must have denoted something still more
primitive, since the same word *hörgr* also denotes a heap of stones at
the summit of a mountain, so that it seems as if it must have meant at
one time an altar built of loose stones. He suggests that Snorri's
remark in *Gylfaginning*, to the effect that a *hörgr* was provided for the
goddesses, may have been based on the fact that women were concerned with an old phallic cult (pp. 287–296). Another possibility
however might be that these shrines were connected with women
because they primarily belonged to the worship of the *dísir*, as the
passage above suggests. It may be significant in this connection to
notice that Þorgerðr Hölgabrúðr is called on at least one occasion
*Hörgabrúðr*.[3]

With the other company of supernatural women, the *nornir*, we
are not at present concerned. They seem, in their connection with
fate and the future, to stand a little apart from the guardian spirits we
have been studying. All these terms for supernatural women, however, are liable to be freely interchanged.

It can be seen now that the evidence for the *fylgja* and the *hamingja*
in Norse literature does not help us very much to find a conception
of the soul. It has been necessary to examine the ideas behind them
fairly closely, however, in view of the way in which the animal and
the woman *fylgja* are often confused.[4] It is necessary too to discover
how many different conceptions seem to be involved, and whether
any of them correspond to the idea of a 'soul'. We have discerned

1 See p. 111 above.
2 M. Olsen, *Farms and Fanes in Ancient Norway* (trans. Gleditsch, Oslo, 1928).
3 *Flateyjarbók*, I, 173, p. 213. For different versions of her name, see G. Storm,
'Om Thorgerða Helgabrud', *Ark.f.n.F.* 1885.
4 As for example in the section on supernatural beings in *Scandinavian Archaeology*
by Falk (trans. Gordon, Oxford, 1937), p. 408 f.

two separate conceptions; one is that of the animal *fylgja*, which might be translated 'fetch'; it accompanies a human being through life, can be seen by others in dreams or in waking hours if they have the gift of second sight; and the life of the owner depends on its well-being. The animal shape in question varies according to the character and standing of the man it accompanies, and there is no idea of it ever surviving after death or passing on to someone else. The other conception, as we have seen, is that of a supernatural woman guardian, who attends an individual until death, and survives him; after his death he is able to enter her abodes, and she then attaches herself to another, often in the same family. She is frequently attended by a company of similar women, generally three or nine in number. She seems to be looked on as the wife of the man to whom she has joined herself. One of the terms used to describe such a guardian is also used generally to mean 'luck', and is regarded as a most important element in the make-up of the individual.

Neither of these conceptions can be held to be that of the soul in man. Both, it is true, are linked up closely with the question of individuality; they are to a certain extent attempts to explain that elusive quality which divides one man from his fellows. But they cannot be looked on as conceptions of the soul, since in neither of the cases concerned are we dealing with any part of man's conscious being; he can move, think and feel independently of his *fylgja* or *hamingja*, closely linked up with his character or fate though they may be. In the case of the second conception, moreover, the evidence suggests that we are dealing here with memories of an actual cult rather than with early attempts at spiritual analysis.

### THE IDEA OF REBIRTH

The evidence connected with the *hamingja* leads us on to what must be an essential part of any study of a belief in survival—that of rebirth. In the chapter on the *Cult of the Dead* one of the most interesting pieces of evidence was the story of Olaf Geirstaðaálfr and the worship of him in his barrow after death. *Flateyjarbók* gives a sequel to this story which concerns us here.[1] Olaf is said to appear in a dream to a man called Hrani, and to beg him to break into his howe. He tells him that he is to carry away the gold ring from the man whom he will find sitting on a stool inside, and the knife and belt that he wears. Part of the directions he receives are puzzling; he is to cut off

1 *Flateyjarbók: Óláfs Saga Helga*, II, 7, p. 7.

the head of the *draugr*, and 'all depends', he is told, 'on whether you put the head straight on the neck'. There is apparently to be a struggle with the howe-dweller, but of this we are not told in detail. What is more individual and interesting about the tale is that Hrani is to make off secretly with the ring, belt and sword, and is to go to Ásta, the wife of Harald the Greenlander, whom he will find awaiting the birth of her child:

...Then you must ask to go and speak with her, saying that it is quite likely that she will be eased thereby. You must ask to decide the name if a boy is born. Then you must put the belt round her. I think it is very probable that there will be a rapid change in her condition. She will give birth to a child, and it will be a boy, both big and thriving. You shall have him named Olaf. I give to him also the ring and the sword Besing....

The son born to Queen Ásta is, of course, King Olaf the Holy. Much later in his saga we learn that Olaf, after he had become king,

rode with his bodyguard past the howe of Olaf Geirstaðaálfr. 'Tell me, lord' [says one of his men], 'were you buried here?' The king replied to him: 'My soul has never had two bodies; it cannot have them, either now or on the Resurrection Day; if I spoke otherwise there would be no common truth or honesty in me.' Then the man said: 'They say that when you came to this place before you spoke so, and said "We have been here before also".' 'I have never said this', said the king, 'and never will I say it.' And the king was much moved, and clapped spurs to his horse immediately, and fled from the place as swiftly as he might (II, 106, p. 135).

Here the belief in rebirth seems to be clearly expressed, all the more convincingly because of the Christian king's determined denial of it later on. Again it will be noticed that the name is important, and with the name it would seem that some part of the dead man enters into the child. The connection with the howe-dweller is of significance also.

There are references to rebirth in the Helgi poems. The lovers Helgi and Sváva are said in the prose note at the end of *Helgakviða Hjörvarðssonar* to be born again, while at the close of *Helgakviða Hundingsbana II* there is a reference to a similar tradition about the later Helgi:

It was believed according to ancient lore (*í forneskju*) that folk were reborn; but this is now said to be old women's lying tales. Helgi and Sigrún are said to have been reborn; he was then called Helgi Haddingja-skati, and she Kara Hálfdanardóttir, as is related in *Káruljóð;* and she was a Valkyrie.

This poem, unfortunately, has been lost; but in the Helgi poems which remain the connection between the valkyries and rebirth has already been made. The most significant passage, perhaps, is that where the second Helgi is said at the beginning of *Helgakviða Hjörvarðssonar II* to receive a name while he sits on a mound. The prose note explains: 'He was tall and handsome; he was very silent, and no name could be found for him (*festiz við hann*).' The poem then tells how his name was given to him by the Valkyrie Sváva, as she rode by in a company of nine maidens. Here then we find a close connection between sitting on a howe and rebirth. It is perhaps not insignificant, in view of this connection, to find that when in the *Sigurðarkviða hin Skamma* Brynhildr is proposing to burn herself with Sigurðr, Högni exclaims wearily:

> Delay her not longer from dying,
> That born again she may never be.          (v. 46.)

We gained the impression in the first chapter that cremation in general—and particularly such cases of suttee as that of Brynhildr—indicated a belief in departure to another world, as opposed to howe burial, where the spirit lingered in the grave. It is natural that rebirth should be connected with the latter practice.

One allusion to rebirth from the *Fornaldar Sögur* may be noticed, because it is connected with the hero Starkaðr, and is referred to in a poem of his quoted in *Gautreks Saga*. He alludes to a belief, quoted against him by his enemies, that marks can be seen on his body which were left on his grandfather, a giant of the same name, after his struggles with Thor:

> They think they see
> Upon me too
> The mark of the giant,
> The eight arms,
> When Hlórriði
> Tore them off
> From Hergrímr's slayer,
> North of the cliff.          (VII).[1]

[1]
| | |
|---|---|
| Sjá þykjast þeir | er Hlórriði |
| á sjálfum mér | fyrir hamar norðan |
| jötun kuml, | Hergrímsbana |
| átta handa, | höndum rændi. |

(The story goes that Starkaðr I was an eight-armed giant, slain by Thor.)

There is an allusion of the same kind in one version of *Þórðar Saga hræðu*. In the *Upphaf sögu* (from *Vatnshyrnu*) we are told concerning the birth of Þórðr:[1]

Afterwards Helga gave birth to a boy, who was sprinkled with water and given a name, and he had to be called (*skyldi heita*) Þórðr after his father. It could be seen on the boy that he had a scar on his left arm, in the place where his father had been wounded. He took straightway the surname which his father had had, and was called Þórðr hræða.

Throughout the sagas many other examples can be found where the giving of the name of the dead to a child is emphasised. Two of these have already been mentioned because of the reference to the *hamingja* which they contain.[2] Of the others, one of the most striking is from the story of Þorstein Uxafótr in the *Flateyjarbók*.[3] This tells how the hero visits a barrow and helps the barrow-dweller to overcome his rival. When they part, the man from the howe tells Þorstein of the coming of Christianity, which, he says,

is much better for those who can take it, but it will go the harder for those whose destinies it may not be, those who are such as I; for we brothers are earth-dwellers. I should deem it a great favour if you could bring my name under baptism, if it should be granted you to have a son.

Here again the connection between the dweller in the howe and the birth of a child to whom the name of the dead is to be handed on is emphasised. In *Vatnsdæla Saga* a dying man, Jökull, begs the man who has slain him 'not to let my name pass away (*niðri liggja*)...if a son be granted to you or to your son' (III). Similarly Þórólfr in *Svarfdæla Saga* begs his brother to hand on his name to a son of his:

...I think my name has not long been upheld, and now it must pass out of use like withered grass...I will that if a son be granted to you you will have him called Þórólfr, and all the luck (*heillir*) which I have had I will give to him (IV).

Again Finnbogi in *Finnboga Saga* (IX) begs his friend to accept his name while he lies dying, for then, he says, 'I know that my name will be known while the earth is inhabited'. Karl, too, in *Svarfdæla*

1 *Þórðar Saga hræðu* (ed. Ásmundarson, Reykjavík, 1900), p. viii. The complete version of the saga merely tells us that when the baby was born during the funeral feast for his father 'the housewife wished him to be called Þórðr; she said she thought he would be a great man if they got the name back again' (I).

2 See p. 132 above.

3 *Flateyjarbók: Óláfs Saga Tryggvasonar*, I, 206, p. 255.

*Saga* (XXVI) demands that his wife, who is expecting a child, shall give his name to it if, as he fears, he dies first. An interesting point to be noticed in *Hallfreðar Saga* (IX) is that after the conversion of Hallfreðr's heathen wife the boy born to them is called Hallfreðr the younger, while his father is still alive.

The custom of naming children after dead kinsmen is certainly very widespread in the *Íslendinga Sögur*. In particular the custom of choosing the name of the grandfather on either the father's or the mother's side is very frequent indeed. Taking an example at random from the saga of Víga-Glúm, we find the following:

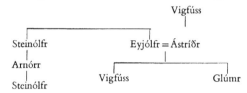

or from *Egils Saga*:

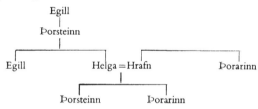

It is not only the grandparents from whom the name is taken. In a valuable study of the evidence for the giving of names in the Icelandic Sagas (*Altisländische Namenwahl*, Palaestra, 176, Leipzig, 1931), Keil has provided us with full statistics of this practice of naming after the dead.[1] He shows that while naming after the grandparents is the most frequent custom, the name may also be taken from a great-uncle, uncle, nephew, cousin, or a father who has died before his child is named. The same practice is followed in the naming of girls, only in this case we have not the same amount of information from the genealogies. Sometimes it is the nickname, or part of it, which is handed down. Keil's evidence shows that it is almost invariably a dead relative whose name is chosen, and particularly one who has recently died. He has only four examples of the name of the living being passed on to children.[2] One is that of Hallfreðr, noticed above;

1 Keil, *op. cit.* p. 26 f.            2 *Ibid.* p. 70 f.

another Harald Hárfagr, who named a son after him in his old age;[1] it seems likely that this forms a parallel case to that of Finnbogi, the third example, who passed on his name with the sense of his own approaching death heavy upon him. The only other example is that of a son of Hálfdan the Black, said to have been named after Harald Gullskeggr.[2] We are told very little about this, but Harald Gullskeggr certainly names his foster-son in his old age, with the intention of letting him succeed to his kingdom, since he gives the realm into the hands of the little boy when he becomes too infirm to rule himself.

The case of Finnbogi appears to be the only one in which the name is not taken from within the family of the newborn child, although there are instances of naming after dead foster-parents. Apparently the name might be changed if it did not seem to suit the child, or at least this is implied by a passage in *Gísla Saga* (xvIII) telling how Snorri the Priest received his name:

> He was first called Þorgrímr after his father, but when he grew up they found him difficult in disposition and unruly, so his name was changed and he was called Snorri.

The name Snorri appears to be derived from *snerra*, a shock or on-slaught; however the departure from the usual custom, that of adding the new name on to the original as a nickname, is puzzling; Keil suggests that the little boy was called after a son of his foster-father, whose name was Snorri too.[3]

The idea that this widespread custom of naming after the dead was directly connected with a belief in transmigration of souls, the spirit of the dead being reborn in the living when the name was used again for a newborn child, was first put forward in detail by Storm, in an article on 'Transmigration of Souls and the Custom of Naming after the Dead' published in 1893.[4] He came to the conclusion that while in the Migration period it was common to find the name of the child beginning with the same letter as that of the parent (alliteration) or containing part of the parent's name (variation), the practice of taking the whole name of a dead relative came in among the Visigoths and Burgundians on the borders of Gaul in the fifth century, and was fully established in Scandinavia by the end of the eighth

1 *Heimskringla: Haralds Saga Hárfagra*, xLII.
2 *Ibid. Hálfdans Saga Svarta*, III.                    3 Keil, *op. cit.* p. 94.
4 'Vore Forfædres Tro paa Sjælvandring og deres Opkaldelsessystem', *Ark.f.n.F.* 1893, p. 119 f.

century. His assumption that this custom was direct evidence for a belief in the transferring of the spirit of the dead to his descendant was generally accepted by scholars until Keil produced his new and exhaustive study on the subject.[1]

Keil's work certainly shows that the system of variation and alliteration continued in Iceland side by side with that of naming after the dead, so that it is incorrect to say that one has replaced the other. Examples of each from the sagas are about equal in number; the practices are absolutely contemporary; and there are plenty of examples of both being used within the same family, although it is roughly true to say that most families incline to one custom rather than the other. Keil further argues that the evidence from Northern Europe gives no support to Storm's theory that the principle of naming after the dead is a later one. A second point made by Keil is that it is incorrect to equate rebirth with transmigration of souls (*sjælvandring*), as Storm has done. If by transmigration we are to understand the Eastern doctrine of the continual progress of the soul through many bodies, not necessarily human ones, then it is true to say that there is no evidence to support its existence in Norse literature, and perhaps the term has been used too carelessly by previous writers. But for a belief in rebirth of some kind there is a good deal of evidence, as we have seen, that cannot be ignored. Finally Keil asserts that the principle of naming after the dead is based on nothing more than pride of birth, and a desire to establish the newborn baby firmly within the family, mingled with that of winning for it the good luck associated with certain names among its dead kinsmen; that, in fact, it is no more than a chance alternative to the variation principle in choosing a name for a child.

This explanation does not appear to be altogether satisfactory. If this were indeed the case, why do we find such reluctance throughout to pass on the name of a living man or woman, since this would offer the closest parallel to the variation system? The argument that this would cause confusion and loss of identity can hardly be urged, since Keil has given examples of the same name being used more than once in the family.[2] Moreover the close and significant connection between the child and the dead man in his grave-mound or the man at point of death cannot be ignored. Even were such passages due to later editing of the sagas, we are left with the origin of such a tradition to explain away. A passage like that quoted above about

1 Keil, *op. cit.* p. 97 f.                    2 *Ibid.* p. 105.

Olaf the Holy is hardly likely to be the invention of a Christian editor, intent on establishing the saintliness of his hero.

It is on the whole doubtful whether we are entitled to assume that the introduction of the custom of naming after the dead—even could we determine with any real accuracy the date of its entry into the North—was really the result of a new belief about the soul. On this point there is a brief but illuminating article by Flom, in *Modern Language Notes* (XXII, 1917, p. 7 f.), to which Keil does not refer. Flom confines himself to the genealogies of the Teutonic kings in the Migration period and earlier. He shows how the custom in choosing names seems to be to seek first for alliteration, then alliterative variation, and then gradually what he calls 'pure variation'—the repetition of either the first theme of the father's name (Heorogar-Heoromund), or the second (Genserich-Hunerich). When in the first part of the sixth century the practice of repeating either the primary theme of the name or the secondary one in alternative generations can be clearly discerned, then it is only to be expected that before long the two themes will be brought together, and repetition of the whole name in alternate generations result. This is in fact the case, and such a gradual development of the principle of repetition certainly does not support the idea that it was introduced among the Teutonic peoples as a direct result of new beliefs about the soul after death. Flom suggests that a belief in rebirth existed early, and attached itself to name-giving long before repetition came in; he reminds us, moreover, of a point that has been neglected in the various arguments about the repetition of names, that it might be thought that a part of the name was in itself sufficient to ensure the 'return' of the first owner; in view of this idea, which he illustrates from Jewish teaching, it is possible that variation may not be as distinct from repetition as Storm thought.

This theory of the origin of the custom of repetition in name-giving in the North seems to be by far the most convincing which has yet been presented. It would seem, then, a mistake to insist that the practice in Scandinavia was consistently based on a belief in the birth of the souls of dead ancestors into the living world again, in the persons of their descendants. But the fact that the custom of naming almost exclusively after the dead is so widespread in Iceland from the time of the settlement onwards, and undoubtedly went on in Norway for a considerable time before this, is of importance in confirming the impression made by certain passages which were examined at the beginning of this section, in which there is a very close connection between the dead and the newly-born. It is suggestive, also, to find that similar practices among the Lapps up to very recent times are undoubtedly connected with a belief in the rebirth of the dead within the family. Unwerth [1] quotes from various authorities to the effect that they were accustomed, in the case of children seriously ill or unable to thrive, to name them afresh, because they believed that in such a case some dead ancestor must be angered because his name had not been given. It is interesting to compare with this the instance of the changing of the name of Snorri the Priest referred to above,[2] although this stands alone, and can hardly be urged as a complete parallel without further knowledge of the circumstances.

Storm suggests that the practice of naming after the dead reached the Teutonic peoples from Gaul. Certainly the idea of rebirth was known in Celtic literature; Meyer [3] has collected a large number of stories alluding to it from Welsh and Irish sources, and adds to these allusions from Latin writers to the belief in rebirth among the Celts.

In looking back over our evidence for rebirth in Norse literature, the chief points which seem to deserve emphasis are the connection with the burial mound and the importance of the name. In the previous chapter we saw how the practice of sitting on a mound seemed to owe something to the notion of inheritance, and it seemed possible that some kind of conception of rebirth is behind this. The evidence in this chapter helps to confirm this, when in several cases we find the burial mound playing an important part in the idea of the dead being reborn into the world. We remember that in one account of a sacred howe it was stated that silver was carried into it whenever a man died or a man was born.[4] Such a conception as this which we have been studying presupposes that a part of man is immortal and survives the death of the body; and this idea is now found to be closely linked with the practice of inhumation. The emphasis on the name as confirming this link between living and dead has evidently some connection with the stories of shape-

1 Unwerth, 'Untersuchungen ü. Totenkult und Ódinnverehrung bei Nordgermanen und Lappen' (*Weinhold, Germ. Abhand.* 37, 1911), p. 37.
2 See p. 143 above.
3 K. Meyer, *Voyage of Bran*, ii, pp. 1–92, 107–119.
4 See p. 104 above.

changing, when the calling of the name of the man lying in a trance could apparently summon back his spirit.

## CONCLUSION: THE IDEA OF SURVIVAL

A survey of the eschatological side of Norse literature renders one thing at least clear—that the Norse mind, in the literature as we have it, does not readily turn to develop imaginative and spiritual conceptions of the life after death. Perhaps it is the reality of the present life, and its importance in the eyes of the creators of that literature which served to keep them from indulging in elaborate and enthusiastic speculation about the future one. The world of the gods is drawn for us here in clear, sure strokes, but of the place of man in that larger world very little has been said directly, and our evidence has had to be collected in fragments and scattered references here and there. Another reason however besides absorption in the present and in the world of action probably lies behind this, and that is the Norse passion for turning the abstract and the symbolic into the actual and the concrete. Symbolism in Norse hands is so well done that it ceases to be symbolism, and becomes a vivid and convincing picture which is sufficient in itself, and is accepted accordingly by the editors. So at least we may suspect, remembering the instance of the ravens of Othin; it is probable that there is much evidence of a similar sort which is hidden from us for want of the necessary information to reveal its meaning.

At the beginning of this study we saw that the practice of cremation, linked up as it seemed to be with the belief in another life after death, implies some kind of conception of an indestructible something which survives the destruction of the body. Of the nature of what is indestructible we are given no indication, yet the elaborate symbolic ceremony at a cremation recorded from the Volga in the tenth century seems to suggest that at that time the doctrine of the soul's survival had been developed to a considerable extent. The other section of evidence which implies a definite conception of the soul as something separate from the body, without which life cannot exist, is that found in the conception of a certain type of shape-changing in which, while the body lies motionless, the consciousness can by an act of will be expelled from it to do the bidding of its owner elsewhere, sometimes traversing great distances, sometimes searching for information, sometimes battling with other disembodied spirits like itself. This is a conception which is capable of deep spiritual development and interpretation; how far it entered into Norse thought it is difficult to say, and it may, of course, have merely come into Scandinavia from outside, with its richer possibilities left unexplored. At least its presence in the literature precludes the notion that the idea of the spirit as distinct from the body never enters Norse thought. In view of some of the mantic conceptions which we find in the literature, I think it probable that these possibilities were explored to a considerable extent, but for this we must wait until a later chapter.

There is certainly a great reluctance in the literature we have been examining to disassociate the personality from the body. The conception of the 'ghost' in Norse literature is a good example of this. We have seen that in the cases where the dead return to visit—and usually to trouble—the living it is never the disembodied spirit but always the animated corpse which is described. The creatures who leave their grave-mounds and cause damage wherever they go, who can usually only be overcome by physical force, and who are brought to an end when the body is destroyed, are the direct ancestors of the vampire rather than the ghost of later belief. Yet they differ from the vampire in that they have not lost their former personality and become wholly and hideously inhuman. The characteristics of Þórólfr Bægifótr,[1] of Hrappr, of Þorgunna, have not changed; they are only, as it were, intensified on the other side of the grave. Even personal relationships are unchanged; Þórólfr is still forced to respect his son Arnkell, and will do no harm to those in his company or leave his new grave on the headland as long as his son is alive. Here we certainly have the idea of the personality surviving death, but only, as far as we can tell, as long as the body itself survives. It is true that a different picture is given in the story of the foster-brothers in the *Egils Saga ok Ásmundar*.[2] Here the dead man becomes as inhuman as the most bloodthirsty of vampires, and there is no remnant of his former affection for his foster-brother. In view of the marked lack of fear of the dead which we find as a whole however, it is unnecessary, I think, to attribute the continued personality of the dead to the interest in character shown throughout the *Íslendinga Sögur*, and to argue that here the *Fornaldar Sögur* have preserved the truer picture.

Also connected with the interment of the body in the earth we

1 For saga references to these ghosts see p. 93 above.
2 See p. 55 above.

have another kind of survival, and here it is that of the soul rather than of the personality. The conception of rebirth combines, as it were, the idea of the indestructible soul and the close connection of this with the body after death. The soul can be freed from the body if summoned by the name—that ever-potent factor in tales of shape-changing—to enter the body of a new-born child, or, in some cases, of a grown man who has changed or added to his name. The well-established custom of naming after the dead, and the traditions connected with the custom of sitting on a burial mound, give some indication of the possible range and familiarity of this conception. The possibility that the continued animation of the restless *draugr* is caused because the soul cannot be freed until it is reborn into the world is one at least worth suggesting as a conception behind the numerous stories of the dead that must be quelled by the living, because it seems to be implied in the story of the birth of Olaf the Holy. Here the *draugr* in the grave of the first Olaf has to be over-come and beheaded and despoiled of its treasures before the spirit of the first Olaf can enter into the second, and Olaf the Holy be born; and it is the desire of the first Olaf, the dead man, that all this should take place. I think it is probable that in the *draugar* who figure so prominently in the literature we have another instance of an originally mystical conception which has become simplified and popularised by being interpreted in a concrete way, partly because of a real inability to comprehend the original, and partly because of the increased possibilities for story-telling in the popularised versions.

The idea of the survival of the souls of the dead in another world is one that is implied rather than directly described in our evidence, but the implications occur so persistently that the conception must origi-nally have been one of considerable importance. The idea of such survival clings to the stories of cremation and suttee; it appears in particular to be connected with Othin, and is indicated in the per-plexing development of the Valhöll conception as a realm of the gods which has survived in the literature. The idea of a journey to a land of the dead is probably of importance also for the doctrine of the disembodied soul, but this we shall have to examine further in the closing chapters. The life lived in the hills after death, as represented in the sagas, appears almost as concrete as the notion of the dead bodies walking out of their grave-mounds, and there is nothing to contradict the idea that it is the animated corpse which leaves the mound or emerges dripping wet from the sea that has destroyed it to enter the open hillside. However we have learnt to distrust the obvious and concrete picture of the future life which Norse literature appears on the surface to present, and the conception behind this belief is likely to prove more complicated and interesting on further investigation.

The idea has been put forward by Frazer and others that the conception of the disembodied soul first originated through dreams, when the image of a person, and in particular of someone who has died, seen in sleep can give rise to the idea that the soul can leave the body and continue to exist after death. Although dreams are very frequently introduced into Norse literature, however, the idea of the spirit of the dead appearing to the living in sleep is almost unknown there, and when it does occur it appears to be inseparably linked up with Christian ideas. The sagas indeed afford an interesting example of how a different interpretation can be put upon such dreams from that assumed by Frazer. On several occasions when characters in the sagas are visited in dreams by the dead, the saga-teller informs us that on waking they were able to catch sight of their visitors as they went away. In *Þorsteins Saga Síðu-Hallssonar* the hero is visited in this way by his dead mother. She gives him good advice, and as he awakes 'he thought he caught a glimpse of her as she went away' (v). Similarly in *Þorskfirðinga Saga* when Agnarr, the dead man from the howe, visits Þorir in a dream: 'Ketilbjörn was awake and had heard all the talk, and saw too where Agnarr went' (III). The dead poet who visits Hallbjörn and gives him the gift of skaldship in the *Flateyjarbók* (p. 108 above) is also seen by the shepherd as he wakes: 'Then he vanished back into the howe, and it shut again; and Hallbjörn awoke and thought he caught a glimpse of his shoulders.' These figures of the dead who enter the dreams of the living are, in fact, as substantial as it is possible to make them.

In reviewing our evidence then, we find that the idea of the disembodied soul is not foreign to Norse literature, but that there is a curious reluctance to state its existence directly, and it tends to be hidden behind other conceptions and is not consequently always easy to perceive. In order to discover more about the Norse view of the soul and its destiny after death, it seems that it will be necessary to leave the evidence relating to the future life and the soul, which in itself is inconclusive, and to study the ideas about the relationship between the living and the dead which are discernible in the literature.

# Chapter VI

## NECROMANCY

O, that it were possible we might
But hold some two days' conference with the dead!
From them I should learn somewhat, I am sure
I never shall know here.
WEBSTER, *Duchess of Malfi.*

In studying the Norse evidence for necromancy, it is significant that the *Íslendinga Sögur* give us practically no information for any such practice. In only one case is a witch or wizard described raising the dead, and this is outside Iceland, since Þrándr, the master of ceremonies, is a native of the Faroes. Indictments against the raising of the dead, however, are found in the earliest written laws of Iceland, so that it could not have been unknown there. One reason for the gap in the evidence may be that the interest in the dead was, as we have seen, more marked in Norway and Sweden than in Iceland—at least such interest as results in a cult of the dead—and we might therefore expect to find necromancy more studied in that direction too. It is also a little doubtful, in examining the evidence, whether the practice of raising the dead is always described in a straightforward way, and whether it will not be necessáry to include some evidence in this survey which does not appear on the surface to be necromancy at all; also conversely whether all the accounts of the consultation of the dead in the poems are to be accepted as records of actual necromantic practice.

The fact that it is necessary to begin with a considerable amount of evidence from the Edda poems means that here we have material of a different category from what has for the most part been dealt with hitherto; and one far more difficult to treat adequately without a wide knowledge of textual history. However it is possible that something may be gained by a collection of the material, and by some examination of the general ideas about the dead to be derived from it. Most of our evidence comes from the Edda, but many passages taken here and there from the prose sagas will need discussion too.

## THE WAKING OF THE SLEEPER

The poems give us several examples of the calling up of the dead, and it is interesting to see whether there is any agreement as to the purpose for which they are summoned. Here the whole matter is taken out of the familiar world, and is represented as taking place within the realm of the gods. The supernatural beings themselves are depicted as eager to establish communication with another realm, the realm of the dead, into which, even for them, there is no immediate and simple entry.

The most experienced practitioner of the art is Othin. In *Baldrs Draumar* he is represented as riding down the road to Hel, and finally summoning a dead seeress from her grave on the east side of Hel's hall. He chants what are described as 'corpse-spells' (*val galdrar*) over the grave 'until perforce she arose, and words came from the corpse' (v. 4). Her first words are of reproach; in thus summoning her he has, she says, 'rendered harder my path of suffering'. She goes on to describe in what, to a modern mind, are the most vivid lines of the poem, how long she has lain dead:

> Snowed on with snow, beaten with rain,
> Drenched with the dew....

But nevertheless she can give to Othin the knowledge he craves, and foretell to him the death of Balder, for whose coming the halls of Hel are decked with gold and stocked with mead. Then at one question which he asks, which to us is practically incomprehensible, as to the identity of a certain weeping maiden or maidens, she realises the true identity of her questioner, and the poem ends on a note of mutual enmity and with a grim prophecy from the *völva* (seeress) of the ultimate fate of Othin at Ragnarrökr.

The poem as it stands is a series of problems; why, for instance, is the *völva's* grave placed inside Hel, the realm of the dead? There is no indication that we are to view this as a second death, and that the seeress has, in the words of *Vafþrúðnismál*, 'died out of Hel'. One would hardly expect it to be necessary both for Othin to take the road to the realm of the dead and for the inhabitant of the grave to be roused up to meet him, unless the place where they meet is to be regarded as a kind of half-way station between the realm of the dead and the realm of the living. Presumably here we are to forget Othin's position as god of the dead, and regard him rather as the representative of the living world of the gods, in contrast to the realm of death to which Balder journeyed, and where Hermóðr followed him for a little while.

Othin's purpose in consulting the dead is clear; she alone possesses that information about the future which can explain the threatening dreams that have troubled Balder, and tell Othin the nature of the fate that will befall his son, and whether revenge for his death will be permitted. This precious information is wrung reluctantly from the *völva's* lips. She declares at intervals:

> I have spoken unwilling (lit. *nauðig*—'of necessity', 'by
>        compulsion'),
> Now must I be silent,

and only the command of Othin—'be not silent, *völva*', followed by renewed questioning, drags more information from her.

Two other poems in the Edda are presented as the prophetic utterances of a *völva*; these are the *Völuspá* and *Völuspá hin Skamma*. In the first of these the speaker declares that she is bidden by Othin (*Valföðr*) to tell what she knows of the past. Here we find the two-fold aspect of mantic wisdom—knowledge of the past being as important and as secret as the knowledge of the future, and both being revealed by one with special wisdom beyond the normal reach of gods and men alike; for the *völva*, having traced the history of the worlds, proceeds to outline their ultimate destiny. She too, like the *völva* of *Baldrs Draumar*, will not continue without repeated questioning, for again we have a refrain which punctuates the poem, after it has advanced a certain way: *Vituð ér enn eða hvat?*—which may be roughly translated: 'Would you know yet more, and what?'[1] The other poem, the *Völuspá hin Skamma*, contains no reference to the reason why the *völva* has been summoned. As we have it, it begins at once with the narrative of events, and ends as suddenly with a reference to the fall of Othin before the wolf, reminiscent of the ending of *Baldrs Draumar*. Here too, however, we have the familiar refrain:

> Much have I told you, and much more can tell,
> Needs must I learn it so; will you know further?

[1] It has been suggested that the last line of the poem should run in the form given in one MS.—'Now *she* must sink', referring to the disappearance of the *völva* into the grave, as in the other poem. F. Jónsson however (*Edda*, p. 20) disagrees, and argues that there are no grounds for supposing that the *völva* in this case has been summoned from the grave. He advocates the reading '*Nú mun hann sökkvask*'.

There is evidently a close connection between these three poems, and even if there is no reason to suggest that the *völva* in either of the two poems last mentioned has been roused from the dead, the fact that this is the background given in *Baldrs Draumar* is in itself of great interest, because it establishes a link between the prophetic utterances of the *völva* and the wisdom of the dead.

The attitude of the dead roused from the grave is not necessarily a hostile one. In *Grógaldr* we have an episode where Svipdagr, before going out on a perilous quest, consults his dead mother and begs her to teach him certain charms to guard him against danger. The poem opens with his summons to the dead, with no indication whether, as in the case of Othin, a journey was first needed to bring him to the grave:

> Awake, Gróa! Awake, good woman!
> Awake at the door of the dead!
> If you remember bidding your son
> Come to your grave cairn.

The reply, like that of the *völva*, emphasises the actual resting place in the grave, and gives no hint of a realm of the dead elsewhere, from which her spirit is recalled:

> What has my only son now at heart?
> What misfortune has come to you
> That you call on your mother, passed into the earth,
> And gone from the world of men?

Here again the reason for calling up the dead is to gain knowledge. Svipdagr protests he has not the necessary wisdom and experience to travel the path 'where none go' to Menglöð. For this journey he needs certain magic spells, and these she teaches him. There are spells for the loosening of burdens, for protection against wandering, joyless, far from the path, and against overwhelming rivers of Hel; spells against lurking foes and against fetters on the limbs; spells which will guard against stormy seas, bitter cold, and ghosts of malignant Christian women wandering in the night; and finally a spell to give the necessary wisdom for the contest with a terrible giant. It seems clear that such spells are intended for no ordinary journey, but for entrance into supernatural realms; this is a question which will need to be discussed further in the next chapter.

It would seem as if in the *Hyndluljóð* we have another consultation of the dead, though this is not as evident as in *Grógaldr*. It begins with an invocation by Freyja to awaken Hyndla, the giantess who 'dwells in a cavern'. She begs her to ride with her to Valhöll, and the scene is set in *valsinni*, the 'road of the slain' (vv. 6 and 7). While Freyja sits on her boar, in reality the disguised Óttarr, and Hyndla upon her wolf, the giantess is persuaded to recite the full list of the ancestors of Óttarr, Freyja's human lover. When the full list is told Hyndla discovers the trick that has been played on her and is furious; she parts from Freyja with bitter words and retires to sleep again. Thus the rousing of the unwilling sleeper, the gaining of the necessary information, the discovery of disguised identity at the end, and the parting with abuse on both sides are very similar to the situation in *Baldrs Draumar*.

Certain resemblances to the theme of the awakened sleeper can be seen too in *Sigrdrífumál*.[1] The poem opens with an inquiry from the woman, whose identity is only given us in the prose, as to who has broken her slumber. Sigurðr replies by telling who he is, and then after a kind of salutation to day and night and the gods and goddesses, she continues:

> Long have I slept,
> Long have I slumbered,
> Long are the woes of men,

a note very reminiscent of the *völva* raised from the sleep of death. The rest of the poem deals with the wisdom which she imparts to Sigurðr; it is again closely connected with spells, this time runic ones, the origin of which she attributes to Othin.

Together with the Edda poems which we have examined, we may also notice a story from Saxo. Harthgrepa, the mysterious fostermother of Hadingus, is on one occasion anxious to learn their future fortunes. They chanced, says Saxo, to pass the night in a house where a funeral was in progress:

> ...Here, desiring to pry into the purposes of heaven by the help of a magic espial, she graved on wood some very dreadful spells, and caused Hadingus to put them under the dead man's tongue; thus forcing him to utter, with the voice so given, a strain terrible to hear
>
> (I. XXIV, p. 27, Elton's translation).

In this strain, as given by Saxo, the dead rebukes the woman who has caused him to speak: 'Contrary to my will and purpose, I must

1 For a discussion of the problems connected with the identity of the sleeper in this poem, see p. 181 below.

declare some bitter tidings.' This has a striking resemblance to the words of the *völva* roused by Othin. As Saxo expresses it, the deed is a recall of the spirit back from Tartarus. However a closer examination renders it doubtful whether such an idea was ever present in Saxo's source; the expression, in particular, 'whoso hath called me, who am lifeless and dead, back from the abode below, and hath brought me into the upper air' rather appears to resemble the words of the *völva*, whose emphasis is on the extreme deadness of her condition, and who gives no hint of a returning soul as something separate from the body. It is noticeable that the dead man foretells the death of her who has roused him, just as the *völva* looks forward with apparent relish to the fate of her tormentor, Othin.

In these poems and the Saxo passage which we have studied, it is clear that there is a certain amount of agreement. The sleeper is aroused from a sleep which may or may not be specified as the sleep of death in order to impart special knowledge to the inquirer. Usually at the end we are told that the sleeper returns to sleep; sometimes, though not always, great indignation is shown because the slumber has been broken, and the concluding words uttered are a prophecy of ill-fortune to come upon the rash intruder. The wisdom which is imparted is of two kinds. Either it consists of a revelation from the future or the past of what is normally hidden—the doom of the world, the fate of the individual or the line of dead ancestors behind a man of noble rank—or else it consists of spells which give power to the possessor, which can guard him against the baleful magic of others, or give him the power to overcome certain perils in his journeyings.

## THE ANIMATION OF THE DEAD

*Baldrs Draumar* does not offer us the only example of the consultation of the dead by Othin. In the vision of the final catastrophe given in *Völuspá* Othin is said to take counsel with the head of Mímir (v. 46). This is explained in *Ynglinga Saga* (IV). Here the Vanir are said to slay Mímir, the wise counsellor who was among the hostages sent to them by the Æsir, because they were angry at being tricked into making the handsome but empty-headed Hoenir, his companion, a chief. The story goes on:

> They seized Mímir, and cut off his head, and sent the head to the Æsir; Othin took the head and anointed it with herbs, so that it should not decay,

and uttered spells over it, and wrought such magic that it spake with him and told him many hidden things.

This is a consultation of the dead of a different nature from that which we have previously examined. Now part of the dead body is worked upon by magic until it is able to converse with the wizard, and then has power to see into what normally is hidden from man. There is, as it happens, a story in the *Flateyjarbók*,[1] said to be taken from a lost poem, of a less reputable cult which bears a strange resemblance to the consultation of Mímir's head. It is practised by a family who live on a headland, at the instigation of the old woman who manages the house; the object venerated is the generative organ of a horse; and the treatment which this receives at the hands of the old woman is strikingly like that which Othin gives to the head of Mímir:

After this she went out and dried it very carefully, and wrapped it in a linen cloth, and put garlic and other herbs with it, so that it would not rot, and laid it in her chest. As the autumn wore on, the old woman took it out every evening and spoke words of worship over it (*með einhverium formála honum til dýrkanar*), and it came about that she put all her faith in it, and took it for her god.... And through the craft of the devil the thing grew in size and strength, until it could stand beside the housewife if she willed it.

The remainder of the story, where the object is carried round the household, and each in turn speaks a different verse to it with the same refrain—'May *Maurnir* receive this idol'—until Olaf the Holy interferes, is extremely interesting. The choice of the object of worship seems to indicate a fertility cult,[2] but the resemblance to the

1 *Völsaþáttr: Flateyjarbók*, II, 265, p. 331 f.
2 On this question see Heusler (*Z.d.V.f.V.* XIII, 1903, p. 24 f.) and Olsen (*Norges Indskrifter med de ældre Runer*, II, p. 652 f.). Heusler believes that here we have an old autumn ceremony, the passing round of the phallic symbol and the speaking of formal verses over it, which may have continued in Norway until the thirteenth and fourteenth centuries with its former significance forgotten. He and Olsen give examples of such ceremonies elsewhere in N.W. Europe. He suggests that it may have been originally a wedding ceremony, and some of Olsen's examples from N. Scotland bear this out.

With regard to the name *Maurnir*, the most reasonable interpretation grammatically seems to be that it is a feminine plural, with the meaning 'giantesses', although neither Heusler nor Olsen is satisfied with this, because they find no evidence for such a cult elsewhere. I would suggest however that here we have a cult associated in some way with the *dísir*, the gigantic supernatural women whom we have seen reason to connect with the autumn sacrifice, and also with worship

tending of the head of Mímir is so marked that the whole reads like a
rather vulgar but delightfully humorous parody on such a theme.
The semblance of life in the dead caused through witchcraft is
particularly significant; one may compare with this the story of the
image of Thor which was so enchanted by much sacrificing that it
was able to talk and walk with its priest and foretell future hap-
penings;[1] and also the wooden man made by Jarl Hákon in whom a
wooden heart was placed, and who through the power of the goddesses was able to talk and walk—albeit a little stiffly—and do the
Jarl's errands for him elsewhere.[2] It is a side of witchcraft of which
we do not know very much, but which must be taken into consideration in studying the evidence for necromancy.

In *Sigrdrífumál* the head of Mímir seems to be associated with the
runes of wisdom—'mind-runes' as they are called. These are said to be

> read and cut
> And thought out by Hroptr (i.e. Othin)
> From the liquid
> Which dropped
> From the skull of Heiðdraupnir
> And the horn of Hoddrofnir (v. 12).

Heiðdraupnir has been suggested as another name for Mímir, but
Hoddrofnir is unknown; it seems likely that there is some connection
with the magic mead described in *Grímnismál* which drops from the
horns of Heiðrún (v. 25). Mímir is certainly mentioned in the next
verse, where we are told:

> Then spoke Mímir's head
> Its first wise saying
> And uttered true words (v. 13).

The whole passage however, and particularly the 'true words' that
follow, is most involved and mysterious. More light might be
thrown upon it by further study of similar conceptions in Irish
literature.[3]

---

of a somewhat erotic type. Heusler is probably correct in his surmise that the
idea of the phallus coming to life is not one originally connected with this cult at
all.

1 *Flateyjarbók: Óláfs Saga Tryggvasonar*, I, 243, p. 292.        2 *Ibid.* 173, p. 213 f.
3 The connection between severed heads, magical practices and prophecy in
Irish sources has been discussed by N. K. Chadwick in an article on 'Imbas
Forosnai' (*Scottish Gaelic Studies*, IV, p. 119 f.). Cf. also an episode in *Eyrbyggja
Saga*, XLIII, where the severed head has the gift of prophecy.

Finally, in connection with Othin and the dead, we have the declaration made in *Hávamál*, where among the powers wrought by means of magic spells we find the following:

> I know a twelfth; if I see from a tree
> A hanged man swaying,
> I can so write and cut runes
> That the corpse walks
> And talks with me (v. 157).

Here again magic enables him who possesses certain knowledge to summon the semblance of life and wisdom beyond his own reach into a dead body. We have the same connection with runes in *Sigrdrífumál*, for it was apparently after the runes were created by Hroptr that Mímir's head first spoke wise sayings.

A picture of the animated dead of a cruder kind is found in the gruesome story of the deaths from the plague in *Eiríks Saga Rauða* (VI) and *Þorfinns Saga Karlsefnis* (V). The dead man Þorsteinn Eiríksson sits up suddenly on the bed and asks for his wife Guðríðr. Then he tells the frightened woman her future destiny; how she will marry again, live in Iceland, and finally after the death of her second husband build a church and become a nun. After he has told her all this, he falls back and speaks no more. In *Eiríks Saga* no reason is given for this sudden disclosure on the part of the dead; but in the other saga the dead Þorsteinn declares he is speaking 'to make amends for my state of life', though how he does so by his words is not clear, while he also asks to be buried inside a church. In spite of the Christian setting in which these incidents are placed, however, the idea of the animation of the corpses and their power to foretell the future seems at bottom to be the same as that in the story from Saxo and the obtaining of knowledge through the hanged claimed by Othin.

Of a slightly different nature is an example of rousing the dead given in the *Hervarar Saga* (IV). The story of the resolute girl Hervör, who goes in spite of warnings and entreaties to visit the haunted island where her father and his brothers are buried in order to obtain the famous sword laid in her father's grave, is among the most vivid and beautiful in the sagas. It is far more romantic in its treatment than the majority of the ghost stories in the *Íslendinga Sögur*, and the swift, impetuous movement of the verses exchanged between Hervör and the dead king is strangely effective against the eery background of the open grave-mounds and the cold fire that blazes round them. The prose story tells us that the howe-dwellers could be seen standing at their doors as Hervör approached. The verses themselves, however, seem to indicate that these dead men needed rousing as much as the sleeping *völva*:

> Awake, Angantýr!
> Hervör rouses you—
> Only daughter
> Of you and Tófa....
> Hervarðr, Hjörvarðr,
> Hrani, Angantýr,
> I rouse you all
> From under the roots.
> In helm and byrnie,
> With keen-edged sword,
> Shield and harness,
> And reddened spear-point....

In reply to these indications and to the demand for her father's sword, which she follows up with threats of bitter curses when there is no response, Angantýr rebukes her for disturbing the dead, though it is a gentler rebuke than some of the others we have encountered:

> Hervör, daughter,
> Why call you so?
> Why such fell curses?
> You do yourself ill.
> Mad must you be,
> All too witless,
> And lost to wisdom
> To rouse dead men.

Hervör seeks the dead with no desire to obtain knowledge; her aim is the possession of the magic sword Tyrfing. Nevertheless Angantýr reveals a certain amount to her concerning the future when he warns her to leave the sword in the grave, since it can only bring evil to all her house. Finally he yields to her stubborn resolve, for she is resolute enough, if need be, to draw the weapon with her own hand from under the dead warrior—

> Wrapped all around
> In sheets of flame—

and she gains Tyrfing for her own.

In this story it is noticeable that Hervör, like Othin in *Baldrs Draumar*, has herself to come halfway before she can gain any contact with the dead. Not only does she come out alone to the grim burial-place, but she wades through the fire that surrounds the howes and forms a barrier between the worlds of the living and the dead. As she herself says in the last verse she speaks:

> I seemed to be lost
> Between the worlds,
> While around me
> Burned the fires.

Thus in the first examples which we considered, the inquirer stood beside the grave to awake the sleeper; in these last examples the living again seeks out the dead body, or part of the dead body, in order to animate it with new life and to draw wisdom from it. It remains to consider one example of necromancy of another kind, found in the *Íslendinga Sögur*.

Here the wizard who wishes to call up the dead neither stands beside the corpse nor seeks out the grave. It would indeed be difficult to do so, since at least two of those summoned have perished at sea. Þrándr, one of the chief characters in the *Færeyinga Saga*, and a man with some skill in magic, undertakes to solve a mystery, and show how Sigmundr Brestison met his death. This is his method:

...Then Þrándr had great fires made up in the hall, and had four hurdles (?) set up to form a square. Then he marked out nine enclosures from the hurdles, in all directions, and he sat on a stool between the fire and the hurdles.[1] Now he forbade them to talk among themselves, and they obeyed him. Þrándr sat thus for a while, and when some time had elapsed, a man came into the hall, soaking wet. They recognised the man as Einarr the Hebridean. He went up to the fire and stretched out his hands to it for a little while, and after that turned and went out. After a while a second man walked into the hall; he went to the fire, stretched out his hands to it, and then went out; and they knew that this was Þórir. Soon after a third man came into the hall; he was a tall man, much covered in blood, and he held his head in his hand. They all recognised him; it was Sigmundr Brestison; he stood still on the floor for a little while, and then went out. And after that Þrándr drew a deep breath and said: 'Now you may see how the man has met his death'....

---

[1] *Færeyinga Saga* XL, p. 59: '*Þrándr hafði þá látit gera elda mikla í eldaskála, ok grindr fjórar lætr hann gera með fjórum hornum, ok níu reita rístr Þrándr alla vega út frá grindunum en hann sez á stól milli elds ok grindanna*' (Jónsson, *Kongelige Nordiske Oldskriftselskab*, Copenhagen, 1927).

Þrándr goes on to explain that the men have appeared in the order in which they died: 'Einarr died first, and either froze to death or was drowned', then Þórir, and finally Sigmundr, who had clearly been killed on land 'since he appeared to us covered with blood, and headless'. Þrándr later proves that his words are true by finding Sigmundr's ring in the house of the man who killed him.

Here an important feature of the raising of the dead is the strange figure drawn on the floor. Unfortunately the description of it is too obscure for us to know exactly what the figure could have been like. Þrándr, it is to be noticed, also throws himself into a trance—or so we are led to infer by the drawing of a deep breath at the end, which is a characteristic feature recorded of those recovering from a condition of trance. Does the spirit of Þrándr, then, leave his body in order to seek out the dead and summon them into the presence of the waiting company, or has he the power, having learned by ways of his own how the men have died, to call up the semblance of them before the eyes of the beholders? Neither explanation would be inconsistent with the powers of witches and wizards as they appear in the *Íslendinga Sögur*, but there are no parallels to this account elsewhere which might serve to explain it.

In this case again, at all events, the dead are apparently summoned from their resting-place in order that information may be obtained from them. Here the knowledge required is of a very simple kind, and consists merely of accurate information as to how they met their deaths. The fact that Þrándr is able to share the sight of the dead and to communicate his discoveries to a large audience is interesting, and it is not unlike the communications of the *völva* in this respect, as will be seen later.

## THE RESTLESS CORPSE

The stories from Norse literature dealing with the raising up of the slain on the battlefield to fight anew have already been examined in an earlier chapter, because they seemed to be important for the better understanding of the Valhöll conception. It was suggested there that the idea of the unconquerable dead who can only be quelled by powerful intervention from the world of the living belongs essentially to the grave-mound, and that it was within the mound that the eternal battle was originally believed to take place.

Some of the stories of the raising of the dead in battle should possibly be included here as examples of a certain kind of necromancy. In this form of raising the dead, however, the motive is clearly not that of obtaining wisdom, but a desire to profit from the considerable physical strength of the *draugr*, and to overcome an enemy by the recuperative powers of such an army. As was pointed out in chapter III, there is no idea of the return of the spirit into the body of the slain to be discerned behind this conception.

The idea is clearly different in nature and origin from the far more complex picture of the awakening of the dead to seek wisdom from them. It must be closely connected with the return of the dead unasked from the grave, with which we have already dealt in the section on survival. Usually in the sagas the attempts of the living are concentrated on keeping the dead within the grave, not on rousing them from it. It is true, as Klare points out in a recent article,[1] that there are certain resemblances between the powers possessed by the *draugar* and those of living witches and wizards; the *draugar* sometimes practise shape-changing, control the weather, see into the future and so on.[2] But the idea of special mantic knowledge possessed by the *draugr* is not, I think, in accordance with the general picture given in the *Íslendinga Sögur*. The *draugar* who cause havoc in the countryside by walking after death are powerful, unpleasant and, on the whole, rather stupid people. Even the redoubtable Glamr in *Grettis Saga* stands and gapes in foolish astonishment when his tug at the hero's cloak is met with stout resistance: 'Glamr looked at the piece that he held, and wondered greatly who could tug so hard against him' (xxxv). The *draugar* may impart advice, when they appear in dreams to those whom they favour, but never wisdom.

On the other hand there are exceptions to the rule when we turn from Iceland, to which most of the stories about the *draugar* belong, to some of the evidence from Norway connected with the cult of the dead. This has already been reviewed, and the story of Þorleifr the poet was of the utmost importance, it will be remembered, for suggesting a connection between the dead and mantic inspiration.[3] It is true that this story cannot be taken as an example of necromancy

---

1 'Die Toten in der altnord. Liter.' (*Acta Phil. Scand.* VIII, p. 1 f.).

2 The examples which he gives for shape-changing as practised by the dead either come from the *Fornaldar Sögur*, or are rather doubtful incidents from the *Íslendinga Sögur*, such as that of the seal that appears through the floor in *Eyrbyggja Saga*, where the inference is by no means clear. If the power of shape-changing is one really characteristic of the dead, then Klare's main hypothesis, that there is no idea of the disembodied soul in Norse literature dealing with the dead, will have to be revised.     3 See p. 108 above.

pure and simple, but the fact that the shepherd sleeps upon the howe of the dead Þorleifr, and endeavours to compose a verse of poetry in his honour, makes it clear that it must be closely connected with it. The mantic inspiration which is given to the living by the dead—in this case the gift of poetic composition—is very significant. But the dead poet who steps from his howe to address the sleeping shepherd is obviously of a very different family from the *draugar* who ravage the countryside, delighting in physical violence to man and beast, and different again from such a being as the more amiable Þorgunna, who leaves her coffin on the way to burial to ensure proper treatment for her bearers.[1]

While communication between the living and the dead in the case of the *draugar* is on the whole personal, that between the inspired dead and the human inquirer tends to be of a different type. The characters of the *draugar*, when we have a chance to gain information about them, are much the same as they have been in life, with certain elements intensified. Hrappr, the *draugr* in *Laxdæla Saga*, always a spiteful busybody, merely becomes a little more violently unpleasant after death; Þórólfr Bægifótr in *Eyrbyggja Saga* still behaves like an ugly, ferocious bully, and is still obliged to respect the character of his upright and generous son, Arnkell; Þorgunna, walking on the way to burial, is quiet, efficient and prudent as she has been in life.[2] They still have their favourites and their enemies among the living, those whom they avoid and those whom they despise. But the relationship between the dead and the living in the passages which have been examined earlier in this chapter is of a different nature. The help which the dead gives is impersonal; the living is not claiming help of a friend, but rather tapping a source of wisdom. No personal confidences pass even between Svipdagr and his mother; he calls, and she responds by a series of spells. With Othin and the *völva*, Harthgrepa and the dead man, the relationship is frankly hostile; the dead speak because they are forced to do so by a power stronger than that of their slumbers. The wisdom which they utter is something quite independent of personal characteristics in this life; it is of the same nature as are the revelations of the *völva* when she recovers from her trance in the accounts of the foretelling of the future in the sagas, and like her they may even be forced to utter the truth against their will.

1 *Eyrbyggja Saga*, LI.
2 For these see p. 93 above.

CONCLUSION

Reviewing the evidence for necromancy at our disposal, it becomes evident that we are dealing with more than one conception of this peculiar relationship between the living and the dead. On the one hand, we have the dead conceived as channels through which knowledge flows to those who have the power and the skill to summon them. The dangers of such a practice are evident, for as well as tapping a source of knowledge the inquirer is also likely to tap a source of bitter hostility, and a prophecy of his own fate may well. reach him together with the knowledge of hidden events which he craves. This happens in Othin's consultation of the *völva*, and in Harthgrepa's speech with the dead in Saxo's story, while Freyja's conversation with Hyndla also ends on a hostile note. This conception of the dead, which is found in the Edda poems and Saxo, is not met with in the *Íslendinga Sögur*, but we do find something very akin to it in the consultation of the living *völva*. The sagas contain accounts of a number of occasions when the *völva* is questioned as to the future of the community or the individual fates of men and women, and in some cases the ceremony where the consultation takes place is described in considerable detail. The most elaborate account of the professional *völva* is given in *Þorfinns Saga Karlsefnis* (IV), where her visit to a little community in Greenland is described; here we are given much information about her dress, her behaviour, and the ritual observed throughout, and interesting parallels are found in a number of other passages throughout the sagas.[1]

From these it can be seen that the living seeress also acts as a channel through which inspiration about what is normally hidden reaches her hearers; she may prophesy concerning the fate of individuals, the whereabouts of lost and hidden things or people, the future of the community, or the coming seasons. The wisdom is again of a quite impersonal nature, and may even reach the inquirer against the will of the *völva*. A striking example of this is given in *Hrólfs Saga Kraka* (III), where the *völva* does not wish to make known the whereabouts of the two young princes whom King Fróði wishes to destroy; she tries to convince the king that her prophecies have

---

1 Other accounts are found in *Vatnsdæla Saga* (X), where a Lapp woman attends a feast in the north of Norway and is consulted in the same way; in *Orms Þáttr Stórólfssonar* (*Fjörutíú Íslend. Þættir*, F. Jónsson, Reykjavík, 1904), V, p. 206; and in two of the *Fornaldar Sögur*, *Hrólfs Saga Kraka* (III) and *Örvar-Odds Saga* (II).

gone astray, and that she has no more to say; but when he 'presses her hard', the information about the boys comes from her lips against her will, until in the end she leaps down from the incantation platform—the only means, apparently, to bring the disclosure to an end. With this we may compare the reluctant speech of the *völva* in *Baldrs Draumar*, who is only prevented from relapsing into silence by the repeated questionings of Othin. The living *völva*, moreover, reveals the knowledge she has gained while recovering from a trance-like condition; and this may be compared to the sleep from which the dead are said to waken when aroused by those who summon them. We find too that the knowledge of the living seer or seeress is represented as something gained at the cost of considerable effort and even pain,[1] and this is also in agreement with the protest in *Baldrs Draumar* that Othin, in demanding information of the *völva*, has 'rendered harder her path of suffering'.

It will be remembered that in the first group of poems we examined it seemed necessary to take into consideration certain poems in which the knowledge was imparted by a woman in reply to questioning, and where it was not clear whether she had been raised from the dead or not. The two important factors seemed to be the imparting of knowledge—which had first to be demanded—and the awakening from some kind of slumber, sometimes described as the slumber of death. It seems at least a possibility worth considering that the situation in these poems is not founded on the actual practice of consulting the dead at the graveside, or even at the deathbed, but rather that of gaining information from the living who have been able, by special powers, to penetrate into the realm of the dead and return from it with tidings of the unknown. This would mean that they are to be interpreted symbolically, and that they are perhaps based on actual ceremonies of which the descriptions of the consultations of the *völva* in the *Íslendinga Sögur* give us a faint glimpse. To see whether there is any real foundation for any such surmise, however, the accounts of the journeys by the living to the land of the dead will have to be examined in detail to see if they too are capable of bearing any such interpretation.

It is necessary to remember also the evidence for interest in the

---

1 Two of the most striking examples of this are the protest made by the Lapps in *Vatnsdæla Saga* (XII) on recovery from a trance in which they have gained information needed by Ingimundr, and that of Þorhildr, a wise woman clearly akin to the *völur*, after prophesying concerning the future in *Ljósvetninga Saga* (XXI).

dead in the grave-mound, shown in the passages studied in the chapter on *The Cult of the Dead*. Undoubtedly there were practices connected with the dead body itself and its last resting-place; the custom of sitting upon a howe, of sacrificing to the grave-mound, of bringing a semblance of life into the dead body by witchcraft, as in some of the evidence we have examined, all point to an attitude towards the dead which seems to be essentially different from that given in the Edda poems and discussed above. Here the dead are revered because they are the dead—with sanctity residing in them, rather than passing through them from some other source. It has been suggested earlier that one element of the greatest importance in this attitude towards the dead is the belief in rebirth. Another factor which might be mentioned is one closely associated with it, that of fertility. This is a factor which may easily be over-emphasised, and on the whole there is not much evidence for fertility cults in Norse literature; for instance the worship of the gods with the exception of Freyr is singularly free from such elements. However the connection between the dead kings in their howes and favourable seasons is significant;[1] sometimes in the accounts of the worship of the howe the same element is stressed; and the gruesome relic worshipped in the *Völsa þáttr* in *Flateyjarbók* must have been connected with the idea of fertility. It will be remembered that Freyr, whose phallic image stood in the temple of Uppsala,[2] was closely connected with the cult of the howe, with rebirth, and the elves.

Mantic wisdom and fertility are not, of course, to be thought of as completely separate. In any society where agriculture mattered intensely because a year of bad crops meant suffering and famine, as in Scandinavia, it is obvious that a knowledge of the coming seasons was one of the aspects of the glimpse into the future which could be of the greatest value. The chief question put to the *völva* in *Þorfinns Saga Karlsefnis* (IV) is whether the bad harvests and the plague from which the community was then suffering would come to an end. It is necessary to make a distinction here, however, between the acquiring of knowledge from the living *völva* or from the apparently dead, and the influence which the dead in the graves were believed to have over the fertility of the earth. The living *völva* might foretell the course of the plague, but in herself she had no powers to make it cease. Similarly the dead who speak have no power to control the future, although they can foretell events to come; they are merely

1 See p. 100 above.　　　　2 Adam of Bremen, IV, 26 (Schol. 139).

instruments through which the knowledge can be obtained. The
influence of Hálfdan's body on the crops, or the power to compose
poetry given by the dead Þorleifr, is a more potent influence of a
different kind.

The third aspect of necromancy is the raising of the slain on the
battlefield; this seems to be connected with the belief in the strength
and ferocity of the animated corpse, which we have discussed above.
We have seen too that it appears to be associated with the battle
inside the grave-mound, and with the belief in Valhöll.

Into three distinct classes, then, the evidence which we have collected seems to fall; and to these may be added the story of the
raising of the dead by Þrándr, which it is hard to fit into any category,
standing as it seems to do alone. The idea of a necromancer calling
back the soul of the dead into the body, or calling up, like the witch
of Endor, the spirit of the dead from another world, cannot be said
with certainty to be found in Norse literature at all, though this is the
interpretation supplied by Saxo. This agrees with conclusions reached
in earlier chapters, particularly after examining the evidence on the
soul, and on the idea of survival.

The laws dating from early Christian times in Iceland have references to the raising of the dead. In the *Ældre Gulaþings Lov*[1] the
practice of those who *utisetu at vekia troll upp, at fremia heiðrni með
þvi* ('sit out at night to rouse trolls, to do witchcraft thereby') is
mentioned, and again in the *Gulaþings Christenret*[2] there is a condem-
nation of *þæir er fræista draugha upp at væickia æda haugbua* ('those
who attempt to rouse *draugar* or howe-dwellers'). Elaborate directions from later times as to the rites to be observed in arousing a dead
man can be found in Jón Árnason's collection of folklore.[3] It is an
odd mixture of such anti-Christian practices as the repeating of the
Lord's Prayer backwards with the remembrances of heathen magic
in the form of carved runes and so on. In spite of the Christian
setting, however, and the late date of the traditions, it is very evident
that it is still the *draugr* which is raised, and that there is no essential
difference between this creature and the *draugr* of the sagas; it is even
necessary to overcome him when raised from the grave by superior
strength, in case the dead man summoned should drag the inquirer
back with him into the grave. It is interesting to note that the

1 *Norges Gamle Love indtil* 1387 (Keyser and Munch, 1846–1895), v. I, p. 19 (XXXII).
2 *Ibid.* v. II, p. 308 (III).
3 *Íslenzkar Þjóðsögur og Æfintýri*, I, Section on *Uppvaknínga*, p. 317 f.

reluctance of the dead to be disturbed is remarked upon, and the dead man is said to protest at the beginning 'Let me lie quiet', a protest which must be ignored if a successful experiment is to be carried out. Here however the dead body rises through its own strength, and there is no hint of necessity for it to be informed either with the spirit of the dead called from some other realm or with an evil spirit from Hell. In the account of the raising of the *draugr*, whose physical characteristics are continually emphasised, and who in reply to questions can tell what his former life on earth has been, we seem to be nearer to the stories of *draugar* in the sagas than to the raising of the dead with their fund of impersonal wisdom in the Edda poems. The evil nature of the dead, who has become practically equivalent to a troll—the word is used in several of the laws—links up with some of the tales of haunting, and with the stories of howe-dwellers gloating over their treasures and devouring living creatures that come their way.

But the evidence for necromancy is incomplete without some examination of the other side—the descent of the living man or woman into the haunts of the dead. It is impossible to separate one conception from the other, indeed, for we have seen that the idea of the visit of the living to the land of the dead is implicit already in some of the stories we have discussed. The evidence for the journey to the land of the dead made by the living must be closely examined before any conclusions can be drawn as to the relationship between the dead and the living which lies behind the stories of necromantic practices.

# Chapter VII

## THE JOURNEY TO THE LAND OF THE DEAD

> For forty days and forty nights
> He wade thro red blude to the knee,
> And he saw neither sun nor moon
> But heard the roaring of the sea.
>
> THOMAS RHYMER.

A short survey of Norse literature soon makes it apparent that the idea of the journey to another world is a familiar one. It is not always easy however to decide on the nature of the world to which entrance is gained by the living. There are of course journeys like that of Hermóðr into the kingdom of Hel to visit the dead Balder, where we are told definitely that the goal of the traveller is the realm of the dead that he may converse with those who have passed from this world. There are also journeys of a different nature, which will need to be studied in connection with these, where the traveller has to brave a number of perils and finally has to pass through a barrier of fire to gain what he seeks; such are the experiences of Skírnir and Svipdagr in the Edda poems. This will lead us on to some of the most puzzling journeys made in Old Norse literature—those to the realms of Guðmundr and Geirröðr in Saxo, Snorri and the *Fornaldar Sögur*. Lastly there are two more types of journey which must be taken into account: the entrance of the living into the grave, and the penetration of the mortal into the realm of the gods.

The field then over which these journeys take us is an extensive one, ranging as they do from the underworld to the kingdom of the gods. Like the way of the adventurers we are studying, our road is beset with manifold perils, for the problem of deciding on the exact relationship between the kingdom of Gymir or of Guðmundr and the land of the dead is anything but a simple one. The most interesting aspect of this subject, that of deciding how far these entries into a supernatural world are based on the mantic vision and are an account of a spiritual adventure rather than a mythological or legendary episode, is precisely the point where the ground becomes most uncertain and the darkness most obscure. Nevertheless it must be faced, however inadequately, since the evidence which has already been studied shows the necessity of some consideration of this kind as a corollary to the investigation of the ideas about the future life and the cult of the dead which has already been made.

## THE JOURNEY ACKNOWLEDGED AS SUCH

The most detailed description of the entrance of the living into the land of the dead, where there is no doubt about the destination, is the account of the ride of Hermóðr to find Balder in *Gylfaginning* (XLVIII). This has already been discussed in the chapter on *The Future Life*, and here we need only notice the nature of the journey. Hermóðr takes Sleipnir, the horse of Othin, to make the attempt. He rides over 'dark and deep valleys' for nine nights; so dark indeed is it that he sees nothing until he reaches the river 'Echoing' (*Gjöll*) and rides on the Gjallar bridge, which is roofed with shining gold. The idea of a closed bridge, 'thatched', as Snorri puts it, with gold, with the mysterious woman Móðguðr stationed there as its guardian, seems rather a surprising one to meet in Norse literature. It may have originated in bridges roofed as a protection against snow, but these are not common in Scandinavia now.

Móðguðr is astonished at the noise made by Hermóðr's coming, which is so unlike that of the hosts of the shadowy dead; while he, she sees, 'has not the hue of a dead man'. Here then we have a conception of the noiseless hosts of the dead which is different from the usual idea in Norse literature, and confirms the suggestion that Snorri was influenced here by some foreign source. Finally Hermóðr is told that Balder has indeed passed over Gjallar bridge before him, and that the way to Hel which he must follow lies 'downward and to the North'. So Hermóðr rides on until he comes to the gate of Hel; and this he has to leap over. Sleipnir however clears the gate with ease, and there is nothing to prevent his rider entering the hall, where he finds Balder.

The chief factors then in the journey to the land of the dead are the borrowed steed, the long ride over dark valleys, the bridge across the river and the woman guarding it, the road leading down to Hel, and the high barrier which has to be leaped by Sleipnir. It is due chiefly to the power of his steed that Hermóðr passes all these obstacles and particularly the last successfully. We shall find that most of these features will recur in other stories to be examined later on.

Another account of the journey to Hel is found in the Edda poem *Vegtamskviða* or *Baldrs Draumar*, which was discussed in the previous chapter. Here it is Othin himself who makes the journey, and again it is Sleipnir who is chosen to carry him. We are told little about the route they follow, except that it was downwards; that a dog with a bloodstained breast met Othin and barked at him as he went by; and that the earth resounded beneath the rider. Othin's goal is apparently the 'high hall of Hel', so that no distinction seems to be made here between Hel and Niflhel, to which Othin in the first verse is said to be riding. The *völva*'s grave is on the east side of Hel. This adds little to our information; but again the journey is performed on horseback; again the road lies downwards; again there is the idea of the noise and clatter of the rider who is alive travelling the ways of the dead, as in the description of the ride of Hermóðr.

The third account of the visit of the living to the land of the dead is the mysterious one found in Saxo in the story of Hadingus.[1] The adventure takes place while Hadingus is at the court of Haquinus, king of the Nitheri, whose daughter Regnilda he has married. A woman bearing hemlocks rises beside the brazier while he is at supper, and invites him to come and see a land where herbs as fresh as those she carries grow in winter. He agrees; whereupon she wraps her mantle round him and draws him down under the earth. 'I take it', Saxo interpolates, 'that the nether gods purposed that he should pay a visit in the flesh to the regions whither he must go when he died.' The way which they follow is first through mist and darkness; then along a well-worn road over which richly clad people are travelling; then through a sunny land where the fresh plants are growing. The next landmark is a 'swift and tumbling river of leaden waters' which contains weapons of all kinds; this they pass by a bridge. Then they meet two armies engaged in a conflict which the woman declares to be unending; these have, she says, been slain by the sword. Finally they reach a wall which the woman tries to leap over, but it is too high for her. She strangles a cock which she carries, and flings it over the barrier; and the bird comes to life immediately, for they can hear it crowing. In this mysterious country Saxo apparently leaves his hero stranded, since after the incident of the cock he goes on to say that Hadingus set off for home with his wife (that is, from the country of the Nitheri).

Here we obviously encounter much difficulty and confusion; but

1 Saxo, I, 31, p. 37 f.

we can recognise some of the familiar items reappearing in slightly different guise. This time the hero is conducted not by his horse, but by a guide in the form of an old woman. Here again, however, the way lies first through darkness; it is downward, beneath the earth; it is necessary to cross a river by a bridge, though here there is no idea of a golden one. Again there is a wall too high for the woman to jump, and when a dead cock is thrown over it is restored to life on the other side. The new factors introduced are the sunny land where fresh herbs grow, the eternal conflict of those who have fallen by the sword, and the idea of renewed life behind the great barrier which Hadingus does not pass.

The identity of the hero forms a series of problems in itself, and their solution may well be important for the better understanding of this strange journey, but it is impossible to discuss these here. They are fully and ably presented in Herrmann's Commentary on Saxo's History,[1] with a list of the literature on the subject. The relationship between Hadingus and the god Njörðr is particularly interesting, for the verses which are said in Saxo to be spoken by Hadingus and his wife are the same which in the *Prose Edda*[2] are given to Njörðr and the giantess Skáði, and there is a certain resemblance, too, between the stories of how each was chosen as a husband. The identity of the Nitheri, whom Herrmann suggests may be the people of Niðaróss, near Þrandheim, is also a problem left unsolved, as is the question of how the visit of Hadingus to the underworld ended. We do know, however, that this is one of three instances where this same Hadingus establishes communication with the supernatural world. The first we have examined in the previous chapter, when Hadingus, by means of Harthgrepa's skill in magic, hears the dead speak. Whether there is any connection between the giantess Harthgrepa of this story, who claims the power to change her size, and the woman who is huge enough to carry the hero to the underworld in her mantle and yet whose 'wrinkled and slender body' (*corrugati corporis exilitate*) is not capable of leaping over the barrier at the end of the journey, cannot be decided from Saxo's information alone. The third expedition to a supernatural realm is that which occurs a little earlier in the story (I, 24); this time Hadingus' conductor is an old man with one eye, who has introduced the hero to the sea-rover Liserus. After the defeat of Hadingus and his new foster-brothers, the old man

1 P. Herrmann, *Dänische Geschichte des Saxo Grammaticus*, II (Leipzig, 1922), p. 89 f.
2 *Gylfaginning*, XXII.

carries him away on horseback, wrapping him in his mantle just as
the woman from the underworld does later. The horse of his guide
passes over the sea; but after one glimpse of the water beneath them
Hadingus is forbidden to examine the road by which they travel.
Their goal this time is the house of Othin, for there can be no doubt
as to the one-eyed old man's identity, and there Hadingus is re-
freshed by a 'certain pleasant draught', and the future is revealed to
him by his guide. Hadingus then, according to Saxo, has special
means of communication with the supernatural world, and this
tradition is not confined to Saxo, since we find the land of the dead
described as *Haddingjaland* in the *Guðrúnarkviða* (II, 23).

We see then that a journey to the land of the dead, directly ac-
knowledged as such, is found in three accounts only. In the first two,
the goal is the hall of Hel, in the underworld; in the third the
journey is more complicated, and it is never actually stated that we
are in the realm of death, although this is the explanation given by
Saxo. However the passage contains a reference to the everlasting
battle, and a mysterious wall behind which the dead are restored to
life; and we have previously noticed close resemblances between
this account and the symbolism employed in the cremation rites on
the Volga, where again we have the idea of a realm of the dead behind a high barrier and where a cock is slain, as here, as a symbol not
of death but of new life beyond the grave. The passage seems to contain a number of separate ideas about the future life, and much in it
remains unexplained, as does also the question of how far there was
any connection in Saxo's sources between this journey of Hadingus
and his ride over the sea to the house of Othin.

From these three journeys, which leave many problems unsolved,
we may pass on to other accounts of entrance gained into a supernatural realm, from which the adventurer is afterwards able to return
to the normal world again.

### The Journey through the Wall of Fire

It will be remembered that in the story of Hervör's visit to the burial
mound of her father and his brothers, examined in the last chapter,[1]
the barrier between the worlds of the living and the dead is marked
by the cold fire that flickers around the barrows. It is mentioned
several times in the verses spoken by Angantýr to his daughter; and

1 *Hervarar Saga*; see p. 159 above.

the climax comes when Hervör declares she is ready to put her hand among the flames and grasp the sword at the dead man's side; at the end she declares:

> I seemed to be lost
> Between the worlds,
> While around me
> Burned the fires.

'She waded', says the saga, 'through the fire like smoke' (IV). Fire was, of course, the recognised sign of a haunted burial mound, whose inhabitant was still active. In *Grettis Saga* the light of a great fire can be seen shooting up from a headland, and Grettir asks what it is, saying that in his country it would be a sign of treasure. He is told 'He who looks after the fire is one that it is better not to be curious about' (XVIII), and when he finally breaks into the howe in search of the treasure he encounters a fierce adversary in the shape of the dead man, Kárr the Old.

Again in an odd story in *Egils Saga ok Ásmundar* (XIII), the broadly comic account of the giantess' excursion to the underworld, which seems full of hints and echoes of more dignified matters, includes the leaping of a wall of fire. It is this which forms the last barrier to be passed in the lowest depths (*undirdjúp*), and Othin himself, here the 'prince of darkness', directs her to it. When she leaps over the fire she is able to obtain the cloak that cannot be burned, the third of the three treasures for which she has been sent.

In view of the fact that the barrier of fire is thus seen to be connected, first with the visit to the dead in the barrow, and secondly with the Underworld, it seems worth while to examine some of the other stories where the passing of this barrier forms an important feature in the journey to a supernatural realm. The two most detailed accounts are to be found in the Edda poems which deal with the stories of Svipdagr and Skírnir.

In the two poems which have to do with the adventures of Svipdagr, *Grógaldr* and *Fjölsvinnsmál*, we have first an account of his visit to his mother's grave, and of the spells which she teaches him, and secondly a description of his arrival outside the hall of Menglöð, and of the successful end of his wooing. Svipdagr seeks out his mother for one particular purpose; he needs her help because, as he tells her in verse 3, he has been sent to travel the way 'that none may go', to seek out the maiden Menglöð. In verse 5 he begs her to chant spells for him, since he fears he will otherwise perish on the way, and deems himself all too young for the quest. The nine spells which are chanted by Gróa in reply to this appeal, then, are presumably for one particular purpose—to assist him in making this journey—and so a study of them may be expected to assist us in gaining knowledge of the way by which Svipdagr is to travel.

The first spell is to enable him to cast off anything harmful. The second is to prevent him from 'wandering, deprived of will, in the ways'. The third is against the power of certain rivers, which might overwhelm him, and is to cause them to sink back into Hel before his advance. The fourth will turn the hearts of enemies who lie in wait for him away from their hostility. The fifth will loosen fetters laid on his limbs. The sixth will calm a raging sea, 'wilder than men know'. The seventh will preserve him from death from the intense cold on the 'high fells'. The eighth will help him, if suddenly over-taken by darkness, against the malignant power of 'dead Christian women'; and the ninth and last spell is to give him eloquence and wisdom when he comes to converse with the wise and terrible giant.

In these spells we are given a fairly vivid picture of the path which Svipdagr is to take. He will encounter hostility on it; enemies will lie in wait for him, some of them actually specified as the dead. He may be deprived of the strength of his will, and wander aimlessly, without the ability to continue on the right path; and he may be bound with fetters. His path will lie over wild rivers, said to flow out from Hel itself, over a stormy sea, and over high mountains where the cold is terrible; and always darkness may overtake him suddenly. At the end of the journey is the giant whom he must outstrip in wisdom if he is to gain his quest. The gap between the two poems, *Grógaldr* and *Fjölsvinnsmál*, is not thus complete; since the nature of the 'spell-songs' of Gróa affords a clue to the journey which Falk in his detailed study of the problems of *Svipdagsmál*[1] seems to have neglected to follow. There is a good deal in this article of Falk's, however, which is of interest for our present subject. Not only does he point out how closely the poems are linked together, as the work of Grundvig on the Danish ballads first indicated, but he also brings out striking parallels with the journey in *Skírnismál*; with the visit of Sigurðr to the sleeping Valkyrie; with *Ung Sveidal* and other Danish ballads; and with the Welsh story from the *Mabinogion*, *Kulhwch and Olwen*. He suggests too a certain resemblance to part of one of the *Fornaldar Sögur*, *Hjálmðérs Saga ok Ölvérs*, and to a much later saga

[1] 'Om Svipdagsmál', *Ark.f.n.F.* VI, 1894, p. 26 f.

in modern Icelandic, the *Himinbjargar Saga*. Evidently the story was one that had a wide circulation; although details may change, the fundamental elements—the young man seized with passionate love and desire for an unknown maiden of whom he hears, often through magic agency; the obstacles that lie between him and her castle; the final and apparently insurmountable barrier which is passed in the end without difficulty because Fate is on the young hero's side; and the young girl who rises to welcome him who has passed through all the encircling defences, and who will henceforth be united to him for ever—these remain the same.

Besides the parallels noted by Falk, we may also add a story from Irish sources, the story of Art, son of Conn,[1] and his wooing of Delbchaem. The banishment of Art by his wicked supernatural step-mother, Becuma, and the perils which he has to overcome before he can enter the bronze stronghold of the maiden, form a close parallel to *Svipdagsmál* and some of the other stories Falk mentions, and is a better example than the Welsh story of how familiar the tradition must have been in Celtic literature.

The explanation which Falk accepted was the then popular one of the sun-myth; while a more modern explanation is that expressed by Olsen in an article on *Skírnismál*,[2] which he takes to be an allegory of the fertilising of the seed in the earth. Whether this be the ultimate meaning or not, there are clearly points in *Svipdagsmál* which deserve investigation for our present study.

In particular, the connection between the dwelling of Menglöð and the land of the dead is brought out by Falk's detailed investiga-tion of the conversation between Svipdagr and Fjölsvinnr. He points out, for instance, the resemblance between the gates Þrymgjöll and Helgrind and the door to which Brynhildr refers as slamming on the heels of the dead; between the fierce hounds that guard the gate and the dog met by Othin in descending to Hel; and, most interesting of all, between the scene in *Fjölsvinnsmál*, where we have the giant watchman, the tree, the cock in the boughs, and the hounds, and that in *Völuspá*, where the giant who sits on the mound playing his harp, the world-tree, the cock and the dog Garmr are brought into close proximity. In the version of the story given in the Danish ballad which is so close to *Svipdagsmál*, it may be noticed that the giant

---

1 Cross and Slover, *Ancient Irish Tales* (Chicago, 1935), p. 491 f. (from rendering given in *Eriu*).
2 'Fra Gammelnorsk Myte og Cultus', *M.o.M.* 1909, p. 17 f.

watchman here is also said to be a shepherd, sitting on a mound. It
certainly seems as if it is the Underworld which is indicated, and we
may add the evidence for the journey thither, through darkness, deep
rivers and a raging sea, and over high mountains, corresponding to
the accounts of the journeys to the land of the dead which have
already been studied, with the emphasis on rivers of Hel and malignant ghosts to bear out the likeness. How Svipdagr accomplished
the journey we are not told, but in the ballad version it is on horseback; *Sveidalsvisen* tells us that the hero:

> rider over det brede hav
> og gjennem de grönne skove,

indicating that it was a horse of supernatural powers that he rode,
like the horse Sleipnir which carried Othin, Hermóðr and Hadingus
into the other world. Finally we notice that the wall of fire is
present also, although it is not much emphasised, for Svipdagr
addresses the giant as one who 'stands before the entrance and keeps
watch on all sides of the threatening flames' (v. 2).

The other poem which deals with a journey to win a bride from a
supernatural realm guarded by a wall of fire is *Skírnismál*, and here
the plot differs from those of all the other stories, because it is not
Freyr, the hero, but his servant Skírnir who accomplishes the journey
and wins the consent of the bride. It has been suggested by Olsen
that the name *Skírnir* indicates that the wooer is only a hypostasis of
the god himself, since the name is formed from one of his titles; the
poem, however, gives no suggestion of this, and there are no references to the story elsewhere to bear it out; *Lokasenna* (42) indeed
refers to the fact that Freyr in giving away his sword to Skírnir left
himself unarmed in the last great battle.

Of the journey made by Skírnir we are not told very much; we
have only the words he speaks to his horse to indicate the perils encountered on the way:

> It is dark without; time for our going, I say,
> Over the dank fells,
> Out to the giant folk;
> We will both come through, or he will have both of us,
> That loathsome giant.

In that brief yet vivid picture there is the idea of a difficult journey
through hostility and danger; and again the darkness and the moun-

tains are mentioned as in *Grógaldr*. Now the wall of fire is more definitely described, in Skírnir's words to Freyr:

> Give me a steed then to bear me through
> The dark and flickering flames,

and from the words of Gerðr we are led to assume that Skírnir leaps either the wall of flame or the great barrier gate that encloses the court, even as Hermóðr on Sleipnir clears the gate of Hel; and like Hermóðr and like Othin he causes the strange realm to shake with the clamour of his coming. Again we have the giant guardian outside, and as in the ballad he is a shepherd sitting on a mound, accompanied by the 'hounds of Gymir'; these are the same fierce guardians as those possessed by Menglöð in the other poem, while yet another parallel can be found in the Welsh story,[1] where the shepherd sits on the mound outside the dwelling of Yspaddaden Penkawr, with a huge mastiff beside him. .

With the penetration of Skírnir within the courts, however, the plot differs from that of *Svipdagsmál* and the Danish ballads. Gerðr is reluctant to give her love to Freyr, and she only consents to do so when Skírnir has called down a series of curses upon her which form perhaps the most puzzling feature of the poem. Olsen has brought out in his article the picture of sterility which is drawn in the fierce and relentless verses Skírnir speaks: Gerðr is to become like a withered thistle, and love and joy are to be denied her. Now there are two other detailed curses which are given to us in Norse literature: the curse of Busla, in *Bósa Saga ok Herrauðs* (IV), and that spoken by Hervör at the grave of Angantýr. That of Busla is easy to analyse: Nature shall be against the king, and the seasons ill; his heart and mind shall be tortured, and his senses dazed; he shall meet with every calamity possible out of doors; and a curse shall fall on all his dealings with women. After this series of threats, Busla calls upon the powers—trolls, elves, giants—to bring ill-fortune upon the luckless Hringr; and she finally snaps his resistance by threatening him with certain runes. The curse of Hervör on her dead father and his brothers is briefer and less embracing;[2] if they do not give up the sword which she demands, their bodies are to be tormented

> As though ants swarmed over you
> In your mounds,

1 Loth, *Les Mabinogion* (Paris, 1913), I, p. 289.
2 See p. 160 above.

and when they still withhold the treasure, she curses them with the curse of utter annihilation:

> I will ordain it
> That you dead
> Shall all lie
> And rot with the corpses
> Lifeless in the grave.

Although the form of the curse imposed on Gerðr resembles that of Busla—physical misery, mental anguish, sterility, and appeal to supernatural powers in the shape of Othin and the Æsir to make it valid, and finally the production of the all-powerful runes—the spirit of it is perhaps nearer to that of Hervör. The maiden Gerðr is already, as we have seen, pictured as residing in a kind of underworld realm of the dead; when the dread curse takes effect, it will bring about a second, more dire annihilation, like that which threatens Angantýr, who is already within the grave. Her joyless existence with Hrímgrimnir is to be beneath *Nágrindr*, the gate of death; and she is to lie 'under the roots' even as do the brothers before they are roused by Hervör. It is interesting to speculate on how far this idea of a second, more dire annihilation could be connected with rebirth; can it be the soul which is unable to pass again into the world of the living which is thought of as sterile, and doomed to pass away completely? The words of the dying man in *Svarfdæla Saga* (v) begging his brother to pass on his name to a child of his after he dies may be remembered here:[1] 'My name...now must pass out of use like withered grass', he says, in words that echo the phrase about the withered thistle in *Skírnismál*. If there were some connection between these two conceptions, the reference to a second death out of the grave (*hel*) into a deeper annihilation (*niflhel*) in *Vafþrúðnismál* (v. 43) would be more understandable.

Among the references to the wall of fire we have left to consider is the story of Sigurðr's ride to the castle of the sleeping Valkyrie, where the chief barrier to be passed is the belt of flames that flicker round her dwelling-place. That fire gleams out, dramatically, in a few of the Edda poems. In *Grípisspá* (v. 15) the seer, Grípir, describes to Sigurðr the king's daughter sleeping in armour on a mountain, whom it is his destiny to awake. In *Fáfnismál* the same picture recurs, and now the wall of fire is added:

1 See p. 141 above.

A hall stands high on Hindarfjall;
All around it is wrapped in flame;
Men of wisdom have fashioned it so
Out of the shining light of rivers [i.e. gold].
On the mount, I know, a war-spirit sleeps,
And around her flickers the lime-tree's foe... [i.e. fire].

In the prose introduction to *Sigrdrífumál* Sigurðr rides towards the mountain and sees what he imagines to be the light of a great fire, 'and the radiance of it reached to the heavens'. This time, however, the fire is explained as being nothing more than a wall of shining shields, within which he finds the sleeping maiden. In *Helreið Brynhildar* it is no longer Sigrdrífa, the unknown Valkyrie, but Brynhildr herself who has stepped into the story. The account which she gives is in accordance with the facts in *Sigrdrífumál*; not only is the Valkyrie shut in with red and white shields by the angry Othin, but the fire, 'the wood's destroyer', is set burning high around the hall.

The part played by Brynhildr in the story of the hero Sigurðr remains one of the many vexed questions in Norse literature. Particularly is the tale of the wooing of Brynhildr and Guðrún by Gunnarr and Sigurðr full of confusion and contradiction; and here the question which stands out most urgently is that of the exact relationship between Brynhildr, daughter of Buðli, bride of Gunnarr, and the Valkyrie asleep on her hill in battle-dress within a wall of flame, whom Snorri calls Hildr, *Fáfnismál* and *Sigrdrífumál* present as Sigrdrífa, an unknown Valkyrie, and *Helreið* and *Grípisspá* identify with the human heroine. The enchanted Valkyrie is absent in the main German version of the story, the *Nibelungenlied*, although the fiery-spirited woman-warrior who can defeat strong men in battle might well be influenced by an earlier Valkyrie conception. The controversy as to the age and interconnection of the many different versions of the story in Norse, Middle High German and Faroese has been a lengthy and complex one, and it would be impossible to outline even the main arguments here. It may suffice for our present purpose, however, to notice that a scholar as fully versed as Heusler[1] in both Norse and German sources reached the conclusion that the story of the awakening of the Valkyrie did not form an original part of the *Sigurðar Saga*, but was added to it later, when the heroine of

1 'Die Lieder der Lücke in dem Codex Regius der Edda' (*Germ. Abhandlungen f. H. Paul*, Strassburg, 1902); 'Altnordische Dichtung und Prosa von Jung Sigurd' (*Sitzungsberichte d. preussischen Akad. d. Wissenschaften*, 1919), p. 162 f.

the Awakening story was identified with the wife of Gunnarr, who helped to compass the hero's ruin. He believed that the source of this story was an early one. Schneider later opposed this point of view, but it is supported and strengthened by the most recent detailed study of the subject, Lehmgrübner's *Die Erweckung der Valkyrie*.[1] After a full and painstaking study of all the available evidence relating to Brynhildr and the Valkyrie, he has been led to the conclusion that the story of the awakening of the sleeper, of which the only first-hand source which we possess is the *Sigrdrífumál*, is a very early one, and formed one of the series of lays recording adventures of the hero Sigurðr-Siegfried in his youth. Afterwards it gradually merged into the Burgundian story of the death of Sigurðr and the slaying of the sons of Gjuki at Atli's court; and by the time of the *Sigurðarkviða en forna*, the earliest lay we possess, the Valkyrie has become Brynhildr the wife of Gunnarr, and a marriage has been arranged for Sigurðr with Gunnarr's sister, Guðrún. One result of this development of the story is the gradual rationalising of Brynhildr the Valkyrie into a more normal heroine, and the relegating of the wall of fire more and more into the background, until in some passages it is even explained away as a glittering barrier of shields. The earlier heroine awakened from sleep may have been nameless; some suggest she was called Hildr; Lehmgrübner himself believes that the name Brynhildr is found in the earliest version. He is also convinced that the story of her rousing belonged to early Germanic as well as to Norse sources.

Besides the story of the awakening of the sleeper, scholars have recognised also an early story bound up closely with it, of the releasing of a maiden from captivity in a stronghold, guarded in some versions by a wall of fire, in others by a dragon, and like it connected with the youth of Sigurðr. Lehmgrübner traces this in various versions of the tale of Sigurðr's wooing; he is of the opinion that the young Sigurðr was the original hero of this story too, who rescued the nameless maiden and won her as his bride.

If we accept this interpretation of the lengthy pedigree of *Sigrdrífumál*, and the belief of Heusler and Lehmgrübner that the story it records was not originally part of the story of Sigurðr and the sons of Gjuki, but was incorporated from a strange tale of the adventure of a young hero, then there is no reason why we should not see it as derived from an account of the seeking of a supernatural woman

1 *Hermaea*, XXXII, Halle (Saale), 1936. See especially pp. 41 f. and 92 f.

from behind a wall of fire akin to those in the poems *Svipdagsmál* and *Skírnismál*. The present form of *Sigrdrífumál* leads us to believe that the gaining of wisdom was the main object of the quest, and this fits in well with the motif of the arousing of the sleeper, which was discussed in the previous chapter. But the fact that this motif appears to have been closely linked from the beginning with what is clearly an example of the supernatural wooing story is very significant, for the connection with the other accounts of the wall of fire and the penetration within it by the hero also becomes marked. The likeness between the situation in *Sigrdrífumál* and that in the other two Edda poems had already been commented on by Grundvig and others, and in Falk's article cited above he points out the resemblance between Menglöð on her mountain Lyfjaberg and Sigrdrífa on Hindarfjall, and suggests that the use of the word *þruma* of Menglöð might even indicate a languor connected with the deep sleep from which Sigurðr has to awaken the Valkyrie. There is also the odd echo of the *svefn-þorn* said to be used by Othin to will the Valkyrie to sleep, found in the name of Menglöð's father, *Svafrþorenn*.[1]

It is interesting to see how these suggestions of early scholars are thus verified by the work of more recent ones concerned with quite a different problem—the connection of the *Nibelungenlied* with Norse sources of the Sigurðr story. It means also that the interpretation suggested earlier in this chapter of the scene in *Sigrdrífumál* is supported by the detailed work of others who had divergent ends in view.

Thus the review of the stories of the supernatural world from which the bride is won reveals tantalising half-resemblances, apparent echoes and imitations, so that the problem of the origin of these traditions is very complicated, and necessitates a study of Celtic legends as well as Norse ones. From the tangle of evidence, however, emerges the idea of a journey to another world which is not entirely outside our concern. Roughly, the way in which it is reached is the same. The steed, above all, must be a special one, with powers which will enable him and his rider to survive the perils of the journey, and it is noticeable that it is often one of Othin's horses which is chosen, for Grani, the only horse that will carry Sigurðr through the wall of

---

1 Some have gone even further than this and pointed out that the father of Olwen in the *Mabinogion* is called *Yspaddaden* ('hawthorn'), a plant which has the name *schlafapfel* in certain parts of Germany (Sijmons & Gering, *Die Lieder d. Edda*, 3, Kommentar, Halle, 1927, 1, p. 140).

fire, is of Sleipnir's stock. Sleipnir himself, it will be remembered, carried Othin, Hadingus and Hermóðr. Skírnir also borrows a horse for the journey, and in the ballad version of the Svipdagr story the hero is given a supernatural horse by his mother. We have seen how the dark fells, the water to be crossed, the final mighty barrier that blocks the way, the dog guardians and the wall of leaping flames, occur again and again. The watchman on the mound, too, is a familiar figure; can it be because the figure sitting on the howe symbolises communication between the living and the dead—that it is, in fact, by way of the mantic vision that the underworld realm can be reached? The emphasis on the journey (often by sea) to the Land of Promise, and the fact that this is said at the same time to be within a mound in the Irish stories, are suggestive.

What do we know of the purpose of this journey made in face of such dangers to the mysterious world reached through the darkness and the flames? In *Sigrdrífumál* it is the obtaining of wisdom, just as in the journey made by Othin himself; in *Svipdagsmál* and *Skírnismál* it is the winning of a bride, and by the introduction of this theme into the story of the consultation of the Valkyrie, the same twist is given to this also. But the winning of the bride in stories of the super-natural world need not necessarily be something separate from the pursuit of wisdom. In the stories which have been examined in the previous chapters, we have seen how the bride-protector, the super-natural woman who attends the hero—*valkyrja*, *fylgjukona* or *dís*—is at once regarded as his wife and as the guardian spirit endowed with supernatural wisdom to protect his fortunes. On the one hand, in-spiration, and on the other, the erotic element, are both undoubtedly present in these stories. It is at least a possibility then that some such conception may be behind these journeys to the Underworld. We remember how it was when sitting on a howe that Helgi first en-countered the Valkyrie Sváva, who became his guardian for the rest of his life, and who was said to be reborn in Sigrún, the wife and guardian of the later Helgi; and in *Grípisspá* (v. 15) we meet with the surprising statement that the sleeping woman on the mountain has been there 'since the slaying of Helgi'—which seems to indicate that here we have the same Valkyrie, reborn or else undying, ready to become the guardian of Sigurðr also. In going further without additional evidence we should be on unsure ground; but at least an examination of the journeys described in these poems shows us that there must be some connection between the strange land to which

the heroes journey and the land of the dead, and that they must therefore be taken into consideration together with our other accounts of
the descent of the living into the land of death.

## THE REALMS OF GUÐMUNDR AND GEIRRÖÐR

The journeys which we have already examined have clearly something in common with the mysterious voyages to the North, said to
be made to the kingdoms of Guðmundr and Geirröðr, and to the
realm of the god Útgarða-Loki. It is not proposed here to make any
attempt to deal with the complicated question of the nature of King
Guðmundr's country, and of the geographical and historical significance of the information which is given us about it in the
*Flateyjarbók* and the *Fornaldar Sögur*.[1] His kingdom is never actually
represented as the realm of the dead; but in several of the accounts a
realm closely connected with the dead seems to lie beside his, and
sometimes his own land is given a supernatural character also, when
we are told that in it lies *Ódáinsakr*—the 'land of the not-dead'.

To turn first to the land of darkness, decay and death that seems to
lie beyond that of the mysterious northern ruler Guðmundr, the
most vivid description of it can be found in Saxo's account of the
voyage of Thorkillus in the Eighth Book of his *Historia Danorum*.[2]
Thorkillus is said to have been given the task of leading the expedition to seek the realm of Geruthus (Geirröðr), rumoured to possess
great store of treasure. He sets out with three hundred men, and they
sail north past Halogaland, seeking, in accordance with the directions
of former travellers, 'to leave the sun and stars behind, to journey
down into chaos, and at last to pass into a land where no light was
and where darkness reigned eternally'. When they come to further
Permland (i.e. Bjarmaland), they go ashore; and it is in this region of
intense cold, pathless forests, wild beasts and foaming torrents, as
Saxo describes it, that Guðmundr encounters them as twilight ap-
proaches. From this time on the travellers are harassed continually by
mysterious prohibitions from Thorkillus, which neither he nor Saxo
ever explains to us. They must refrain from speaking to the people of
these parts; they must abstain from any of the food of the country;
they must not lay hands on the people or the cups in which the drink

1 This is too extensive a subject to be treated here and it is in any case being worked
on in detail by Mrs Chadwick, the person best fitted to elucidate its obscurities.
2 Saxo, VIII, 286, p. 344 f.

is served; and they must have nothing to do with the women of Guðmundr's household.

Beside Guðmundr's realm runs a river, crossed by a golden bridge; and this too they are forbidden to pass over, since Guðmundr tells them that it divides the world of men from that of monsters, and no mortal foot may cross it. Yet they are finally ferried by him to the far side of another river, when he finds himself unable to persuade them to taste any of the delights of his realm, and land in what seems to be a region of monsters indeed.

They make their way to a great walled stronghold; fierce dogs guard the entrance to it, and the heads of warriors impaled on stakes grin at them from the battlements. The dogs, whose presence reminds us of the guardians of the underworld, are quietened by a horn smeared with fat which Thorkillus throws to them. The gates are impassable, like those of the Underworld in the Edda poems, but this northern Odysseus finds a way of entry by means of ladders, and so the walls are scaled. The description of the interior of the stronghold is a strange picture of decay, of riches and glittering treasures surrounded by foulness and dark horror, that is closer to the tales of entries into burial mounds by robbers than anything else in Norse literature. They seem to be surrounded by dark phantoms; there is mud and a horrible smell of corruption on every side, and as they enter the innermost chamber where Geirröðr himself is rumoured to lie, the horror becomes greater; there is more filth and squalor, and a stench so frightful that they can hardly go forward. Moreover the roof is made of spearheads and the floor covered with snakes, as in the grim underworld of *Völuspá*. It is inhabited by monsters, some apparently fighting with clubs and others playing a kind of game with a ball of skin, while doorkeepers stand at watch on the threshold. These creatures do not seem, however, to be alive and in motion; they resemble rather the motionless guardians of some great burial-place, servants laid like those in the royal tombs at Ur, in fitting postures round their master. Finally the adventurers come upon Geirröðr himself, and see an old man with his body pierced through, sitting beside a mighty rent in the rock with three women with broken backs beside him. Then they see the treasure—great 'butts', as Elton translates the Latin *dolia*, with hoops of gold and silver chains hanging from them, magnificent horns ornamented with gold and gems, and a heavy bracelet. Some of the men venture to touch these, but to touch is fatal, for immediately the coveted things turn into snakes or weapons and kill the rash intruder. Finally however Thorkillus himself is so tempted by some rich clothes laid out in a side chamber that he lays hands on a splendid mantle—and at once the whole place springs into life and the apparently dead creatures rise up and attack them. There is a terrible fight, and at the end only twenty of the company escape alive, and are ferried back to Guðmundr. Before they leave his realm altogether, one of the leaders is tempted to woo one of Guðmundr's daughters; and this causes his death, for he is drowned in the river as they leave the country.

In the second excursion of Thorkillus [1] he aims at discovering the dwelling-place of Útgarða-Loki, whom King Gormr worships as a god, and to whom they had prayed successfully for favourable weather to bring them home from Guðmundr's realms. Here the expedition is to certain rocky caverns in a land of unbroken night. They enter a narrow entrance in the rock, striking lights to assure them of the way, and again iron seats and serpents meet their eyes, and there is a slow stream winding over the floor which they have to cross. Then the floor slopes upward, and they find Útgarða-Loki bound with enormous chains, with hairs as long and stiff as spears. One of these hairs is plucked out by Thorkillus, and he and his companions make their way out, but many are killed by the poison from the snakes as they go, and the poison is said to follow them until they move their ship out of the harbour, killing all those who do not cover themselves with hides. This journey bears some resemblance to the former one, in the tomb-like cavern, the darkness and the foul smells. This time however the central theme is like that found in folktale, that of 'the boy who plucked three hairs from the Devil'. It does not seem to add anything very new to the conception of the journey into the unknown land, except the name Útgarða-Loki, which has replaced Geirröðr.

The story of the visit to Geirröðr is evidently in the same tradition as one which Adam of Bremen tells of a journey made by certain Frisians. [2] They too suffer from terrible cold and darkness before they reach an island, surrounded by high cliffs like the walls of a town. They go ashore to investigate, and find men hidden in underground caverns—presumably these seem to be dead, since no attempt is made to stop the intruders—at the entrance of which there is an amazing array of treasure, including many rare vessels of gold. They

1 Saxo, VIII, 292, p. 352 f.      2 Adam of Bremen, IV, 41, Schol. 159.

seize as much as they can, and try to reach the ship, but they are pursued by gigantic figures, accompanied by huge dogs, which tear one of the crew to pieces. The rest reach the ship in safety, though without their booty, and the giants wade out to sea, shouting threats after them, as they sail away.

Here the cold, the darkness, the high cliffs like a wall, the rocky caverns, the golden treasures consisting in particular of drinking vessels, the giants and the fierce dogs that avenge the robbery, are all in accordance with Saxo's account, especially the idea that there is no sign of hostility until the adventurers are leaving with the treasure.

It may be noticed that in the *Prose Edda*[1] also we have two accounts of journeys made by Thor; once to the realm of Útgarða-Loki, and once to that of Geirröðr the giant. Here the idea of the land of death is so little emphasised in either case that they hardly concern us. However the mighty stronghold of Útgarða-Loki, so high that Thor and his companions have to set their heads far back before they can see the top, and the gate at which entry is only gained when the great Thor condescends to creep through the bars, remind us of some of the other journeys. The Útgarða-Loki of this story—which clearly owes a great deal to the masterly hand of Snorri himself, so satirically and wittily is it told—is an adept at *sjónhverfing*, the deceiving of the eyes, and he tricks the strong but simple Thor at trial after trial of strength. Only the mighty horn which Thor tries in vain to empty, because the sea runs into it, and the Miðgarðs serpent, which appears as a grey cat, call to mind momentarily the drinking-horns and the serpents in Saxo.

In the second journey Thor has to ford the river Vimur; here he has his first brief but decisive encounter with one of Geirröðr's daughters; but the verse which he speaks is one of greater dignity than the crude situation in Snorri warrants, and reminds us of the spell in *Grógaldr*, where Svipdagr is given magical strength which, like the god-might of Thor, can make the hostile rivers in his path roll back into Hel. Of the scene in the giant's hall no details are given, except that when Thor sits down he finds that the giant's two daughters (according to Saxo there should be a third) are under his chair, but he forces them down and breaks their backs. Geirröðr like Útgarða-Loki then calls for sports, and hurls a ball of glowing iron at Thor; but the god returns it with such a will that it cuts through a pillar and through Geirröðr himself, before tearing a piece

1 *Gylfaginning*, XLV; *Skáldskaparmál*, XVIII.

out of the wall; and to this story of Thor's exploits Saxo makes reference in the account of Thorkillus' voyage.

The idea of a visit to Geirröðr's realm was evidently a favourite theme, for it is dealt with again in the *þáttr þorsteins Bæarmagnis* in the *Fornmanna Sögur*. This time it is Guðmundr himself who makes the journey, accompanied by the hero, who is of minute size beside the gigantic king and his men. Geirröðr and his jarl Agði are represented as wicked and troll-like, in contrast with the white-skinned and benevolent Guðmundr, and here *Guðmundr* is said to be a title adopted by each of the kings of Glasisvellir when they ascend the throne. Again a river lies between the two realms, and is of no ordinary nature; it is called *Hemrá*; and it is interesting to notice that no horse will ford it save those ridden by Guðmundr and his two sons. The water of the river is fatal to the touch, and þorsteinn has to cut off his toe after the river has touched it. In the hall of Geirröðr there is again ball-throwing, and this time the ball is 'a seal's head glowing with heat, with sparks flying from it and the fat dropping off like glowing pitch'. Again, too, elaborate drinking-horns and a contest in drinking play an important part. Finally Geirröðr is slain by the agency of þorsteinn, and the black and sinister Agði retires into a howe. The resemblance between the situation here and that inside the howe in the story of þorsteinn Uxafótr has already been noticed. Apart from this, however, there is no direct and obvious connection with the kingdom of the dead, and the same may be said of other stories in the *Fornaldar Sögur* in which Guðmundr and Geirröðr are represented as neighbours. We may notice that nearly all the stories, however, agree in placing Guðmundr's realm in the far North, and in emphasising the fact that the way to reach it is through mist and darkness and intense cold.

There is also a strange tradition recorded of Guðmundr in the *Hervarar Saga*:

...Guðmundr was the name of a king in Jötunheim....He and his men lived out many men's lifetimes, and because of this heathen men believed that in his kingdom was Ódáinsakr, and everyone who came there turned his back upon sickness and age, and would not die. After the death of Guðmundr, his men worshipped him and called him a god (1).

The evidence for Ódáinsakr in Norse literature is slight and tantalising. Rydberg[1] built up a fascinating but wild theory around it,

1 *Teutonic Mythology* (trans. Anderson, London, 1889).

equating it, among other places, with the land behind the high wall in the story of Hadingus, and the land beyond the golden bridge next to Guðmundr's realm in Saxo; but we have unfortunately no grounds for accepting these suggestions, pleasant though they might seem, without more weighty evidence. Apart from the reference in Saxo to Fialler, governor of Scania, who is said to have been driven into exile and to have retired 'to a spot called Undersakre, unknown to our people' (IV, 105), we are limited to the strange *Saga Eiríks Viðförla* in the *Fornaldar* collection, which caused even Rydberg to despair because of the preponderance of Christian influence. The introduction of Ódainsakr into the teaching of the king of Constantinople is, however, interesting. In chapter II he teaches the hero, Eric, the Christian conception of the cosmos, consisting of Heaven above the air, where God and angels and good men dwell; the earth, a dungeon in comparison; and *helviti*, the deep pit below the earth where Satan lies bound, and where sinful men are tormented eternally. Besides these three divisions, the king allows a fourth—Paradise—which he places beyond India, the 'outermost land on the southern half of the earth'. It cannot be reached by men, he says, because a wall of fire forms a barrier between it and the world of mortals (II).

But Eric has made a vow to discover the country 'which heathen men call Ódainsakr', but Christian men 'the land of living men' (*jörð lifanda manna*): and accordingly he sets out for India. As he and his companions come closer to the mysterious land, they journey through a region where 'the stars shine by day as well as by night', and where lumps of gold can be found. Then they travel through a dark forest, and gradually it grows brighter as they emerge from the trees, until they see a stone bridge leading to a beautiful land on the other side of a river. The country across the river seems to be full of blossoms and sweet odours, but a great dragon with gaping jaws bars the way,[1] and it is only when Eric and one companion have the courage to leap through his mouth that they are able to reach the fair country: '...It seemed to them as if they waded through smoke, and when they passed out of the smoke they saw a fair land....' Here then the dragon head evidently stands for the wall of fire of which the king spoke, and the same expression ('she waded through

1 This was a familiar medieval conception of the mouth of Hell; it served as a means of depicting it in the Miracle Plays, and may be seen in the Cædmon MS. (Junius XI, facsimile ed. Gollancz, Brit. Acad. 1927), p. 16.

the fire like smoke') is used of the passing of the flaming barrier by Hervör. Later on in the saga Eric has an interview with his guardian angel, and is told that although this country is near Paradise, it is not the same, 'for from Paradise all life comes, and there the spirits of righteous men shall dwell; and this place is called the land of living men' (IV).

This country, which recalls at once the Fortunate Isles of Greek mythology and the land across the sea in Irish traditions, is part of a conception which has evidently lingered on in a few passages when its main significance has been forgotten; and it stands apart from the main stream of conceptions about the future life. The journey to it, however, consisting of travel through darkness, over a river by a bridge, and through a wall of fire, links it up with the journeys which we have already examined, those concerned with the supernatural wooing and with the voyage northward.

## The Entrance into the Burial Mound

The entrance of the living adventurer into the burial mound has already been discussed to some extent in the chapter on *The Future Life*. Before leaving the subject of the journey into the land of the dead, however, it is instructive to notice the resemblance between the form these stories take and the account of the penetration into the realm of Geirröðr in Saxo.

In *Grettis Saga* (XVIII) the howe of Kárr the Old stands on a headland, and after dark it is surrounded by a fire. Grettir goes out to the headland, and tries to break into the howe. He finds it a very difficult task, but finally he makes his way through the wall of earth and comes to the inner wall, which is of wood; this too he tears down, and by this time it is growing dark. Grettir then has himself lowered by a rope into the darkness of the burial mound; 'it was dark there', says the saga, 'and the smell was not pleasant.' He makes his way gingerly forward, and comes upon the bones of a horse, and then he stumbles upon a chair, and finds the occupant. The old man is seated upon the chair, with much treasure in gold and silver around him, and a casket full of silver at his feet. Until Grettir attempts to return to the rope with the treasure, all is still in the mound, and the figure in the chair shows no sign of activity, but as the young man turns away with the gold, he is gripped tightly from behind, and the silent grave becomes a terrible scene of battle. Grettir and his unseen opponent sway here and there in their wrestling, and everything that comes in their way is broken; first one and then the other is beaten to his knees, until at last as they struggle among the horse's bones Grettir makes a mighty effort and throws the howe-dweller backwards with a resounding crash. He cuts off his head with his sword and sets it between his thighs, and then he makes for the rope with the treasure, and since his companion has fled in terror he climbs up without help.

In the light of what we have already studied, this story now seems a very familiar one. Here we have fire burning around the barrow, and besides the fire the wall of the barrow itself proves an obstinate barrier which it requires great effort to break through. Inside, as in the dwelling of Geirröðr and Útgarða-Loki, there is darkness and a foul smell of corruption, bones of a dead animal, and a huge figure sitting on a chair, surrounded by a splendid treasure in gold and silver. When the interloper tries to make off with this, the apparently dead figure comes to life, and attacks him with terrible ferocity. Grettir has to overcome him, cut off his head, and climb out by the way by which he has entered. This story does not by any means stand alone, for there are many tales of breaking into howes in the sagas, and all are roughly of the same pattern. In the entrance gained by Hörðr into the mound of Sóti in *Harðar Saga* (xv), in Gestr's entrance into Raknár's mound in *Bárðar Saga Snæfellsáss* (xx) and in Hrómundr's entrance into the mound of Þráinn in *Hrómundar Saga Greipssonar*, to name three of the most elaborate accounts, the difficulty of opening the mound, the darkness, the foul smell, the seated figure guarding his treasure, and the pandemonium and fight with the inhabitant on the way out, all occur as before.

The entry into the grave-mound by the living is not always for the purpose of robbing the dead. In the story of *Egils Saga ok Ásmundar* (vi) the foster-brother enters voluntarily into the tomb for three nights to fulfil a vow, and the fight between himself and the howe-dweller occurs when the dead Aran attempts on the last night to devour his companion as he has previously devoured the horse, hawk and hound buried with him. In the *þáttr þorsteins Uxafóts*, it will be remembered, the hero again enters voluntarily into the tomb; in fact he is invited in by one of the inhabitants. Here the close parallel to the help given by Þorsteinn Bæarmagn to the fair, red-clad Guðmundr against the black and troll-like Agði has been noted,[1]

1 See p. 81 above.

emphasising the relationship between the dwelling of Geirröðr and the burial mound.

The whole question of how far the journey to the land of the dead was based on the entrance into the burial mound is not likely to be an easy one to answer. They are evidently closely related, but there are two ways in which the relationship may have come about. The practice of robbing burial mounds was undoubtedly well known in Viking times, and is indeed wherever barrow burial on a large scale is used. The darkness, the evil smell, the seated figure surrounded by treasure, would certainly be very real and obvious factors in such a robbery; and traditions about the power of the dead inhabitants and the vengeance taken on robbers would be inevitable, since they even attach themselves to stories of modern archaeologists to-day. The journeys to the land of the dead, then, might be based on such entry as was known to be obtainable into the actual grave. Another possibility however is that these stories, which seem to belong to a definite literary tradition, may be rationalisations of a more complex and perhaps more mystical conception. And it is perhaps most probable that both processes have been at work together.

We are left, at any rate, with what seem to be two separate conceptions, although there is a certain similarity between them, and although it is common for stories to contain elements from both side by side. There is the story of the long journey through many dangers, on a supernatural steed or with a supernatural guide, and finally the passing of a difficult barrier to reach the goal, which is set in a realm closely connected with the realm of the dead. Secondly there is the story of penetration into the world of corruption and physical death—the grave itself—where wonderful treasures are to be found by the brave man, but where the price to be paid is likely to be heavy. Two differences stand out in the two conceptions; in the first case the importance of wisdom and supernatural knowledge is stressed and physical strength alone is useless—indeed physical qualities seem for the most part to be ignored altogether, for it is the spells of Gróa, the curses of Skírnir, the prophecies made to Sigurðr, and above all the help of Fate, that are of avail. In the second case the idea of wisdom hardly enters into the question at all, and it is by physical prowess that the enemy has ultimately to be overcome; even the knowledge of Thorkillus has to be supplemented by hard blows before the company can escape from the realm of Geirröðr. The other difference that may be noticed is that in the second case the gain from the adventure is far more material than in the first. A supernatural bride, the knowledge of supernatural lore, speech with the loved dead—these may be set against the heaps of gold and silver treasures which the realms of Geirröðr and of the howe-dwellers provide. Some doubt as to whether these were originally regarded as strictly material is thrown, however, by the story of Olaf Geir-staðaálfr, where the overcoming of the dead *draugr* and the seizing of his treasure in the approved fashion are represented as the means by which the first Olaf was able to be reborn into the world.

## CONCLUSION

We can see that in few of the stories which we have studied is there any attention paid to the gods. Only Othin is not forgotten, for Hadingus, as we saw, was carried to his hall by the horse Sleipnir, who so often bore riders to the realm of the dead, and there given a miraculous draught, while the future was revealed to him. There is reference to another king who went to seek Othin in *Ynglinga Saga* (XI, XII), where King Svegðir is said to make a vow to visit the house of the gods, and to find Othin the Old. He seems to have made a journey to South Russia on this quest, which took him five years. Apparently it was not successful, although he is said to have married a wife of the Vanir, for on his return he went towards East Sweden, still in search of the home of the gods. Finally he is said to have been invited into a great stone by a dwarf, who told him that here he would meet Othin. Sveigðir, says Snorri contemptuously, was very drunk at the time, and he leapt immediately into the stone, on which it closed behind him.

It is tantalising to think of all the possibilities which might lie behind this brief, crudely told story. It seems likely that the king who disappeared from men and retired into a rock is linked up with the tales of men like Bárðr of Snjófell, who disappeared into the mountains.[1] The idea of the voluntary journey of the king eastwards in search of Othin and his subsequent retirement from the world of men, however, is not quite like anything else in Norse literature. We have it is true the somewhat garbled account of the voyage north-eastwards in search of Útgarða-Loki, who is said to have been the god worshipped by Gormr; though in Snorri he is giant rather

---

[1] H. R. Ellis, 'Fostering by Giants in Saga Literature', *Medium Ævum*, June 1941, p. 70 f.

than god, and in opposition to the deities of Ásgarðr. It is for the most part among the giants rather than the gods that the guardianship of the land of the dead seems to be placed. Geirröðr, Gymir, Fjölsvinnr and the huge barrow-dwellers are the main figures that hold sway there, although the figure of Othin is usually kept within reach, even if it is only in the theories of the scholars who are fond of suggesting that Svafrþorenn or Fjölsvinnr are only synonyms for the most mysterious of the rulers of the land of the dead.

The main result gained from such a survey as this is indeed a new realisation of the complexity of the problems involved in such a subject. Very few of the journeys we have studied are presented simply and directly as journeys to the land of the dead, yet it has been shown that they have some connection with the kingdom of death and with one another. They are mingled with the idea of breaking into a burial mound, of sailing north to a supernatural kingdom, and of calling up the dead at the grave, and the idea of a land of perpetual life is found strangely counterbalancing the land of perpetual death. We are not dealing here with anything which can be summed up as the expression of a belief, real or fictitious, in the way that the life lived in the hills, for instance, might be; it is rather a case of confused traditions, whether literary or religious, passing into the literature, and possibly in some cases of symbolism whose significance has been misunderstood or passed out of mind.

Certainly the amount of evidence seems to indicate that at one time there was a considerable amount of interest in the commerce between the world of the living and that of the dead. We may recall the impression of this gained in previous chapters. The evidence for the future life in Norse literature seemed, it will be remembered, to deal rather with journeys towards an underground realm than with any continuous life lived there after death. Life within the grave-mound, however, was of great importance. When we came to examine the evidence for a cult of the dead, the idea of the relationship between the dead and living was strengthened; for the two conceptions of rebirth and of mantic inspiration through the dead necessitated close communication between the two worlds, and again the emphasis was laid on the burial mound. In the chapter on *Necromancy* we examined one side of this relationship, the possibility of consulting the dead, and of summoning them into the world of the living again. Here we found that together with the idea of the dead being called up there was bound also that of the living proceeding half-way to meet them; and in the case of the awakening sleeper, it was hard to say whether we were indeed dealing with the dead awakened from the sleep of death, or with the living who had been able to gain entrance into the world of the dead and to return with its wisdom. In the present chapter, where we have concentrated on the other side of the picture, it can be seen that the conception of the living proceeding at considerable cost to themselves into some kind of underworld of the dead is very frequent in Norse literature, although it is hard to say exactly what the conception of this underworld may be. Moreover in certain accounts the emphasis on supernatural wisdom, through which the journey may be made, and on the immaterial gifts to be gained through it, is marked.

The impression gained from a first approach to Norse literature, then, namely that the Norse mind was not particularly interested in the clear-cut conception of another world beyond the grave, is to a certain extent confirmed. As far as can be perceived, the emphasis in the literature lies always on the journey thither: the dangers or the glory of the road by which the spirit may travel, and not the permanent joy or anguish that comes with the attainment of the realm of death. The ready flames that bear the dead man to Othin, the steed that can traverse the dark valleys on the way to Hel—it is on these that the attention is riveted, and it is not unfitting that the funeral ship should remain in the mind as symbolic of the heathen grave in Scandinavia. And when we have once realised this change of viewpoint, which is opposed to the Christian attitude to death although it is not difficult to find parallels from the teaching of the mystic and the seer farther East, it becomes possible to understand something of the paradox apparent in Norse literature. There is no concrete and consistent picture of the other world there, and yet certainly no lack of interest in the dead and in death, for in Norse mythology do not the very gods themselves fall fighting at Ragnarrökr, while the deity supreme over war and poetry, twin inspirations of the literature of the heroic age, is the god of the dead also? Further, since our minds are directed continually toward the road rather than the goal, we are faced with a way which is not trod by the dead alone, but which the living also may follow. The land of the dead according to Norse heathen thought is not a wholly undiscovered country, and from it the traveller who has learned the old wisdom aright may return to the world of men.

So far the endeavour has been to survey the evidence relating to the way of the dead in the literature, and it includes, as we have seen, something of the larger question of the relationship between the two worlds of the dead and the living. The resemblance which was noted in the last chapter between the converse which in certain of the poems was held with the dead and the consultation of the living seeress recorded in the prose sagas suggests a new line of approach. The examination of mantic practice and ceremonial in Norse literature, and particularly in the sagas, might throw more light on the obscurities of the poetry of the mythology. To do this here, however, would be to move outside the scope of this book, since it is impossible to discuss such evidence without taking into account the whole subject of Norse witchcraft, which on the surface at least has little connection with the cult of the dead. Whether there may be a deeper relationship than is at present recognised I hope to consider in a further study. For the moment the conception of *helveg*, the road to Hel, gained from a close examination of the literature, is sufficiently consistent to stand alone. As our knowledge of pre-Christian thought in Old Norse literature increases, we shall the better comprehend its deep significance.

# Conclusion

It now remains to review briefly the main points of significance which can be discerned in the course of this study.

First, the evidence for a belief in survival after death appears to fall into two outstanding divisions. There is on the one hand the conception of an existence after death in the realm of the gods. Connected with this we find the practice of cremation, of suttee and certain kinds of sacrifice; the god Othin seems to be of great importance; and one side of the Valhöll conception is dependent upon it. The impression left by the literature is that entry into the realms of the gods was to some extent at least a matter of aristocratic privilege; that it was kings and rulers and high-born men who took an interest in Othin and whom he, as the leader of the gods, delighted to honour, and that for the people in general this realm of the gods had little real interest or significance. Contrasted with this on the other hand, we find the conception of a continued existence within the grave-mound itself; there is evidence for a cult of the dead developing out of this, with emphasis on fertility beliefs, rebirth and mantic inspiration; and one side of the Valhöll conception, that of the everlasting battle, appears to be bound up with it too. Freyr and the elves have some part to play here, but there are certain links with Othin also. We thus have two separate conceptions which have left traces in the literature; there can be survival either through a life lived with the gods after the end of the life on earth, or through rebirth out of the grave. An additional problem arising out of the evidence is the nature of the belief in a life lived in the hills after death, which appears to have been a family cult of some kind.

Secondly, the evidence studied in the course of this investigation leaves us with the impression of some kind of cult connected with supernatural guardian women, who give help to certain men through life and are destined to receive them in their abodes after death. They have become linked with the idea of Valhöll, and have influenced the peculiarly Norse notions of the *hamingja* and *dís*. They appear also to be connected with the belief in rebirth, and with the motif of the supernatural wooing which forms part of the evidence for the journey to the land of the dead. The information which we possess about one local cult, that of Þorgerðr Hölgabrúðr in Halogaland, is relevant here.

Thirdly, the impression given by the evidence which deals with the relationship between the world of the dead and that of the living is that behind the stories and allusions dealing with the raising of the dead and with strange adventures in a supernatural world there may be a deeper significance than has been hitherto recognised. The grave-mound we have seen to be regarded as the place of mantic inspiration; and it seems possible also that the emphasis on the help and wisdom to be won from the world of the dead by the seeker who knows the way is based on a belief in the nearness and potency of the other world, prevalent in Scandinavia in pre-Christian times. There is evidence in the literature, and certain archaeological indications to bear it out, that there was at one time a definite cult connected with the dead and with the grave-mound. Certain cryptic stories preserved in the literature and certain of the mythological poems may become more comprehensible if they are interpreted as expressions of the inward and spiritual significance behind the outward and visible symbolism which the saga evidence has preserved for us.

As to any attempt to give to these concepts a definite historic setting in time or a geographical foothold in certain regions of the North, this cannot be satisfactorily achieved without much further work on rather different lines. The evidence which has been collected is not wanting in suggestion for this. The archaeological data surveyed at the beginning served to show the long and complex ancestry behind such practices as cremation, ship-funeral and howe-burial in Scandinavia. They served also, in conjunction with the literary evidence, to point the way to Sweden and particularly to south-eastern Sweden as the region from which the cult of cremation and sacrifice connected with Othin, and later the cult of the dead in the howe associated with Freyr, entered Scandinavia. Elaborate cremation ceremonies took place in the royal graves in Uppsala in the Migration period, and they were still continuing in Swedish settlements in Russia as late as the tenth century. Already in the Migration period the howe was of importance, and rich inhumation ceremonies on a vast scale were going on in Norway in the Viking Age. The cults of both Othin and Freyr evidently travelled westwards, and were carried by way of Norway, a chaotic mixture by now of divergent beliefs, recollections and literary traditions, out with the early settlers to Iceland. It is necessary then to increase our knowledge of the early kings of Sweden if we are to discover more about the range and nature of the cults in which the Swedish royal families took part.

The earliest literary sources to which we can turn for information about religious beliefs in the heathen period are the works of the skaldic poets. Such skaldic verse as is accessible shows clearly that at the time of Harald Hárfagr ideas about Othin and the future life, about the *dísir* and the valkyries and the various denizens of Ásgarðr, were familiar property to the poets at the king's court and to those who gained a reputation in Iceland in the early years of the Settlement. More detailed investigation of the work of the skaldic poets, about which all too little is known, would probably do much to elucidate the religious conceptions extant in the ninth and tenth centuries in Scandinavia, and would also be likely to give much needed information as to the origin of many of the most puzzling religious and mythological traditions, which have entered the literature as a result of mistaken attempts at interpretation by writers like Snorri and Saxo of the work of the skalds.

The traces of outside influence on Norse thought which have become noticeable in the course of this study indicate yet another direction for future investigation. There is a striking parallel to be observed between the accounts of shamanistic ideas about the soul, recorded from Northern Europe and Asia, and the conception of the journeying of the spirit outside the body which plays an important part in Norse literature, and is undoubtedly significant in connection with the widespread interest in Norse heathen thought in the journey of the living into the realm of the dead. Further close resemblances in Norse heathenism to the beliefs and practices of North-eastern Europe and Asia are evident when the nature of witchcraft in the literature is investigated in detail, as I hope to prove at some future date. One important road for such influences might be south-westwards from the lands of the Lapps; another that north-westwards from the Norse settlements in Russia. We know that there was considerable movement along both in the heathen period, and more accurate knowledge about this might be of great value. Finally there are influences from the opposite direction to be considered, from the lands 'west over sea', and particularly those Celtic lands in the western ocean which had still preserved something of their own peculiar culture up to the time when the Viking invaders reached them. We have seen how from time to time parallels from early Welsh or Irish literature help to throw light on little understood details in

Norse mantic practice, and further investigation on these lines might prove valuable.

The chief claim which can be made for such an introductory study as this is that it points the way to roads along which investigation may go on, and ends with suggestions rather than conclusions. I have been primarily concerned with answering the questions raised at the outset, namely how far pre-Christian ideas about life after death are discernible in Old Norse literature, and how consistent a shape they take there. Among the most impressive of these ideas I would place the conception of the disembodied soul, and the emphasis on the relationship between the world of the living and that of the dead. This is far more important and significant than any notion of a more or less concrete realm of the dead which can be discerned in the literature, whether for warriors or kings or for the common folk. The agreement between certain of the Edda poems and ideas and practices recorded in the prose literature is also suggestive and illuminating for our better understanding of the obscurities of Norse mythology.

In dealing with Scandinavian ideas about the dead I have touched on the fringe of an immense subject, that of the development of religious thought in the north of Europe in the period before the advancing sea of Christianity and the heritage of the Ancient World engulfed Scandinavia, a period when the road to Asia still lay open, and when the heathen culture of the West had not yet been overwhelmed. The religion of that vexed and vigorous age, when men's thoughts about the other world and the practices in which their priests and seers took part were constantly changing, is likely, from what traces we can discern of it in the literature, to merit not only our interest but our respect also. The rich and powerful literature of Old Scandinavia which has preserved memories of it for us has many treasures not yet yielded up, and not the least among these are the utterances of the poets and prophets of a heathen faith on the relationship between the familiar world and the realm of the spirit.

# Index

Printed in Great Britain
by Amazon